The Florida Life of Thomas Edison

UNIVERSITY PRESS OF FLORIDA

Florida A&M University, Tallahassee
Florida Atlantic University, Boca Raton
Florida Gulf Coast University, Ft. Myers
Florida International University, Miami
Florida State University, Tallahassee
New College of Florida, Sarasota
University of Central Florida, Orlando
University of Florida, Gainesville
University of North Florida, Jacksonville
University of South Florida, Tampa
University of West Florida, Pensacola

D1218761

Seminole Lodge, circa 1915. No30950.
*Courtesy the State Library and
Archives of Florida.*

The
Florida Life
of
Thomas Edison

Michele Wehrwein Albion

University Press of Florida
Gainesville
Tallahassee
Tampa
Boca Raton
Pensacola
Orlando
Miami
Jacksonville
Ft. Myers
Sarasota

13 12 11 10 09 08 6 5 4 3 2 1

Library of Congress Cataloging-in-Publication Data
Albion, Michele Wehrwein.
The Florida life of Thomas Edison / Michele Wehrwein Albion.
p. cm.
Includes bibliographical references and index.
ISBN 978-0-8130-3259-7 (alk. paper)
1. Edison, Thomas A. (Thomas Alva), 1847-1931—Homes and
haunts. 2. Inventors—United States—Biography. 3. Electric
engineering—Florida—Fort Meyers Metropolitain Area—
History. I. Title.
TK140.E3A635 2008
621.3092—dc22 [B]

The University Press of Florida is the scholarly publishing agency
for the State University System of Florida, comprising Florida
A&M University, Florida Atlantic University, Florida Gulf
Coast University, Florida International University, Florida State
University, New College of Florida, University of Central Florida,
University of Florida, University of North Florida, University of
South Florida, and University of West Florida.

University Press of Florida
15 Northwest 15th Street
Gainesville, FL 32611-2079
www.upf.com

In memory of my grandmother, Beatrice Wehrwein,
who taught me to respect the past,
and to my children, who look to the future.

Contents

List of Maps ix

The Edison Family's Winter Visits to Seminole Lodge, 1885–1947 xi

Abbreviations xv

Preface and Acknowledgments xvii

1. A Florida Adventure 1

2. The Edison and Gilliland Estates Rise 12

3. Honeymoon in Florida 19

4. Waiting for the Light 28

5. Waiting for the Inventor 42

6. The Wizard Returns 51

7. Transformations and Torments 62

8. Roughing It with Famous Folks 74

9. Neighbors, Welcomed and Not 97

10. A Mind in "Cold Storage" Thaws 105

11. Inventor at Work and Play 115

12. Rubber Research and Road Trips 125

13. A President Comes to Call 137

14. Honors and Exhaustion 145

15. The Last Hurrah 166

16. A Widow at Seminole Lodge 178

Epilogue 192

Notes 195

Bibliography 227

Index 233

Maps

1. The Edison Winter Home, Guest Home, and Grounds xix

2. Edison's 1885 Journey 4

3. Edison's Journey up the Caloosahatchee 7

4. Edison's 1886 Honeymoon Journey 20

5. Edison's 1886 Vision for the Edison and Gilliland Estates 25

6. Atlantic Coast Line Railroad Map of Florida, circa 1904 59

7. The Edisons' 1906 Journey to Lake Okeechobee 64

8. 1914 Camping Trip 77

9. Collier and Henry Counties Separate from Lee, 1923 111

10. 1925 Trip along the West Coast 118

11. The Tamiami Trail 134

12. 1929 Day Trips 141

The Edison Family's Winter Visits to Seminole Lodge, 1885–1947

YEAR	ARRIVAL DATE	DEPARTURE DATE	EDISON FAMILY	OTHERS
1886	March 15	April 26	TAE, MME, Marion Edison	Ezra Gilliland, Lillian Gilliland, LM, MVM
1887	Early March	May 4	TAE, MME, Marion, Thomas Jr., and William Edison	
1888–1890	No visits			
1891–1892	Late January	April	Samuel Edison	James Symington
1893	January	March or April	Samuel Edison	James Symington, William Kennedy Dickson, Theodore Lehmann
1894–1897	No visits			
1898	February	March	Thomas Edison Jr.	Henry Gill
1899	No visit			
1900	No visit*			
1901	February 27	March 25	TAE, MME, Edith Edison, ME, CE, Theodore Edison (TE)	Grace Miller
1902	March 3	April	TAE, MME	Grace Miller[?], MVM
1903	February 21	April 1	TAE, MME, CE, TE	Fred Ott
1904	February 25	April	TAE, MME, ME, CE, TE	Grace Miller[?]
1905	No visit			
1906	February 28	April 8	TAE, MME, ME, CE, TE	Madeleine's classmates and teacher from Oak Place School

(continued)

(Continued)

YEAR	ARRIVAL DATE	DEPARTURE DATE	EDISON FAMILY	OTHERS
1907	February 27	April 22	TAE, MME, TE	Ira Miller and family
1908	Mid-March	April 28	TAE, MME	
1909	February 18	unclear	TAE, MME, ME, CE, TE	
1910	February 3	April 20	TAE, MME, ME, CE, TE	Grace Miller[?]
1911	No visit			
1912	March 13	April	TAE, MME, ME, CE, TE	Fred Ott, Madeleine's friends
1913	No visit			
1914	February 22 or 23	April 17	TAE, MME, ME, CE, TE	Lucy Bogue; Bessie; Henry Ford (HF); Clara Ford (CF); Edsel Ford; John Burroughs; John Harvey Kellogg; Richard, Margaret, and Muriel Colgate; Fred Ott
1915	No visit			
1916	Unclear	April 23	TAE, MME	
1917	No Visit			Henry Ford**
1918	Unclear	April 1	MME, CE, Carolyn Hawkins Edison (CHE)	Lucy Bogue
1919	January	April 20	MME, TAE, Madeleine Edison Sloane, Ted and Jack Sloane	
1920	February 27	Late March or early April	TAE, MME	William and Mary Miller Nichols, Rachel Miller
1921	No visit			
1922	March 22	April 20	TAE, MME, CE, and CHE	Edith Potter, Fred Ott, HF and CF
1923	March 15	June	TAE, MME, Ted and Jack Sloane	HF, Harvey Firestone
1924	February 27	April 11	TAE, MME	Harvey Firestone, Grace Miller Hitchcock, Edith Potter, Elizabeth Miller
1925	February 5	April 16	TAE, MME, TE	HF, Harvey Firestone

YEAR	ARRIVAL DATE	DEPARTURE DATE	EDISON FAMILY	OTHERS
1926	February 5	April 20	TAE; MME; Madeleine Edison Sloane and Jack, Ted, and Peter Sloane	HF, CF, Edith Potter, Fred Ott, Harvey Firestone
1927	February 19	May 3	TAE, MME	Fred Ott, Edith Potter, Dr. John Hammond Bradshaw
1928	January	June 13	TAE, MME	John K. Small, Harvey Firestone, HF, CF, Emil and Elga Ludwig
1929	January 16	June 14	TAE, MME, CE, CHE	HF; CF; Edsel Ford; Herbert Hoover, Lou Hoover, and Herbert Hoover Jr.; Harvey and Idabelle Firestone; Fred Ott
1930	December 5	June 11	TAE, MME, CE, CHE, Marion Edison Oser	HF, Hamilton Holt, Harvey and Idabelle Firestone, Roger and Elizabeth Firestone, Grace and Halvert Hitchcock, Fred Ott
1931	January 21	June 15	TAE, MME, CE, CHE	Harvey and Idabelle Firestone, HF, CF, Fred Ott, William and Mary Nichols, John Harvey Kellogg, Lucy Bogue
1932	February 25	April 17	MME	Grace Hitchcock, Edith Potter
1933	March 1	April 26	MME, Peter and John Sloane, CE, CHE	Edith Potter, Mrs. Osterhut
1934	February 18	April 21	MME, CE, CHE, TE, Thomas Edison Jr. and his wife, Theodore and Ann Edison	John V. Miller, Grace Miller Hitchcock, Lucian Hitchcock, Mary and Will Nichols
1935	No visit			
1936	February 26	April 30	MME, Edward Hughes	Mary Nichols, Grace Miller Hitchcock

(continued)

(Continued)

YEAR	ARRIVAL DATE	DEPARTURE DATE	EDISON FAMILY	OTHERS
1937	March	April 21	MME, Edward Hughes, Peter Sloane	Grace Miller Hitchcock
1938	February 16	unclear	MME	Grace Hitchcock, Edith Potter
1939	February 18	May 3	MME, Edward Hughes	John Miller, Grace Miller Hitchcock
1940	March 21	May 2	MME	Grace Miller Hitchcock, Muriel Colgate, John Miller and wife, HF, CF
1941	February 18	April 27	MME	William and Mary Nichols, Grace Miller Hitchcock
1942	April 8	May 1	MME	Muriel Colgate, Grace Miller Hitchcock
1943–1946	No visit			
1947	February 13	April 11	MME, Madeleine Edison Sloane, CE, CHE	Grace Miller Hitchcock

*The Edisons visited Tampa, Florida, in 1900, but did not travel farther south.

**Beginning in 1917, Henry Ford stayed in his bungalow next door to Seminole Lodge.

Abbreviations

CE	Charles Edison
EFWE	Edison and Ford Winter Estates, Fort Myers, Florida
ENHS	Edison National Historic Site, West Orange, New Jersey
HFMGV	Henry Ford Museum and Greenfield Village, Dearborn, Michigan
LM	Lewis Miller
MME	Mina Miller Edison
MVM	Mary Valinda Miller
TAE	Thomas Alva Edison
TE	Theodore Edison

Preface and Acknowledgments

When Thomas Edison selected Fort Myers, Florida, for a winter home in 1885, it was an unusual choice. The Gulf Coast was an obscure place, beautiful and exotic but geographically isolated. As a frontier community, it lagged behind the rest of the nation in everything from basic sanitation to transportation to lighting technology. It had no fashionable resort hotels, no cultural offerings, simply nothing to attract the traditional tourist.

It was the Gilded Age, a time when newly wealthy Americans demonstrated their fortune and social standing by what economist Thorstein Veblen called conspicuous consumption. Taking a holiday became part of the trend. The well-to-do went to fashionable and expensive resorts in Florida because they could. Like summering in Newport, a Florida holiday became de rigueur.

But Edison avoided the up-and-coming grand hotels in Florida for a more rustic setting. Although Edison was already a world-famous inventor whose acclaim granted him access to sophisticated vacation spots, he made a conscious decision to winter in southwest Florida. It was precisely because he was not a typical wealthy tourist seeking to prove his social standing that he chose Fort Myers. He wanted to escape to a place where he could be himself.

If Edison had been a typical tourist, a recluse in his tropical Shangri-La, the story would have ended there. But Edison and later his wife Mina became active citizens, interacting with neighbors and building long-term relationships. Over the years there were periods of joy, absences, misunderstandings, and broken promises. Yet beneath it all lay deep mutual feelings of affection between the Edisons and their community. In other locations, Thomas and Mina Edison were respected and admired. In Fort Myers, they were loved.

As the years progressed, the Edison children began to appreciate the solitude and freedom of Seminole Lodge. Soon famous friends--Henry and Clara Ford, John Burroughs, and Harvey Firestone--joined the Edison family, also seeking relaxation and a chance to communicate away from the pressures of society and the media. They all found welcome and refuge.

In the midst of his leisure paradise, Edison launched scientific undertakings. During World War I, he worked for the navy in Key West. As a result of that experience, after the war, at an age when many retire, he began a search for a domestic source of rubber. It was a quest that would consume him for the remainder of his life.

The Edisons' many experiences in Florida form a broad tapestry with many threads. A number of fine studies have presented Thomas Edison's great accomplishments. This book endeavors to combine Thomas and Mina Edison's work and leisure in Florida with other elements of their lives to provide a comprehensive picture of the inventor, his wife, and their family in their winter community.

Researching the history has been challenging. There are literally millions of documents about Edison's inventions, but clues to his personal life are more elusive. In an era of letter writing, he corresponded infrequently. However, the records of his secretaries often contain marginal notes that, though brief, reflect Edison's opinions. Mina's correspondence with other family members helps fill in the gaps. When these sources are combined with newspaper articles, magazine interviews, and oral histories, a more complete picture emerges.

I am deeply indebted to many individuals who made this book possible. Howard Segal, professor of history and director of the Technology and Society Project at the University of Maine and the author of numerous books in the field of the history of technology, provided encouragement and advice.

Research assistance came from a variety of talented individuals. Writer David Sloane, a grandson of Madeleine Edison, generously shared his research and expertise. The Thomas A. Edison Papers, specifically Director Paul Israel and Rachel Weissenburger, answered questions, provided documentation, and suggested direction. Also of valuable assistance were Leonard DeGraaf of the Edison National Historic Site and Pam Miner, Rebecca Jones, and other staff at the Edison and Ford Winter Estates.

Others who made contributions include Susan Carter of the Henry B. Plant Museum; Rodney Kite-Powell, curator of the Tampa Bay History Center; Victor Zarick of the Southwest Florida Museum of History (formerly the Fort Myers Historical Museum); Michael Widner of the Collier County Public Library; Sue Vincent of the Dover Public Library; Marjorie Marcotte; Jim Benson; John (Doe Doe) R. Stewart; Lori VanWagner; Susan Kouguell; Ariane McCarthy Hofstedt; Brad Wehrwein; Joachim Schatton; and Meg Fairbairn.

Thanks also to the wonderful staff at the University Press of Florida, especially the nearly infinite patience of Eli Bortz, Susan Albury, and Kate Babbitt.

Last, but by no means least, thanks to my family: my husband Jim, and children Zoe, Noah, Sarah, and Matthew, whose delayed gratification made this book possible.

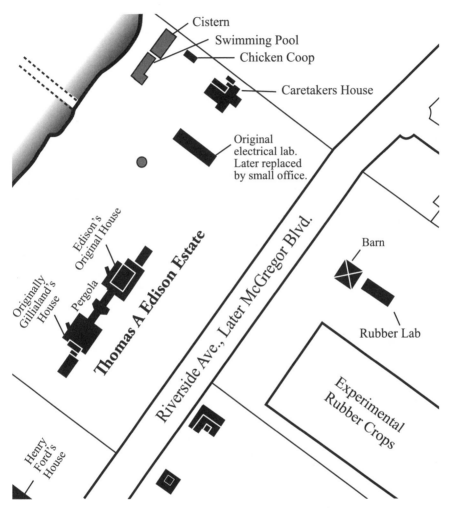

Cistern
Swimming Pool
Chicken Coop
Caretakers House
Original electrical lab. Later replaced by small office.
Edison's Original House
Pergola
Originally Gillialand's House
Thomas A Edison Estate
Riverside Ave., Later McGregor Blvd.
Barn
Rubber Lab
Experimental Rubber Crops
Henry Ford's House

Map 1. The Thomas A. Edison estate and surroundings

A Florida Adventure

"This is the end of the world, jump right off."
Sign at the Shultz Hotel

March 1885

In 1885, nearly everyone in the western world knew the name Thomas Alva Edison. The *New York Sun* called him a magician, the Napoleon of Science, and the Inventor of the Age.[1] The praise and awe was well earned. At 38, Thomas Edison was a world-famous inventor, a celebrity, and indeed, a wonder.

Edison was born in Milan, Ohio, in 1847. His beginnings offered no predictor of his future success. He failed miserably in school, was called "addled"[2] by his teacher, and withdrew after only three months of formal education. Tom was educated at home by his mother until he embarked on a career as a boy telegrapher. From the ages of 16 to 21, he roamed the United States and Canada tapping out messages in Morse code on a telegraph key. The messages were transported all over the country in minutes, not the days or weeks it took to send conventional mail. Yet the telegraph was not fast enough for Edison. He tinkered and discovered methods of sending more than one message on the same telegraph line. By the time he was in his early 20s, he had also made improvements to stock tickers and the telephone.

Edison built a laboratory complex in a rural New Jersey community called Menlo Park in 1876. After a year of success at the new lab, the youthful inventor produced something so unique that he surprised even himself. In a period of a few weeks he conceived of the phonograph. The surprisingly simple machine used a stylus to record words or music on tinfoil wrapped around a cylinder. For the first time in history, sound could be recorded, replayed, and preserved for the future.

Edison went on to experiment with electric lighting. Although the light bulb brought him even greater fame, it was the systems he created around the incandescent lamp that ensured the new technology's success. He established a business infrastructure that manufactured generators, called dynamos, to make direct-current electricity; systems to transport power over wires; and other systems to enable the technology to operate successfully outside a laboratory environment.

By the early 1880s, Edison had been awarded over 500 American patents[3] and had earned the nickname the Wizard of Menlo Park.[4] The name stuck even after he closed the Menlo Park facility in 1882.

While Edison's career was a great success, his personal life suffered. He married Mary Silwell on Christmas Day in 1871. A family story tells that an hour after the wedding, he went off to his laboratory, consumed with solving a puzzling defect in a stock ticker. It was midnight before he realized he had abandoned his new bride.[5] Though the story is likely apocryphal, Edison was renowned for working long hours. Leisure time with his wife and their three children was infrequent. There would always be time for family later, after he had achieved all of his goals.

For years Mary suffered from physical ailments and depression. When her physician insisted that she give up the responsibility of managing her household in 1883, the family moved into a New York hotel. The following year she became hysterical when her father fell ill and passed away. Then on Saturday, August 9, 1884, Mary died. She was 29. The official cause of death was congestion of the brain.[6]

The following morning, Edison was home when his daughter Marion awoke. "I found my father shaking with grief, weeping and sobbing so he could hardly tell me that mother had died in the night," she later recalled.[7] Suddenly he was a widower with three children. Marion was 11 and the boys, Tom and William, were 8 and 6.

Edison had a family to support and a business to operate, and he did not allow himself to be paralyzed by grief. He focused on making improvements to the telephone, a device Alexander Graham Bell had invented the previous decade. In the span of months, Edison submitted nine patent applications. He cemented his role as a telephone innovator at the World Industrial and Cotton Centennial, where his telephone improvements were included in a Bell Telephone exhibit.[8]

Accompanying him to New Orleans was an old friend he had worked with as a young man. Now, in 1885, Edison and Ezra T. Gilliland collaborated to improve telephone communication systems. Gilliland brought to this partnership his expertise as head of the experimental department of the Bell Telephone Company. After the Centennial, Edison, Marion, Gilliland, and Gilliland's wife Lillian, traveled together from New Orleans to Jacksonville, then on to St. Augustine, Florida.[9]

Northern Florida had been a destination for winter travelers since before the Civil War. American journalist and publisher Whitelaw Reid called it the "grand national sanitarium." Along the east coast of the state from Jacksonville to Sanford, grand hotels offered northerners a warm place to rest and recreate. Caring for invalids and their companions became the mainstay of the economy, prompting the state's unofficial motto, "We live on sweet potatoes and consumptive Yankees."[10]

During the Gilded Age, the character of Florida tourism changed. In the post–Civil War boom, Americans found new wealth and sought to cast off their humble backgrounds. A long winter excursion to Florida became fashionable, not just for an ailing aunt but also for the young heir or heiress. By the 1880s, Florida was the place to be and be seen.

Edison's experience was consistent with this trend. In years past, he had sent his ailing wife Mary and their son to Florida to convalesce. Later, in 1884, he traveled with Mary at her doctor's suggestion. Mary rebounded, feeling well enough to collect orange blossoms and pick strawberries while the ever-restless Edison went hunting.[11] His March 1885 journey to St. Augustine was different. Edison was not in Florida for health reasons but to get away and explore.

The inventor's adventurous quest was immediately quashed because the weather was unseasonably cold and dreary.[12] Instead of exploring in the warm sun, he was bundled up in his spring overcoat,[13] waiting for the clouds to part.[14] Likely the weather fueled melancholy memories of his last visit with his wife.

Edison and Gilliland eventually set off on a hunting expedition. The inventor remembered the game he had seen along the Indian River the previous year.[15] A contemporary guidebook boasted, "It is only necessary to penetrate a short distance into the country in any direction in order to find game incredible in quantity and variety."[16]

The two men said goodbye to Gilliland's wife and young Marion, who remained at the hotel. The two men took a carriage from St. Augustine to Jacksonville[17] to the north, and climbed aboard a train crossing the state. A guidebook claimed that it would take them to the state's sparsely settled west coast in eight and three-quarter hours.[18]

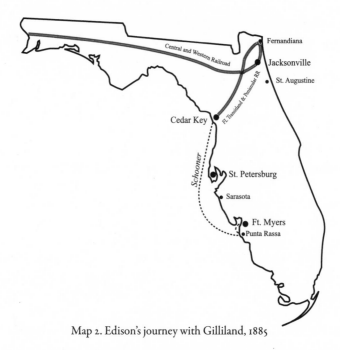

Map 2. Edison's journey with Gilliland, 1885

The guidebook was wrong. Years later Edison still remembered the harrowing journey:

> This railroad was in deplorable condition. The ties were rotten and the rails in some places were strap iron. . . . We ran off the track three times. At one place we were detained a day and a half. At another place we ran off the track and there was no operator at the station. I happened to have with me a pocket telegraph instrument. I cut into this station wire and got connection with Jacksonville. They sent on a little train to help us on our way.[19]

Cedar Key was literally the end of the line. Edison and Gilliland stayed overnight in a modest hotel. In the morning, they explored the small town inhabited by fishermen and employees of the Faber Pencil Company. The mill prepared cedar trees to be shipped north and made into pencils. The inventor was fascinated by the enterprise. Thirty years later he still remembered the cost of the logs, how long the logs were, and the men who guarded the yard with Winchester rifles.[20] Then he and Gilliland went to the docks and hired a small fishing sloop called the *Jeannette*.[21] Once aboard, they traveled south along Florida's gulf coast.

Since leaving New Orleans, Edison and Gilliland had been struggling to create a system of induction telegraphy for relaying messages to and from moving railroad cars. If it worked, every train in the nation would be able to send reports of accidents and dispatchers could send help immediately.[22] But neither man could concentrate on the project as they beheld the unspoiled beauty of the region.

They traveled south, passing Tampa Bay and Sarasota. It seemed like a paradise with mile after mile of sandy beaches, stately palm trees, and lush tropical vegetation. Dolphins danced in the wake of the boat as sawfish and other game fish darted back and forth in the clear blue waters beneath them. Even Edison, who had progressive hearing loss, could hear teeming masses of birds squawking overhead.[23]

As it happened, they found a tour guide on board. Sixteen-year-old Nicolas Armeda had been indentured as a cabin boy when his father, a Spanish immigrant and sailor, was lost at sea. By the time Edison met him, plucky Nick had skipped out on his captain and hired himself out as a guide and deckhand to skippers along the coast.[24]

Nick told Edison and Gilliland about Punta Rassa, where the sloop would next make landfall. The low peninsula at the mouth of the Caloosahatchee River was a way station for the region's cattle trade. Steers were driven from inland towns like Kissimmee, Bartow, Fort Meade, and Arcadia to the coast, sometimes hundred of miles. Once at Punta Rassa, they were herded aboard four-masted schooners for transport to booming cattle markets in Key West or Cuba.

The cattle trade was highly profitable through the 1870s, but it declined the following decade. Ranchers withheld shipments to Cuba in 1884, hoping prices would rebound, but they did not. During Edison's visit, the pens at Punta Rassa were bursting with cattle and their owners, many of whom had not been paid in a year, desperately hoped to get a good price.[25]

At Punta Rassa, Edison and Gilliland quickly learned that the cattle business dominated the local economy. They might have imagined themselves transported to the Wild West. Rough-and-tumble cowhands wearing chaps and broad-brimmed hats sat tall in the saddle. They snapped long-handled whips, called drags, at the restless steers being herded to the docks. The resulting noise, an ear-piercing pop, could be heard for miles. The cowboys seldom hit the steers, but if a snake was nearby, one crack was all it took to separate the creature from its head.[26]

At night the cowboys bedded down at one of two nearby "hotels." The oldest, called Summerlin House, had been established in 1874. George Shultz, a New Jersey native, owned the second establishment. He had arrived in 1867 to take charge of the local telegraph service. The relay station was contained in a cavernous barn-like structure near the cattle pens. Shultz offered the cowboys a dry place to sleep away from the bloodthirsty mosquitoes. At first they hung hammocks between the rafters. Later Schultz supplied cots. Soon he and his wife were offering hot meals and calling the establishment a hotel.

When Edison and Gilliland selected the Shultz Hotel, they soon realized that "hotel" was a relative term. A sign announced, "This is the end of the world, jump right off."[27] The floors were unvarnished rough-hewn wood. Guests washed in tin washbowls and there was no indoor plumbing. The cattlemen and fishermen who stayed at the hotel were coarse and sometimes less than law-abiding. The eleven rooms where they stayed were called "Murderers' Row."[28]

The hotel had one unorthodox, if not downright peculiar, tradition. Each morning, the male guests, who frequently included wealthy industrialists, dressed for the day then put long white dressing gowns over their clothes. As a passerby described it, "When our boat whistle blew, about twenty big fat men in nightshirts and straw hats strolled down to the dock. They looked exactly like a flock of dignified penguins."[29] Edison was a self-made man with a certain disdain for polite society. Without a doubt, he found his stay at the Shultz Hotel refreshing.

In the morning, Edison sat on the verandah smoking cigars with the hotel proprietor. George Shultz had a walrus moustache and a generous build and was generally clad in overalls and canvas shoes.[30] While they were relaxing in the sun, Edison observed a family getting into a sloop and going up the nearby river. He asked Shultz where they were going. "Up the Caloosahatchee," he replied.[31] He then told Edison about the river and some of the small towns on its banks.

Years before, Fort Myers had been the site of a military fort. At first, soldiers were garrisoned there to monitor the local Seminole Indian tribes. During the Civil War, a garrison of Union forces tried to keep Florida cattle out of Confederate hands. By 1885, a collection of cattle folk, fishermen, and some businesspeople were living in the small village.[32] Edison's curiosity was peaked. He and Gilliland decided to see the town for themselves. They climbed aboard the *Jeanette* to take the fifteen-mile journey up the river.

From the mouth of San Carlos Bay, they entered the Caloosahatchee River. Edison was astounded by the immense size of the alligators; some were twelve

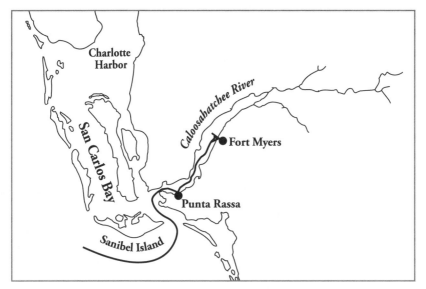

Map 3. Edison's journey up the Caloosahatchee River in 1885

feet long. The rookeries exploded with exotic birds that included snowy egrets, great white herons, and great blue herons. Edison recalled seeing flamingoes.[33] As they ascended the river, the banks became mangrove swamps and coastal marshes and deer drank at the shoreline.[34] They passed coconut groves and pineapple plantations. In a few hours, the sloop went a short distance above Fort Myers and circled back.[35]

Fort Myers was a frontier outpost. Years later, Edison recalled, "It was a small cattle village consisting of not more than 40 houses."[36] The main thoroughfare was a dusty irregular path with clumps of weeds flanked by a small collection of unpainted wood-frame buildings. The town had no electricity or gas for lighting or cooking. Wells supplied water, and outhouses served as the only toilet facilities.[37]

Gilliland and Edison became acquainted with the town by walking up and down the unpaved main street. The three general stores in Fort Myers carried everything from alligator skins to canned goods. One hotel and two boardinghouses offered lodging to cowboys and travelers. There were livery stables and blacksmith shops to attend to horses. A rugged saloon called the Golden Palace offered libations. Cows roamed freely up and down the thoroughfare, eating anything unprotected by a fence.[38] Edison and Gilliland had to tread carefully to avoid stepping in their droppings.

For two days the men explored the town and Edison talked with the crackers[39] about the cattle trade. They watched frontier families arriving in oxcarts from distant cabins to do their weekly shopping. Especially interesting were the Seminole Indians, who wore colorful clothes and traded alligator hides and exotic bird plumes for cooking pots and knives. After cattle, the goods the Seminoles brought from their inland communities were the economic mainstay of the region.[40]

Seminole Neighbors

During the 1500s, Native Americans known as the Calusas populated Florida. Spanish conquest and disease decimated their culture. By the early 1700s, the Calusas were extinct.*

During the next century, European settlers pushed other Native American tribes out of Alabama and Georgia and into Florida, where they became known collectively as Seminole Indians. As Florida's population increased and settlers wanted more land, conflict with the Seminoles escalated.

By the time Edison arrived in southwest Florida, three wars had been fought between the Seminoles and settlers. Though never defeated, the Seminoles were pushed into the region's most uninhabitable swamps and wetlands, where they survived by hunting and trading. The Seminoles limited contact with white settlers as much as possible.** Edison and Gilliland observed the Seminoles in their colorful clothing but probably would not have talked with them.

* Brown, *Florida's First People*.
** Missall and Missall, *The Seminole Wars*.

Ever curious, Edison talked with nearly everyone he met. He probably heard about the big Christmas celebration that had taken place a few months before. Shooting contests were held on Christmas Day. Prizes included portions of a side of beef and a pair of boots. The final event was a jousting tournament where the most accomplished horseman won the right to crown a young woman the Queen of Love and Beauty.[41]

During the week before Edison and Gilliland's arrival, the town, led by cattle baron Samuel Summerlin, had celebrated the inauguration of President Grover Cleveland. They had released a hot-air balloon, had an oyster bake, and experimented with homemade fireworks. After setting fire to a barrel of kerosene on a raft in the river, they had filled an anvil with gunpowder. When it exploded, iron fragments--some as large as six pounds--were hurled dangerously through the town. One passed through a local store's front wall and continued through a counter and a meal barrel before lodging in the back wall. Fortunately no one was hurt.[42]

To learn more, Edison and Gilliland likely read the town newspaper, the *Fort Myers Press*. The weekly paper, which had only been in publication for four months, printed national stories on the front page and local news inside.

During the week of their visit, the paper reported that the village's only photographer had packed up and left town and that one of the general stores had changed hands. It also recorded the comings and goings of schooners, sailboats, and steamships. The *Press* announced that Key West "has achieved a decided advantage in civilization. It is lighted with gas." And a couple of opossums had invaded the offices of the newspaper. Since no one wanted to eat them, they had been released into the woods.[43]

After reading the newspaper, Edison probably sought out Stafford C. Cleveland, publisher, editor, and owner of the *Fort Myers Press*. Cleveland's ill health had necessitated his move to a warm climate. He had planned to establish a newspaper in another region but had been waylaid by his schooner captain, who owned a Fort Myers dry goods store. Believing the town needed a newspaper, the captain had brought him to the town fathers, who had enticed him to stay and set up his presses.[44] Soon, Cleveland had become one of the town's most ardent promoters.

Edison and Gilliland spent the night at the Keystone Hotel, a three-year-old, two-story wooden structure named in honor of the owners' native state of Pennsylvania. The Keystone had twenty guest rooms, a large dining room, a parlor, and a detached kitchen.[45] Years later Edison remembered his first impression of the hotel: "It was built high up on stilts and rooms were 50 cents a day with meals 25 cents each."[46]

On his second day, Edison visited Huelsenkamp & Cranford, the town's first realtor.[47] The rustic office contained four chairs with the hairs still on the cowhide seats, a homemade table, and a shiny cuspidor for spitting tobacco.[48] The modest office was in direct contrast to the firm's extravagant advertising claims that Fort Myers was "the Italy of America. . . . Equaling if not surpassing the Bay of Naples in grandeur of view and health giving properties!"[49]

C. J. Huelsenkamp was more than happy to produce a list of available properties for Edison.[50] One parcel was a thirteen-acre tract on the west side of the

Caloosahatchee River. Known as the Summerlin Place, it was owned by Samuel Summerlin, one of the sons of the region's most prosperous cattle barons.

In the 1840s, Samuel had traded an inheritance of twenty black slaves for 6,000 cattle.[51] The herd had expanded during the Civil War when his father won a contract to supply the Confederacy with beef. Though Samuel's father had been known as the "King of the Crackers," the Summerlin family made for unconventional royalty. They worked hard and lived simply, doling out wages for their men from a large bag of gold Spanish doubloons heaped on a rude wooden table.[52]

At first glance, the thirteen-acre Summerlin plot may not have impressed Edison. It had only a small wood-frame home and the land was typical of the region, a mass of sand with dense clumps of palmettos, scrub grasses, and slash pines. The two best features were a stretch of over 600 feet of river frontage and a large clump of bamboo.[53] Edison knew a great deal about the tropical plant because he had used it as a filament in his incandescent light bulbs.

Edison returned to Huelsenkamp's office, where he and the agent agreed on a purchase price for Summerlin's land. Edison handwrote the terms of the contract, which included a down payment of $100, a purchase price of $3,000, and a stipulation that Huelsenkamp needed to get clear title to the property.[54] Although Summerlin had paid only $500 for the property a decade before, Edison thought he had made a wonderful deal.[55]

Town Founder Major James Evans

During his first visit to Fort Myers in 1885, Edison met the town's founder. Major James Evans had come to the region in 1859 and purchased property, but had vacated during the Civil War when the town became a Union outpost. After serving as a major in the Confederate Army, he returned to repurchase the property from the U.S. government and establish the town.[*]

Evans was 62 when Edison arrived. Evans taught the inventor about the region's tropical plants. Years later Edison remembered his sense of humor: "I said to him one day, 'How does it happen that your trees grow so rapidly?' And he replied, 'I put lots of fertilizer in the holes before planting and they are trying to get away from it.'"[**]

[*] Grismer, *The Story of Fort Myers*, 275.
[**] Interview with TAE, n.d. (ca. 1917), Edison General File, ENHS.

For two marvelous days, Edison and Gilliland toured the town, talking to the residents and asking them questions. Everywhere they went, local folks were awed by the inventor's presence. Then he and Gilliland departed, climbing aboard the *Jeannette*.[56] As suddenly as he had appeared, the wizard was gone.

The Fort Myers weekly newspaper quickly recounted Edison's visit, calling him a "distinguished electrician" and a "Ph.D." The *Jeanette*, the fishing sloop Edison had chartered, became an "elegant yacht." The *Press* announced Edison's intention to purchase the Summerlin property, saying "he will fix [it] up handsomely and make it a pleasant abode." What came next was truly shocking: "He will also bring along a forty-horse-power steam engine and set up his workshop and laboratory, for a portion of the year."[57]

Only a week before, Fort Myers had been a little-known backwater hamlet. Now Thomas Edison was planning to establish a laboratory and produce an invisible power called electricity. For the region's citizens, who relied on kerosene lamps or tallow candles to light their homes, Edison's visit offered magical and mythical wonders. With Edison as a resident, perhaps electricity was a harbinger of even more exciting things to come.

Secret Travelers

On Edison and Gilliland's return trip from Fort Myers, they tried to find lodging in Tampa, Florida, but the hotel was full. Another guest named Herbert J. Drane offered to share his room. The travelers, who never gave their own names, gratefully accepted. The following morning after they departed, a colleague scolded Drane for sharing his room with strangers.

Embarrassed, Drane was determined to learn their identity. He traced their steps to a skipper on the Tampa docks, who reported that one of the men "wanted me to move a carload of lumber to Fort Myers.... I think he's crazy. Only a crazy man would ship lumber here from [Maine] when we've got more lumber here—good lumber too—than we'll ever be able to use." The skipper then told him the "crazy man's" name was Thomas A. Edison.*

* "When Mr. Edison Visited Tampa," *Tampa Tribune*, December 28, 1947; "Edison Slept on Spare Cot in Crowded Tampa Hotel," *Tampa Sunday Tribune*, November 7, 1954; "Edison Slept Here," *Tampa Tribune*, May 9, 1955. Also Herbert Jackson Drane, unpublished autobiography, 23–24, Lakeland Public Library, Lakeland, Florida. Because the four accounts differ, I have selected the most historically likely details.

2

The Edison and Gilliland Estates Rise

"Mr. Edison Means Business."

Fort Myers Press

April 1885–February 1886

In the shops and on the dusty streets of Fort Myers, everyone talked about Thomas Edison and his plans. A laboratory would be a tremendous boon to the economy. Edison would hire local people and order supplies from area stores. Soon, hearing that Edison was wintering in Fort Myers, other famous people would purchase estates nearby. The potential seemed limitless.

There were detractors too. The town had been disappointed before. Hamilton Disston, an English immigrant from Philadelphia, had been awarded a state contract to drain the Everglades in 1881. His plan included carving out wide canals, depositing the fertile soil on swampland, and creating new farms.[1] Although Fort Myers was the base of operations, the town never really boomed. By the 1880s, the dollars had begun to shrink.[2] Was Edison's plan to build a winter home and laboratory just speculation?

Spring came and went and Edison did not purchase the property. Huelsenkamp sent him a deed and a certified abstract.[3] In July of 1885, he dispatched a telegram: "If you desire property prompt action is required."[4] In August, Huelsenkamp contracted with a surveyor named Col. J. P. Perkins to make a map of the riverfront acreage. The plan transformed the cow path that divided the property from east to west into a wide drive. The west side would contain residential structures and Edison's laboratory. Support buildings, barns, and stables would be located on the east side.[5]

In September, Edison's 1885 visit was described in an article in *Blackwoods*, a nationally circulated magazine. It called Fort Myers a "Rip van Winkle settlement" and described the inventor's plan to establish a laboratory. The article warned that "Mr. Edison's plans are not like the laws of the Medes and Persians: they may have changed several times before next winter.[6] But he was a social attraction for Fort Myers and St. Augustine while he lasted."[7]

When Edison still had not signed the deed by September, Huelsenkamp tried to force his hand. He claimed that Summerlin wanted to withdraw the deal because of the delay. The agent further claimed to have convinced Summerlin to reduce the purchase price to $2,700. He asked again, "Do you wish us to take charge of the property?"[8]

What were Edison's plans? Gilliland was collecting estimates for construction of the inventor's home in Florida, but was he just going through the motions? Was the entire plan a lark? Why had Edison not yet signed an agreement?

In mid-September Gilliland sent Edison a newspaper clipping. Three masked men had robbed a man just outside Fort Myers, nearly killing him.[9] Gilliland remarked, "You will observe the writer goes for [Fort] Myers pretty rough."[10] Edison forwarded him one of Huelsenkamp's old letters with a margin note asking, "Gilliland, what do you say[?] Edison."[11]

Although a formal agreement was not recorded for several months, Edison was indeed committed to a winter home and laboratory in the wilds of southwest Florida. The surprising element was that Edison was not alone. As the final Perkins plan reflected, he and Gilliland planned to divide the acreage into three parts. On the first parcel, Edison would establish a Florida laboratory. On the second portion, he would build a vacation home. The last piece would be sold to Gilliland, who would erect a winter home of his own.

This agreement took their association to a new level. In addition to being business partners, Edison and Gilliland would vacation together. For the inventor, the arrangement was unprecedented. In his past friendships, he had been the dominant partner. His relationships with business colleagues tended to be intense and brief. Never before had Edison maintained a successful long-term relationship with an equal.[12]

That summer, the two men fine-tuned their plans. While staying at Woodland Villa, Gilliland's cottage in Winthrop, Massachusetts,[13] Edison reflected on the decision to create a winter retreat. In his short-lived diary he wrote, "We concluded to take short views of life and go ahead with the scheme. It will make a savage onslaught on our bank account." He noted wryly that Gilliland had "remarked that now all the wind work[14] is done there only remains some little details to attend to, such as 'raising the money.'"[15]

When they were not working, Gilliland and his wife Lillian acted as matchmakers for the widower. Although his fame had made him one of the nation's most eligible bachelors, Edison's personal habits made this a challenge. Lillian's niece recalled, "Well, he was dirty . . . about his person. He wouldn't take a bath. They had to force him to take [one]." The Gillilands and their guests dressed for dinner, and Edison's dirty and rumpled suits would not do. When Edison was a dinner guest, the maid would lay out a tuxedo for him after drawing him a bath.[16]

The Gillilands hosted weekend dinners and music performances at Pelham Manor, their home in Westchester County, New York. Edison, clean and neatly dressed, was often the guest of honor. They paraded suitable young women before the widower. Daughter Marion immediately made her selection. "I picked-out the step-mother I wanted right away, more because she was a blond like my mother, than for any other reason." The inventor had other ideas. "I had the impression, however, that my father was in love with the Ohio girl."[17]

The "Ohio girl" was Mina (pronounced My-nah) Miller of Akron, a petite 19-year-old. Like his first wife, Mina had a generous figure. Unlike her, Mina was educated. After high school she attended Mis Johnson's Young Ladies School in Boston. The finishing school prepared young women for marriage and society.[18] Mina Miller was also beautiful with an olive completion, dark flowing hair, and deep, dreamy eyes. Now, in Gilliland's home, the bachelor inventor found himself smitten.[19]

The uncharacteristically romantic style of his diary reflects his new love interest and perhaps a fear that he would be rejected. He wrote, "[Gilliland] and I . . . study plans for our Floridian bower in the lowlands of the peninsular Eden, within that charmed zone of beauty, where wafted from the table lands of the Oronoco and the dark Carib Sea, perfumed zephyrs forever kiss the gorgeous flora. Rats!"[20]

In the weeks that followed, Edison and Gilliland drew up the basic plans for their combined estate. Gilliland took them to Alden Frink, a relatively obscure Boston architect. Over the summer Frink prepared specifications for a "dwelling house & Machine Shop." Ever frugal, Edison ordered the design of only one house, which would be copied in reverse to create the second. The architect's fee was $200. As they would with all future bills, Edison and Gilliland divided expenses into three parts. Gilliland paid for his home, in the sum of $80. Edison paid $120: $80 for the design of his home and another $40 for the laboratory.[21]

Though they were opulent by Fort Myers' standards, the plans for the Edison and Gilliland homes were modest compared to the estate homes of contemporary wealthy industrialists. The men chose simple two-story rectangular buildings with small additions for kitchens and servants' quarters. They were to be built of wood, not brick or stone. And because southwest Florida was so undeveloped, nearly everything would have to be shipped to the building site.

Gilliland sent the final plans to the Kennebec Framing Company, which sold "Ready-Made Buildings Furnished for Shipping to Foreign Ports."[22] The company, located in Fairfield, Maine, compiled multiple large shipments of planks, boards, shingles, windows, and sashes. Each order was organized into parts, which the company claimed were "planed, sized, cut and marked to place, thus enabling any practical workman to put the same together without difficulty."[23]

Other Maine businesses provided building supplies. Lime and cement came from Rockland.[24] A Bath, Maine, company provided 55,000 bricks for foundation piers and 66 bushels of hair to be used in horsehair plaster walls.[25] Another company supplied 100,000 pounds of coal.[26] The home furnishings came from New York. From Baumann Brothers, Edison and Gilliland bought rocking chairs, settees, end tables, beds, and washstands.[27] James McCutcheon & Co. furnished bedspreads, pillow shams, towels, and napkins.[28] From the firm of Lewis & Conger came pie plates, ladles, brooms, chop knives, and washboards as well as at least two refrigerators, which were actually iceboxes.[29]

When all the invoices were tallied and the exorbitant costs of shipping were figured in, Edison and Gilliland had each spent about $12,000 on their winter homes and furnishings.[30] The workers who built the house were paid between $1.50 and $2.75 per day.[31]

Edison also paid about $16,000, to outfit his laboratory.[32] He ordered hardware and tools—table saws, lathes, couplings, pulleys, injectors, braces, wire, and engine oil. Then there were invoices for over a thousand dollars' worth of chemicals.[33] He placed an order with a New York stationery company for $68.79 in pens, pencils, erasers, pads, and blotters.[34]

Edison's choice for lighting the homes was sentimental. Instead of new fixtures, he opted to remove old ones from the abandoned Menlo Park laboratory in New Jersey.[35] The elaborate chandeliers, called electroliers, resembled gaslights and were among the first electric fixtures ever made. The manufacturer was Bergmann & Co., a New York firm where Edison was a silent partner. It was fitting that these historic fixtures would again make history by illuminating the wilderness of southwest Florida.

Lighting in Fort Myers

There is no underestimating the excitement generated by Edison's plan to light his new home and laboratory with electricity. In December, the *Fort Myers Press* reported that "at the present rate of progress Fort Myers will be ready for electric lights and street railways before the winter is over."*

At that time, there were no electric generating plants south of Tampa. Few in the region would have known what a light bulb was, much less seen one illuminated. Poorer citizens used foul-smelling lard lamps or tallow candles, while the more affluent used kerosene. Cooking was done in fireplaces or woodstoves, which brought fire hazards and unbearable heat in the summer. Edison's electric light bulb and the idea that tiny wires could bring light and heat inside a home did indeed seem magical.

* Untitled article, *Fort Myers Press*, December 12, 1885.

Generating the electricity to light the electroliers would be challenging. Fort Myers had no electric plant, so Edison ordered his own dynamo to generate electric power.[36] It was among the items lost in February when the *Fannie A. Milliken*, a 200-ton schooner carrying the laboratory furnishings and equipment, was grounded on the way to Fort Myers. Fortunately, the lost cargo was insured and a duplicate shipment was sent later that month.[37] Gilliland and Edison divided the costs of all items they had ordered together. Their individual charges illustrate differing vacation plans. The inventor aimed to work, but Gilliland intended to play. He spent hundreds of dollars refurbishing a steam launch, the *Lillian*, named for his wife.[38] He ordered fishing poles, gear, and buckets of tackle[39] as well as hunting gear—a Whitney rifle, a dozen holsters and belts, and large quantities of ammunition.[40] Orders for special lumber and tenpins indicate that he also planned quiet days of bowling.[41]

While Gilliland was ordering supplies and Edison's New York staff was coordinating shipments to Fort Myers, Edison was wooing Mina Miller. In August, he met her family at the Chautauqua Institute in New York. Her father, Lewis Miller, was one of the co-founders of the Methodist retreat center. At the time, young Mina was probably engaged to the other co-founder's son. By the end of September, she had broken the engagement and Edison had asked for her hand in marriage by tapping his proposal on her hand in Morse code. She accepted, and they set the date for February. The wedding would take place at her parents' home in Akron, Ohio, and be followed by a Florida honeymoon.[42]

Preparing the winter estate for Edison's honeymoon visit would be difficult. Most supplies were not ordered until the fall of 1885. Edison's employee, Eli Thompson, accepted shipments, inventoried orders, hired workers, and supervised the construction. He arrived late in November, leaving a narrow window of three months for all work to be completed.[43]

Through the *Fort Myers Press*, the townsfolk of Fort Myers kept track of every shipment and improvement to the property. On December 5, the support posts for Edison's dock arrived.[44] A long dock was essential to all further construction on the estate because supplies could be off-loaded directly onto the property instead of at the main street in town. The 350-foot pier was constructed by Joseph Vivas, a Mexican-born carpenter from one of Fort Myers's founding families.[45] Once completed, it extended far enough into the river for schooners and Gilliland's steam launch to dock at the end.

In February, newspaper editor Cleveland made one of his frequent inspec-

Fort Myers Cashes In

As the townspeople hoped, the establishment of the Edison and Gilliland estates gave a boost to the local economy. Steam ships like the *Manatee* and *Chimo* as well as the schooners *Julia Bailey* and *Lilly White* delivered furnishings, lab equipment, and building supplies. Hardware and other goods not included in the huge shipments from New York were purchased at Towles & Hendry Dry Goods and Blount's General Store.

Once the supplies arrived or were procured locally, men from all over the region were hired for construction and landscaping jobs. Most made between $1.50 and $2.75 a day, working six days a week.* Workers sent by Edison from New York found lodging at the Shultz Hotel, at Summerlin House at Punta Rassa, and at the Frierson boardinghouse in Fort Myers. All in all, Edison did indeed mean business.

*"Pay Role [*sic*] Edison & Gilliland, Myers [*sic*] Fla., April 5–10 [1886], ENHS.

tions of the estate, reporting that "today all is changed, buildings and other improvements having sprung up with a rapidity that rivals the growth of the mushroom." Most of the fencing, essential to keeping out cattle, was installed, and G. W. Bassler, a landscape gardener from Philadelphia, had laid out the grounds.[46] There were fruit trees—limes, lemons, and coconuts—as well as ornamental Spanish bayonets. The progress that had been made on the homes was stunning:

> They stand facing the delightful Caloosahatchee, from which they are distant about twelve or fifteen rods, and are separated from one another by a space of nearly four rods, through which runs a broad avenue or driveway leading up from the entrance. Between the buildings and this driveway, Mr. Bassler has placed two splendid specimens of the century plant. The houses are two-story buildings, square roofed with a broad plaza running around three sides, while a large kitchen is attached to both. The interior is still unfinished and but a small portion of the side-boarding has yet been completed, but the painters have commenced their artistic work on the roof and have given an indication of how the structures will look when all is completed. Dictated by good common sense Mr. Edison has had a large fireplace built in each house, thus providing against the chilly weather which even the people of South Florida are subject to during the months of December and January.... Wires are also now being put in that the buildings may be lighted by electricity.[47]

After a year of waiting and hoping, Edison was indeed going to be a resident of southwest Florida. Two stately homes were rising out of the sandy soil. Edison's laboratory would bring the region fame. All would be illuminated by Edison's mysterious electric light.

As the town awaited the famous inventor's return, the newspaper reported giddily, "Really the people here must be pardoned for believing that Mr. Edison means business, and will do what he said he would do. Further, the people here believe that many of Mr. Edison's friends and acquaintances and thousands of other people will follow his illustrious example: come and see this lovely summerland, be delighted with it, purchase land here, build and make Fort Myers their headquarters also. Next!"[48]

3

Honeymoon in Florida

"Hurrah for Thos. A. Edison!"
Fort Myers Press

February and March 1886

On February 28, four days after their wedding in Akron, Ohio, Thomas A. and Mina Miller Edison arrived in Jacksonville, Florida. In a letter to her parents, the 20-year-old bride complained, "People stare at us so; all knowing that the person with me is Mr. Edison who has just been married . . . [and it] causes quite a stir."[1]

They checked into the St. James, Jacksonville's premier hotel. The block-long establishment could lodge more than 300 guests and offered every amenity. It had its own barbershop; news, book, and flower stands; and ticket and baggage offices. The honeymooners could take advantage of libraries, wine rooms, billiard rooms, modern elevators, sumptuous parlors, and breezy verandas. If Edison ran out of his favorite cigars, the hotel had its own cigar shop.[2]

The St. James also offered its guests the latest technology. There were no old-fashioned gas lamps. Stunning electric lights illuminated the dining rooms and electric bells summoned staff.[3] Both were a credit to Edison, who not only had invented the incandescent bulb but had also established entire system to light buildings and neighborhoods.

From the telegraph office of the St. James, Mina sent word of their safe arrival to her parents.[4] Her husband dispatched a message to his New York staff. Another telegram went to Ezra Gilliland, who was in Fort Myers with Lillian and Edison's daughter. Edison requested a report of the progress on his estate but found the reply disappointing. The houses were incomplete. Gilliland assured him that he was seeing that the work was done as quickly as possible. In the meantime, they were staying at the Keystone Hotel.[5]

Although the St. James Hotel was quite comfortable, Mina Edison found it lacking. "This is a miserable hotel and a worse city," she lamented to her mother. The flies kept her new husband awake. She longed to move on to the next leg of their journey: "We have seen nothing yet resembling the jungles we read [about] and see illustrated in books. That is still in store for me."[6]

Mina's disappointment might have been post-wedding letdown or her growing realization that her husband's first priority was his work. As they traveled by train to Florida, Edison and his New York employees constantly exchanged telegrams. On the day the newlyweds arrived in Jacksonville, Edison made sketches in his notebooks and directed his staff to patent a system for sending three telegraph messages simultaneously.[7] As Mina was learning, Thomas Alva Edison was an inventor first, a husband second, even on his honeymoon.

The next day they were off to St. Augustine, lodging at the San Marco Hotel,[8] where Edison had stayed with Marion and the Gillilands the previous year. The hotel offered a panoramic view of Anastasia Island, the Matanzas River, and Castillo de San Marcos, which was then known as Fort Marion. The fortress, which had been built during the era of Spanish rule in Florida, had become a major tourist attraction. A contemporary guidebook noted, "It is especially popular with romantic, newly-married tourists."[9]

After a week in St. Augustine, the Edisons were again on the move, traveling

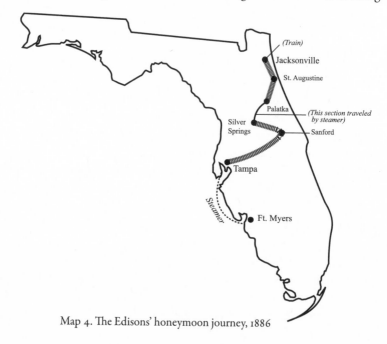

Map 4. The Edisons' honeymoon journey, 1886

thirty miles southwest to Palatka. Edison had been to the charming town with his first wife, Mary, in January of 1884 when it was a busy village with shops, tourist hotels, and wide oak-lined boulevards.[10] A fire the following November had reduced much of the town to ashes, and it had lost its prominence as a major tourist destination.[11]

The Daily News, the Palatka newspaper, lost no time in announcing the Edisons' arrival. "American's [*sic*] greatest living inventor, Thomas A. Edison of electric fame of New York is at the Putnam accompanied by his bride."[12] They stayed at the Putnam Hotel for two days before leaving for a planned trip on the Ocklawaha.

A contemporary guidebook insisted that "every visitor to Florida should make the famous excursion 'up the Ocklawaha.'" It continued that anyone who did would "likely [never] forget a night-journey upon what has been well called 'The Mysterious River.'"[13]

Writers captured the spirit of the river in contemporary literature. Edward King, who wrote for *Scribner's Magazine*, asked, "What poet's imagination, seven times heated, could paint foliage whose splendors should surpass that of the virgin forests of the Ocklawaha?"[14] Henry James, who had spent decades in Europe, was more cynical, calling the Ocklawaha, "Byronically foolish." In one sentence he waxed poetic about its "velvety air, the extravagant plants, the palms, the oranges, [and] the cacti," but then he complained about its "cheap and easy exoticism," finally ending by comparing it to "a corner of Naples or Genoa."[15]

Edison likely chartered a steamer or a private cabin to ensure the couple's privacy during the six-hour journey. Ocklawaha boats were peculiar-looking crafts of two stories with "the appearance of having been placed in service just before completion."[16] What the steamships lacked in elegance, they made up for in power, making tight turns and plunging into small tributaries obscured by trees and hanging Spanish moss.

Mina's wish to experience the jungle was fulfilled as the little steamer navigated through curtains of vegetation. They were surrounded by the sounds of birds, cranes, herons, water turkeys, curlews, and storks. Many of the birds sported bright plumage that contrasted brilliantly with the verdant green of the jungle. Large turtles and alligators surfaced to watch as the steamer chugged up the river.

As darkness fell, the Ocklawaha became mysterious and romantic:

It is grand, impressive, strange, tropical—now gloomy and awe-inspiring, now fairy-like and charming, and again weird and wild. The great forest-trees of that region are all of immense size, oaks, gums, magnolias, cypress, etc., interspersed with a perfect network of immense vines, too tangled for description, brilliant with vegetation—leaves of all colors, flowers of all shapes, sizes and hues, and loaded with great clusters of mosses.[17]

After an evening in the jungle, the steamer docked in Silver Springs. There, tourists could take a rowboat onto the small clear lake, which was so translucent that pebbles sixty-five feet below were plainly visible and one could drop a dime and follow it all the way to the bottom.[18]

After the Ocklawaha, the Edisons returned to Palatka for a day. While Mina wrote to her parents,[19] Edison telegraphed his New York staff about selling stock, delegated work to various staff members, and followed up on a model of a railway truck he had designed before the wedding.[20]

From Palatka, the couple traveled south and stayed in Sanford before crossing the state on the South Florida Railway. Aboard the train, they passed mile after mile of scrubland. Here and there they saw truck farms and a few dusty towns before reaching the end of the line in Tampa.[21] Even after all this traveling, their journey was not over. They stayed overnight at the Plant Hotel, a modest establishment on the corner of Ashley and Mason Streets. In the morning, the Edisons and their baggage were put aboard a steamer called the *Manatee*[22] for the last leg of their journey. They found themselves among farmers, cattle ranchers, and a few tourists bound for Fort Myers, the Edisons' new home.

While the Edisons were honeymooning, the town fathers in Fort Myers considered plans to welcome the famous inventor and his new wife. They opted for a public reception where the whole town would greet them when they disembarked. But Eli Thompson or Gilliland likely interceded. The *Fort Myers Press* was told that "it would be much more acceptable to [Edison] for our people to make a sixty foot avenue from our city to his place on the Caloosahatchee." Editor Cleveland supported the idea: "It would not cost more than $100, a good part of the job being already completed. Let something be done in this direction."[23]

On Monday, March 15, 1886, the steamer *Manatee* chugged up the Caloosahatchee River, and without ceremony Thomas and Mina Edison disembarked. Out of respect, the citizens of Fort Myers were true to their word and did not greet the couple. But their exhilaration could not be completely contained. The newspaper announced gleefully, "Hurrah for Thos. A. Edison!"[24]

Because the winter homes were still incomplete, the Edisons went directly to the Keystone Hotel, where the Gillilands and Marion had been staying for three weeks.[25] After her complaints about the St. James Hotel, Mina must have been absolutely aghast at the conditions of the Keystone. It had a small dining room and a parlor but no electricity, gas, or indoor plumbing.[26]

After settling in, they were off to inspect their new home. The 60-foot path suggested by the newspaper was not yet realized. Years later, Mina remembered the rough one-mile ride with her feet dangling from a donkey cart.[27] "There was a trail of sorts going to town, over palmettos, through shrubs, with the sand up to the hubs of the cart in many places."[28]

When they arrived, twenty-five men were laboring on the two homes.[29] One structure was nearly finished and would be habitable in a few days. The other was still weeks from completion. The grounds showed little signs of progress. Mina recalled that "there were no trees, not even a blade of grass—just piles of sand."[30]

The Edisons stayed at the Keystone for three nights, and then on Thursday, March 18, moved into their new and rather crowded home. Because only one structure was complete, space was at a premium. Lillian and Ezra Gilliland, Mina and Thomas Edison, and Marion Edison and her traveling companion likely shared the small upstairs bedrooms. The house also had to accommodate Mina's maid, Louise,[31] and at least two other domestic servants.[32]

Even after the homes were completed, they lacked many of the amenities to which the Edisons and their guests were accustomed. Mina lamented, "No running water, no sewerage, no ice. Tough beef—no other meat—making it almost imperative to have food shipped from the north."[33]

The generator was not installed, so there was no electricity. Further, the detached kitchen provided no protection from the wind. Mina remembered, "There were many times when the bread and other foods were blown right out of [our] hands and carried out of sight."[34]

Wizard without the Light!

Ironically, Thomas Edison, inventor of the incandescent light and electrical systems, illuminated his Fort Myers honeymoon nights with either kerosene lamps or candles. Although electric wires were installed in both the Edison and Gilliland homes, the generator necessary to create the electricity to run them was not operational.[*]

[*] Marjory Stoneman Douglas, "Mrs. Thomas A. Edison, at Home," *McCall's Magazine*, October 1929.

Complicating matters was Edison's daughter Marion's open distain for her new stepmother, who she viewed as "too young to be a mother to me but too old to be a chum."[35] Marion, who was nicknamed "Dot," was only seven years younger than Mina. By contrast, her father was nineteen years older than his bride. The relationship between Mina and Marion would always be contentious.

The same day they moved into their new home, Edison decided it was time to get back to work. Even without a laboratory, the inventor made technical drawings for incandescent lighting and continued to consider long-distance telegraphy for the railroad.

Mina Miller Edison was wise beyond her years. After only three weeks of marriage, she realized that if she wanted to connect with her husband, she would have to do it on his terms. Nearly every day for the next two weeks, she joined him in discussions about future experiments. They even performed an experiment together. Edison hypothesized that shocking an oyster with an electric current would paralyze its shell muscle and force the shell to fly open. The inventor recorded their dismal results: "Dead failure."[36]

Edison, who had been in constant contact with his New York staff, now communicated less frequently. The staff's exaggerated complaints sound like those of a jilted lover: "We haven't heard a word from him. It is three weeks since he married and he has taken no notice whatever of us in all that time. We have written to him; we have telegraphed him. We get no response. He has cut us dead. We ask him questions requiring immediate attention and that is the last of it. We are running the concern without him. He ignores the telegraph and despises the mail."[37]

A few weeks later, Mina's parents came for a post-wedding visit. Their exhausting trip took them by train (an engine and one car) to Arcadia. They then traveled by horse and buggy over rough trails that had no houses for miles. One night they stayed at an abandoned shanty. Since there were no beds, Lewis Miller placed a door on the floor for his wife to sleep on.[38] After a 24-hour journey they finally arrived.[39] Unaware of their ordeal, the newspaper boasted that "it will greatly surprise us if [Mr. Miller] too does not decide that this is a delightful place in which to spend his winters."

When the Millers arrived, the two homes were habitable and the laboratory was nearly finished. The cadres of workers building the homes had departed, leaving the residents in peace and privacy.[40] Edison continued to experiment and made an elaborate plan for Eli Thompson to beautify the grounds of the Edison and Gilliland homes. The plan was an expansion of the map Col. Perkins had made.

Edison's notes demonstrate his growing understanding of the plants and crops of the region. But his knowledge was incomplete. He had no idea what he was undertaking when he declared that "I want to *carry* everything to extreme *excess* down here."

He set the estate on a grid system with symmetrical avenues and focal points balancing the Edison and Gilliland homes. The laboratory, "Summerlin's 'old house,'" and outbuildings were placed to the side. Around the buildings, Edison planned to experiment with various types of grass seed and eventually achieve a luscious green lawn. (This would prove to be a losing proposition until the advent of reliable sprinkler systems.)[41]

On the river side of the property, he proposed ornamental plants like cabbage palms and flowers around the two homes. Perhaps in homage to his incandescent light, a large clump of native bamboo would provide a focal point near the river. He planned orange and grapefruit groves in the corridor between the homes and the road, and Poinciana trees along the road for privacy and shade.

On the other side of the road that divided the property there would be a hedge of lemon and lime trees. Behind the hedge, Edison planned extensive

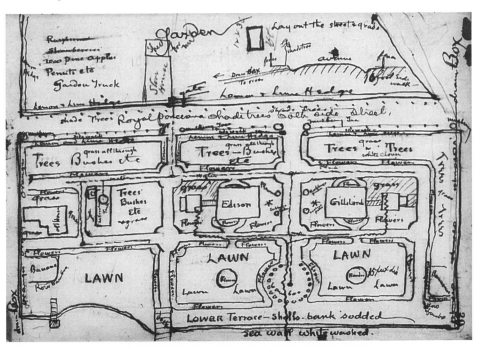

Map 5. Edison's plans for the grounds of his winter home, 1886.
Courtesy Thomas A. Edison Papers, Rutgers University.

truck gardens with a variety of fruits. He wanted strawberries, red and black raspberries, mulberries, gooseberries, and currant bushes. There would be more fruit trees: peaches, mangoes, alligator pears, sapidillas, pomegranates, custard apples, guavas, pear cherries, plums, and apricots. Then there would be nuts: pecans, almond, Brazil nut, English walnut, and filbert trees and peanut plants. There were also experimental crops of castor beans, cotton, and tobacco.

He gave specific instructions to Thompson to protect and care for the plants. He wanted two hives of bees to pollinate them and a fence around the gardens to protect them from roaming cattle. He wanted them to be well fertilized: "We propose to have our grounds the best manured in florida." Further, he told Thompson to put in coconut bales to "hold the manure + prevent it going clear through to *China*."[42]

For weeks, the citizens of Fort Myers had observed the Edisons, Gillilands, and Millers from a distance. In late March, the Fort Myers town elders prevailed upon Edison, and the town's newly formed band performed privately for the Edisons and their guests. On the night before the Edison-Gilliland-Miller party left Florida, the band, which consisted mostly of brass instru-

Daughter on the Honeymoon?

Edison sent a telegram to Mina Miller just days before their wedding, telling her, "Better not send the girl with Mr. Gilliland, but take her with us if agreeable to you[.] They left tonight six train."[*] Many have assumed that "the girl" was his daughter Marion and that the telegram was informing Mina that her stepdaughter was going to accompany them on their honeymoon from Ohio to Florida.

But the girl in question was likely one of Mina's maids. Marion did not attend the wedding in Akron. She stayed with the Gillilands, arriving in Fort Myers on February 25th, just one day after the wedding.[**] Thomas and Mina traveled to Florida alone, except for their servants. Once in Fort Myers, the honeymoon included Marion as well as Ezra and Lillian Gilliland and Lewis and Mary Valinda Miller.

[*] TAE, telegram to MME, February 18, 1886, CEF, EFWE.

[**] Untitled article, *Fort Myers Press*, February 27, 1886. An invoice for the Keystone Hotel states that Gilliland, his wife, and "Misses Johnson + Edison" stayed for three weeks, while "Mr. Edison, wife + Maid" stayed for three days. The invoice was paid on March 23, 1886. ENHS.

ments and a couple of drums, serenaded them. At best, the group's music was amateur. (They had been banned from playing within the city limits a few months earlier.) Yet Mina, who was herself a gifted pianist, complimented them generously, calling their music ethereal.[43]

The weather became warmer and the northern visitors prepared to depart. In the midst of packing, Mina arranged to send a couple of small live alligators to her younger brothers as souvenirs.[44] On March 26, the party headed up the Caloosahatchee, where they met teams of draft animals. The Edisons, the Gillilands, and the Millers then made their way overland to the Florida Southern Railway at Bartow.[45]

Their adventures in Florida were not entirely over. The party stopped at a spring in Bartow. Everyone headed straight for the bathhouse except Edison, who thought that the rickety pier looked unsafe. Sure enough, it fell away, plunging everyone into the shallow bubbling waters. It was a comical sight to see rescuer Edison paddle out in a boat to reach those unable to trudge ashore in the knee-deep water. They all went to a nearby hotel to dry their clothing.[46]

Back in Fort Myers, as life resumed its normal pace, some very exciting rumors started to circulate. The story was so fantastic that it could not be true. But it was true. In August, the *Fort Myers Press* reported that "Mr. Thomas A. Edison has promised to light the town by electricity next winter."

4

Waiting for the Light

"When will Edison light our town?"
—Fort Myers Press

1887–1888

The tone of life in Fort Myers changed in the months after Edison promised to light the town. There was a great feeling of possibility in the air. But preparing the town for electrification was a long struggle. The inventor agreed to supply the generator, but the townsfolk had to pay for the poles and wires.

Money was tight. Taxes were high, and the town had to replace the local schoolhouse, which had recently burned to the ground.[1] Somehow they raised the funds for the equipment. It was ready and waiting for the inventor to arrive.

The townsfolk felt a new confidence as the *New York Tribune* and the *New York Sun* carried stories mentioning Edison's Fort Myers home. Even Florida newspapers, which frequently disparaged competing communities, praised the village on the Caloosahatchee. The *Fort Meade Pioneer* announced that "Mr. Edison is very much in love with his Florida home. He likes the gentle climate of tropical Fort Myers much better than that of Jacksonville and St. Augustine."[2]

But troubling news soon reached the little town. Edison was extremely ill. He had had an operation to remove two abscesses below his left ear.[3] It was reported that he had also developed a cold in the muscles of his chest, which in turn had reached his bronchial tubes. His condition had intensified and affected his heart.[4] A trip to Fort Myers was becoming less likely.

Meanwhile, Mina was having her own difficulties. In addition to her worries about her husband's precarious health, she was concerned about their marriage. In the beginning, it was a novelty for Mina to work at Edison's side in the laboratory. He appreciated her interest in his experiments. But once they settled in back home in New Jersey, everything changed. Within a few months, Mina made entries less frequently in his technical notes. The inventor spent more and more time working away from home. While he was ill, she had to balance the roles of caregiver and gatekeeper for those who kept Edison's business concerns running. On top of it all, she was pregnant.[5]

Compounding Mina's feelings was the daunting prospect of caring for Edison's three children from his first marriage. Eleven-year-old Thomas Jr. and 9-year-old William were wild and generally ill-mannered. Marion, now 14, was a constant worry. After her mother's death, Marion had taken on an adult role, caring for her father when he was sick, running errands for him, and accompanying him to racy minstrel shows and all-male clubs.[6] Marion later commented, "I think I must have been my father's favorite child, probably because I was the oldest and most mature."[7]

From Mina's perspective, Marion's activities and demeanor were dangerous. She feared that if Marion did not learn to take her place in polite society, her future prospects would be dim, despite her father's famous name. With the help of her Miller siblings, Mina tried to reform her stepdaughter, bringing on what Marion would later refer to as the "most unhappy [years] of my life."[8]

February arrived, and Edison's health was still precarious. Although he could barely sit up, his doctors encouraged him to go to Florida.[9] He endured an arduous journey by train and steamer, arriving in Fort Myers on February 15, 1887. The *Fort Myers Press* reported his appearance aboard the steamer *Alice Howard* with a party of eight people.[10] Gilliland was among that group, as were Mina and Marion.[11]

Thanks in part to pleasant weather, Edison's health improved within a few days and soon he was hard at work in his new laboratory. His aim was to install its generator. Once the dynamo was operable, the laboratory as well as the Edison and Gilliland homes would have electricity. In the midst of his labors, Sidney Smith, a reporter from the *New York World*, arrived for an interview.

The reporter wrote, "His face was slightly sunburnt, and he was dressed in dark clothes, white flannel shirt . . . [and] a jaunty tie. A wide-brimmed straw hat crowned the whole and completed the costume." Smith was surprised that Edison appeared so healthy. He said, "I understand from some reports that you have been compelled to seek rest and forego your electrical researches for the present."

Edison's reply was indignant, "Rest! Why I have come down here to work harder, if anything. I will tell you how I rest; I am working on at least six or seven ideas. When I get tired of one I switch off to another."

Smith asked, "Then I [can] say emphatically that you are well?"

"I never felt better in my life. The air here is perfect; the weather, as you see, is beautiful, and the days are a constant succession of blue skies and warm sunshine, and to all this I owe my rapidly returned health."[12]

Edison's hard work was paying off. On March 10, the local newspaper reported that the inventor had successfully illuminated his laboratory with electric light. He re-created the scene for journalist Smith, who reported, "Watching the films of wire inclosed [*sic*] in their little glass cases, forty or more of them being placed in every possible nook and corner, it would seem that they gradually changed color from black to red, gold, and finally burst out to obscure even the brilliant sun of Fort Myers."[13]

A more public display of electric lights occurred on March 27. That Saturday, people from communities along the Caloosahatchee made their way down the path to the Edison and Gilliland estate. As dusk descended, they fixed their eyes on the elegant electroliers in the twin homes. Then, like magic, they began to glow. There was no match, just the flick of a switch.[14] Suddenly, southwest Florida seemed less a rural outpost and more a region ready for a bright modern future.

After the Edison and Gilliland estate had been successfully illuminated, the *Fort Myers Press* asked the logical question: "'When will Edison light our town?' We answer we do not know, but hope to announce the fact in a short time."[15]

Lighting the town was turning out to be more challenging than Edison had anticipated. When the 1886 laboratory delivery was lost in the shipwreck, a duplicate inventory was sent to Fort Myers, but through an oversight, the municipal generator was omitted from the shipment. In January, Edison's employees realized their error and ordered a new generator from the Edison Machine Works in Schenectady, New York, but delivery glitches delayed the dynamo again and again.

In mid-March, Edison's assistant, Charles Batchelor, joined him in Fort Myers. Presumably, he was there to help Edison set up the generator and establish the lighting system for Fort Myers. While they waited for the dynamo, they organized the laboratory, experimented with a new motor design Edison had devised, and made plans for the inventor's New Jersey laboratory.[16]

Time passed and still there was no generator. Edison delved into other projects. He was fascinated with electricity and magnetism and made multiple drawings of pyrogmagnetic or magnocaloric motors for future experiments.[17] Through telegraphed messages, he kept in constant contact with his New Jersey staff, making decisions on domestic and foreign patents and dealing with other legal concerns.[18]

He also found time for fun. Edison acted as host to William Halsey Wood, a New York architect. In 1885, Wood had stayed at the Shultz Hotel shortly after Edison and Gilliland passed through. During his visit, Wood won great acclaim. Using just a rod and gearless reel, Wood had captured a 5-foot 9-inch tarpon weighing 93 pounds. The story made headlines not only in the *Fort Myers Press* but also in the northern papers.[19] Edison admired Wood's fishing success and hoped to catch one himself.

While Edison, Mina, and Marion were in Florida, Mina's father Lewis Miller was at Glenmont, the Edison's West Orange, New Jersey, home.[20] He was spending some time with Edison's sons Thomas and William. Like their older sister, the boys were in great need of instruction. Since their father paid them little attention, Mina had enlisted her father. As the father of eleven children, an inventor, the co-founder of Chautauqua, and a Sunday school teacher, Miller was a ready-made mentor.

In early April, Edison was in his new Fort Myers laboratory up to his elbows in flour. He had an idea that if he crushed rocks that contained ore, he could use large magnets to extract the metal. He constructed a miniature ore-milling machine and experimented, using the flour to simulate iron-ore filings.[21]

Though Edison was working hard and had told a *New York World* reporter that he was completely healthy, in reality, he was far from fit. He had developed another abscess below his ear, which would require an operation.[22] The inventor confessed to one of his northern employees, "I am feeling dizzy in [the] head."[23]

Mina had her own problems. Still tired from pregnancy, she struggled to deal with stepdaughter Marion and worried about the Edison boys. Her husband spent more and more time working, even on vacation in Florida. When Lewis Miller arrived with young Thomas and William a few weeks later, she spoke to him privately. She told him that she felt that she "did not have [Edison's] full affection"[24] and implored him to talk to her husband.

Miller would have ample opportunity to speak to Edison. Mina and Marion left shortly, leaving the Florida estate an all-boys club. Edison, Miller, and the boys decided to go on a camping expedition.[25] The group valiantly battled swarms of mosquitoes and snakes. They even did some hunting. Edi-

Advice from Father

When Mina asked her father to join them in Florida, she hoped he would encourage the inventor to become a better husband and father. During the stay, Lewis Miller formed an easy bond with Edison. His awe of his son-in-law is evident in his letter to Mina. "I have had a better opportunity to get acquainted with Mr. Edison than ever before. The more I see of him the more I am impressed with his greatness and good heart."

In the same letter he told her, "I am convinced that if you will not force a different impression by your apparent feelings that all is not right[,] You can have a delightful home. You have it in your power to make all around you happy and delightfull."* Miller's letter implied that he would no longer act as a mentor to the boys and that he certainly would not lecture his son-in-law. Like a proper Victorian father, Miller put the responsibility of making a happy marriage squarely on Mina's shoulders.

* LM to MME, April 26, 1887, FH001AAA, TAEM161:486, ENHS.

son proved to be a questionable marksman. He succeeded in shooting an alligator, but it was already dead.[26]

Following her departure, Edison did not write to his wife. He talked about her with his father-in-law and doodled her name in various styles in one of his laboratory notebooks, but he did not reply to her frequent letters. Even Marion, who had limited affection for her stepmother, suggested, "I real[l]y think you ought to write her very often if you don't intend having a cyclone soon."[27]

The generator to light the town of Fort Myers finally arrived in mid-April. The newspaper remarked, "As Mr. Edison is very busy and his stay short we have our doubts as to whether he will light Fort Myers by electricity this year or not. They are very busy at present at the laboratory, and can hardly spare the time to put up lamps & c."

It was too late. The ever-optimistic *Fort Myers Press* knew that even the Wizard of Menlo Park could not electrify an entire town in the remaining two weeks of his stay. The editor admitted defeat but added, "However the plant will be put in good season next winter and we'll all rejoice."[28]

On May 4, 1887, Thomas Edison, Ezra Gilliland, Lewis Miller, the Edison boys, and the staff of servants and employees began what was becoming an annual ritual. They packed up their trunks, made arrangements for closing the homes and care of the grounds, and departed. The newspaper reported they would come earlier and stay longer next fall. What none of the parties knew was that everything was about to change.

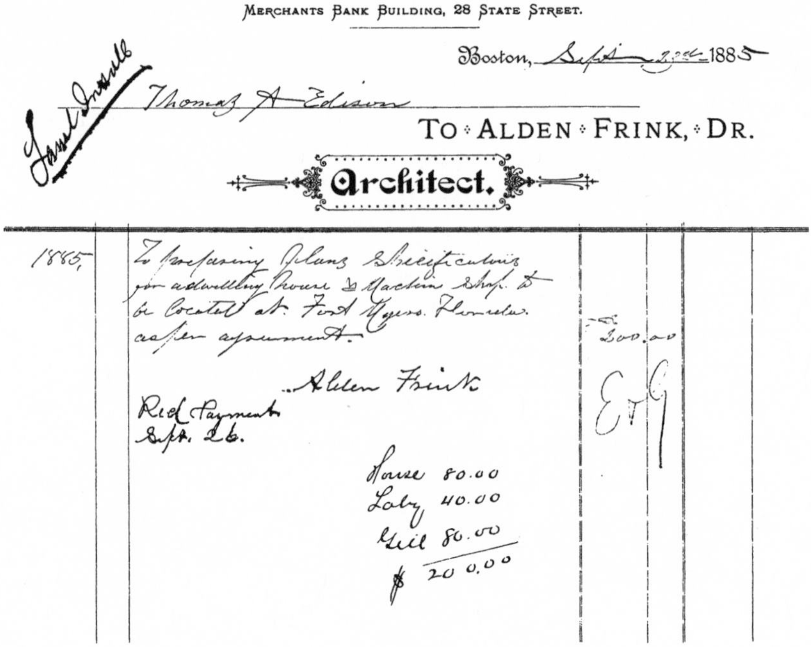

Boston, *Sept 23rd* 1885

Thomas A. Edison

TO · ALDEN · FRINK, · DR.

Architect.

1885	To preparing Plans & Specifications for a dwelling house & Machine Shop to be located at Fort Myers, Florida as per agreement.		200.00
	...Alden Frink		E.J.G
	Rec'd Payment Sept. 26.		
		House 80.00	
		Laby 40.00	
		Gul 80.00	
		$ 200.00	

Figure 1. Invoice from architect Alden Frink, September 23, 1885. *Courtesy Thomas A. Edison Papers, Rutgers University.*

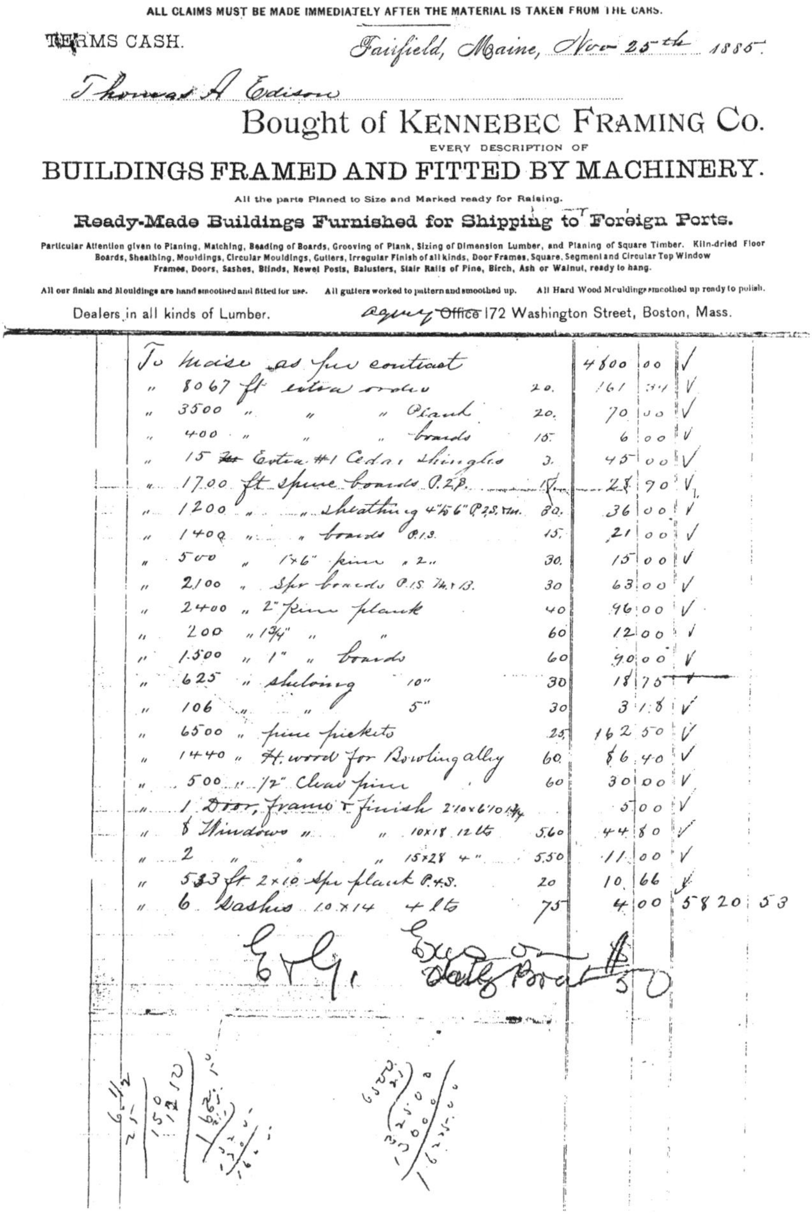

ALL CLAIMS MUST BE MADE IMMEDIATELY AFTER THE MATERIAL IS TAKEN FROM THE CARS.

TERMS CASH.

Fairfield, Maine, Nov 25th 1885.

Thomas A Edison

Bought of KENNEBEC FRAMING Co.
EVERY DESCRIPTION OF
BUILDINGS FRAMED AND FITTED BY MACHINERY.

All the parts Planed to Size and Marked ready for Raising.

Ready-Made Buildings Furnished for Shipping to Foreign Ports.

Particular Attention given to Planing, Matching, Beading of Boards, Grooving of Plank, Sizing of Dimension Lumber, and Planing of Square Timber. Kiln-dried Floor Boards, Sheathing, Mouldings, Circular Mouldings, Gutters, Irregular Finish of all kinds, Door Frames, Square, Segment and Circular Top Window Frames, Doors, Sashes, Blinds, Newel Posts, Balusters, Stair Rails of Pine, Birch, Ash or Walnut, ready to hang.

All our finish and Mouldings are hand smoothed and fitted for use.   All gutters worked to pattern and smoothed up.   All Hard Wood Mouldings smoothed up ready to polish.

Dealers in all kinds of Lumber.   Office 172 Washington Street, Boston, Mass.

To House as per contract			4800	00
" 8067 ft extra order	20.		161	34
" 3500 " " " Plank	20.		70	00
" 400 " " boards	15.		6	00
" 15 Extra #1 Cedar Shingles	3.		45	00
" 1700 ft spruce boards O.2.P.	14		23	90
" 1200 " Sheathing 4 5 6" P.2.S.1m.	30.		36	00
" 1400 " boards O.13.	15.		21	00
" 500 " 1x6" pine 2"	30.		15	00
" 2100 " Spr boards O.1S. 14 x 13.	30		63	00
" 2400 " 2" pine plank	40		96	00
" 200 " 1¾" "	60		12	00
" 1500 " 1" boards	60		90	00
" 625 " sheloing 10"	30		18	75
" 106 " " 5"	30		3	18
" 6500 " pine pickets	25		162	50
" 1440 " H. wood for Bowling alley	60.		86	40
" 500 " 12" Clear pine	60		30	00
" 1 Door frame & finish 2'10 x 6'10			5	00
" 8 Windows " " 10 x 18 12 lts	5.60		44	80
" 2 " " 15 x 28 4"	5.50		11	00
" 533 ft 2 x 10 Spr plank P.4.S.	20		10	66
" 6 Sashes 10 x 14 4 lts	75		4	00	5820	53

Figure 2. Invoice from the Kennebec Framing Company, November 25, 1885.
Courtesy Thomas A. Edison Papers, Rutgers University.

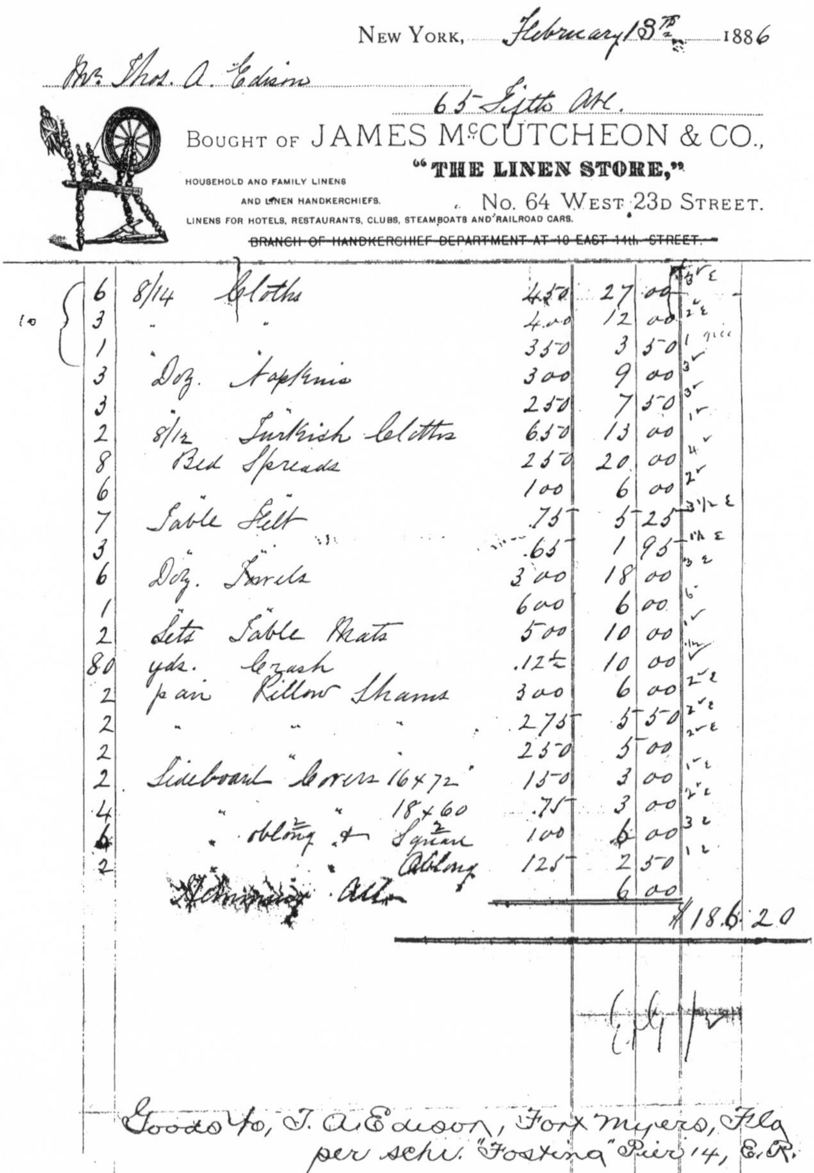

New York, *February 13th* 1886

Mr. Thos. A. Edison

65 Fifth Ave.

BOUGHT OF JAMES McCUTCHEON & CO.,
"**THE LINEN STORE**,"

HOUSEHOLD AND FAMILY LINENS
AND LINEN HANDKERCHIEFS.   No. 64 WEST 23D STREET.

LINENS FOR HOTELS, RESTAURANTS, CLUBS, STEAMBOATS AND RAILROAD CARS.

BRANCH OF HANDKERCHIEF DEPARTMENT AT 10 EAST 11th STREET.

6	8/14	Cloths	4.50	27	00
3	"	"	4.00	12	00
1			3.50	3	50
3	Doz.	Napkins	3.00	9	00
3			2.50	7	50
2	8/12	Turkish Cloths	6.50	13	00
8		Bed Spreads	2.50	20	00
6			1.00	6	00
7		Table Felt	.75	5	25
3			.65	1	95
6	Doz.	Towels	3.00	18	00
1			6.00	6	00
2		Sets Table Mats	5.00	10	00
80	yds.	Crash	.12½	10	00
2	pair	Pillow Shams	3.00	6	00
2	"	"	2.75	5	50
2			2.50	5	00
2		Sideboard Covers 16×72	1.50	3	00
4		" 18×60	.75	3	00
6		" oblong & Square	1.00	6	00
2		" Oblong	1.25	2	50
				6	00
				$186	20

Goods to, T. A. Edison, Fort Myers, Fla
per schr. "Fostina" Pier 14, E. R.

Figure 3. Invoice from James McCutcheon & Company, February 13, 1886.
Courtesy Thomas A. Edison Papers, Rutgers University.

No. 23.

Figure 4. Drawing of electrolier, from the 1883 Edison light fixtures manufactured by Bergmann & Co. *Courtesy Thomas A. Edison Papers, Rutgers University.*

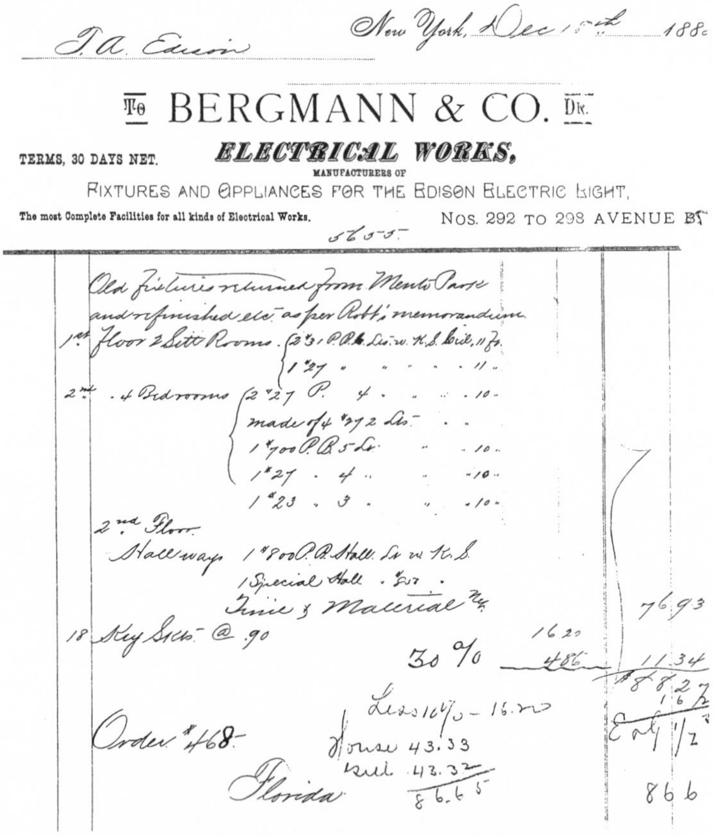
T. A. Edison

New York, Dec 18th 188

To BERGMANN & CO. Dr.

TERMS, 30 DAYS NET.

ELECTRICAL WORKS,

MANUFACTURERS OF

FIXTURES AND APPLIANCES FOR THE EDISON ELECTRIC LIGHT,

The most Complete Facilities for all kinds of Electrical Works.

NOS. 292 TO 298 AVENUE B.

Old fixtures returned from Menlo Park and refinished etc. as per Robb's memorandum

Order #468

Florida

Figure 5. Invoice from Bergmann & Co. for refurbishing of "old fixtures from Menlo Park," which were sent to Florida, December 18, 1885. *Courtesy Thomas A. Edison Papers, Rutgers University.*

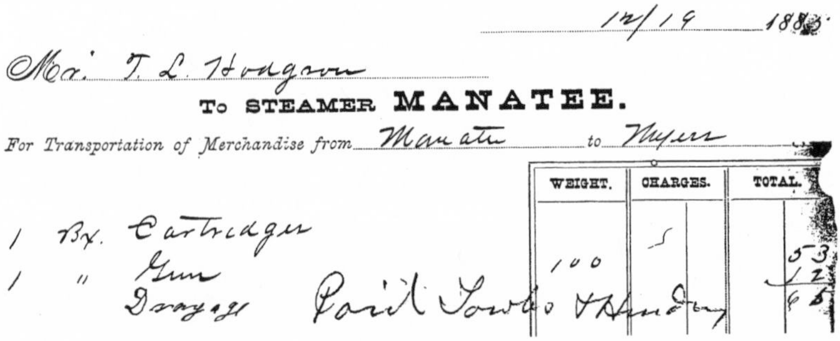
12/19 188

Mr. T. L. Hodgson

To STEAMER **MANATEE.**

For Transportation of Merchandise from Manatee *to* Myers

	WEIGHT.	CHARGES.	TOTAL.
1 Bx. Cartridges			
1 " Gun			
Drayage			

Figure 6. Invoice from the steamer Manatee for transporting materials to Florida, December 12, 1885. *Courtesy Thomas A. Edison Papers, Rutgers University.*

Figure 7. Drawing of an excursion on the Oklawaha, circa 1880s. PR15105.
Courtesy State Library and Archives of Florida.

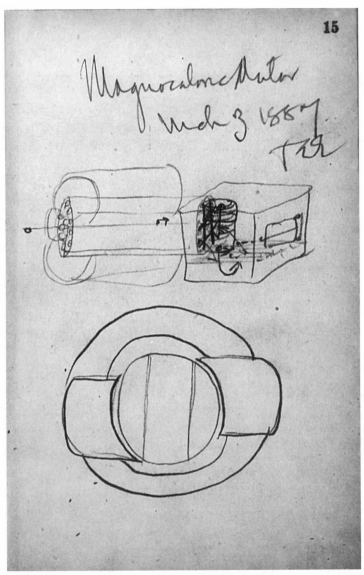

Figure 8. Edison's drawings of a magnocaloric motor, March 3, 1887. *Courtesy Thomas A. Edison Papers, Rutgers University.*

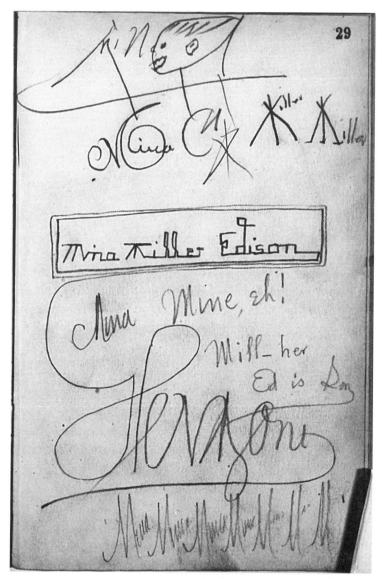

Figure 9. Edison's doodles of "Mina Miller Edison," March 1887. *Courtesy Thomas A. Edison Papers, Rutgers University.*

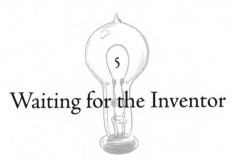

Waiting for the Inventor

"The Crackers are again howling for taxes..."
—William Hibble

1888–1899

It promised to be the perfect year for Edison and Gilliland to make their annual visit to Florida. Their homes were completed, inside and out, and everything needed for a comfortable stay was ready and waiting. The laboratory was fully equipped for Edison's research and for fulfilling his promise to Fort Myers. As the newspaper reported, "There sets the powerful dynamo that is to be used in lighting Fort Myers by electricity, and we believe the lamps, wires and everything that is necessary is on hand."[1]

Edison had also received a tempting invitation from William Halsey Wood, the architect who had caught the record-sized tarpon in 1885. He offered to completely equip the inventor with tackle and gear. Wood assured Edison that he was not merely being polite but was making "a boni-fide request that you accept this invitation with the certainty [that] should you capture a tarpon, it will give me as great a pleasure as it would be to yourself."[2]

It was indeed the perfect year to winter in Florida, but Edison would not make the journey. His wife, Mina, had miscarried, quite late in her pregnancy. Within weeks she was pregnant again and would not risk difficult travel.[3]

Another "baby" helped keep Edison close to home. In a letter, he explained, "I have just completed the erection of a new Laboratory here [in West Orange, New Jersey], which is the largest of its kind in the world. Next winter I intend going to Florida to continue some experiments which I am making there."[4]

People in Fort Myers were disappointed. Not only were the townsfolk gen-

uinely interested in seeing the famous inventor and his famous friends, they
also wanted their electric lights. Fearing that an outbreak of yellow fever the
previous year had kept the inventor away, the health inspector of Lee County
wrote Edison, "There is not the slightest danger now in coming."[5]

Despite their disappointment, the people of the region expected him to
return the following season. They knew him to be an upright man, and they
were sure that he would honor his promise to light up the town. The newspaper predicted, "Fort Myers will be a lively place next winter."[6]

Again in 1889, the great inventor stayed away, as well as the year after that.
In fact, Edison would not grace the sandy streets of Fort Myers, sit on his ve-
randah admiring a stunning tropical sunset, or work through the night in his
Florida laboratory until a new century dawned. The cause was not family or
work but something personal and painful. It was betrayal by his best friend,
Ezra Gilliland.

During the fall of 1887, the relationship between Edison and Gilliland had
shifted. While working on plans for the mass production and marketing of the
phonograph, the two had frequently disagreed. For the first time, Gilliland
had acted more like a partner than a subordinate, which had rankled Edison.
When Gilliland realized that the two would never be true equals, he began to
look for ways to provide for his own economic future. With Edison's approval,
he had secured a deal to acquire venture capital for the phonograph. Without
Edison's knowledge, he had seen to it that he personally profited from the sale,
about $200,000.

Even though the deal earned Edison half a million dollars, the inventor
thought that Gilliland's actions were duplicitous and completely unforgivable.
He vowed to cut all ties with his former friend and by January of 1889 had filed
a lawsuit against him.[7] The *Fort Myers Press* soon reported, "Mr. Gilliland will
not be down this winter. The firm of Edison & Gilliland has been dissolved,
Mr. G. retiring."[8]

Within the space of a few weeks, his close friend, the man who had introduced him to his wife and run the affairs of his business, virtually disappeared.
Yet his presence would linger; Gilliland's house was located just a few yards
away from Edison's. The twin structures were now a painful reminder of the
failure of Edison's most intimate friendship.

Gilliland made the first move concerning the estate, writing to caretaker
William Hibble to ask for a full report of all expenses.[9] Hibble divided all costs
for the homes equally, but soon Gilliland balked at paying his half of repairs to
the long wharf on Edison's property. Hibble reported that Gilliland was not

only planning to vacation in Florida, he was also thinking of building his own dock.[10]

Edison's personal secretary, Alfred Tate, soon conveyed his boss's instructions: "If Mr. Gilliland carries out his intention and goes to Fort Myers, Mr. Edison wishes you not to permit him or any of his party to enter the Laboratory or to go about the premises belonging to Mr. Edison. Neither must any of Mr. Edison's property be used by them for any purposes whatsoever."[11] Gilliland would have to travel to Fort Myers by boat, disembark at the town's dock, and then travel by road to reach his home. More important, by denying access to the laboratory Edison made it impossible for Gilliland to use the dynamo. No dynamo meant no electricity.

Hibble soon realized he did not want to be positioned between the disputing parties. He would have to make a choice. It made more sense to be in the employ of a world-famous inventor than in the employ of an obscure industrialist. "I should feel better satisfied from the fact I was sitting on one stool,"[12] he said, choosing Edison.

Hibble wrote to ask if Gilliland had any interest in the site's windmill. If not, he would cut the pipes. Located on Edison's part of the property, the windmill generated the power that pumped water from the new well, which was also on Edison's property. Without access to the well or the windmill, there would be no water. Tate told Hibble to cut the pipes.[13]

While Gilliland's estate lay without electricity or water, Edison ordered Hibble to perform repairs and regular maintenance on the Edison home, preparing it for his return. Soon Mina, who was now mother to an 18-month-old girl named Madeleine and pregnant with her second child, began to take more responsibility for managing repairs and improvements. In February, she instructed Hibble to paint the house "pretty colors in yellow and white such as they are now painting some of the [West] Orange [New Jersey] houses."[14]

A few months later, indoor plumbing was installed in the Edisons' home. Hibble found the project no easy task. It was likely the first flush toilet in the region, and he had trouble finding "a man who understands the work."[15] He also requested wire mesh screening for the windows and doors. With indoor plumbing and protection from mosquitoes, the home would be very comfortable indeed when the inventor next came to visit.

Unbeknownst to Edison, his Florida estate was under threat of foreclosure. In March of 1890, he received a postcard from one of his Fort Myers neighbors. The *Fort Myers Press* had announced the sale of his estate for $60.53 in back taxes.[16] Previously, the New Jersey staff had been slow in dispatching funds, but not this time. Mina immediately sent Hibble a check for the taxes.[17]

The fact that Edison's property was listed for back taxes is surprising. It appears that he was never informed of the overdue payment. Gilliland was also among the list of delinquent property owners. Perhaps Edison's Fort Myers neighbors were tiring of waiting for him to return and light the town. Caretaker Hibble clearly viewed the actions of his neighbors as suspect. "The Crackers are again howling for taxes (that is about all they can do, collect taxes)."[18] He also complained that "it is their creed to bleed the Yankees, but leave enough blood to keep them alive for future operations."[19]

As the 1890s began, the predictions in the *Fort Myers Press* of Edison's imminent return had become less frequent. Instead, it reported on other visitors to the home. In 1891, 1892 and 1893, Edison's father, Sam, visited with his traveling companion, James Symington. The warm weather invigorated Sam, who was in his late 80s. Symington sent Edison frequent reports about Sam's health. "He will persist in working and sweating six or seven hours in the hot sun every day and has done so for the last eleven days."[20]

Symington's descriptions of Sam's hard work hoeing and weeding Edison's property included frequent complaints that Hibble was not maintaining the estate. In April 1891, he wrote a long letter condemning the caretaker. He charged that Hibble and his wife were enriching themselves at Edison's expense and recommended that the couple be terminated immediately.[21]

Then Symington, who was in his 70s, suggested that he and his family replace the Hibbles. "I have a wife and two daughters. [There are] no smarter neater women in the land." Symington added, "Another most important point. Your father feels that the cold of the Northern winters is too much for him." Symington reported that Sam wanted "to spend every winter of his remaining life in the South. Now if you appoint me here would it not be easy for him to come down and stay with us all winter[?]"[22]

The work of Hibble and his wife was examined and found to be wanting. By June, they had been fired, but Symington was not considered for the position. Instead, Edison appointed his old friend Major James Evans to oversee the estate.[23] Evans in turn hired Ewald Stulpner, a Dutch immigrant,[24] to serve as caretaker and deal with day-to-day maintenance and upkeep of the homes and grounds.[25]

When Sam Edison and Symington returned to Fort Myers in 1892, Symington continued his complaints about the management of the estate. The following year he grew positively irate that Edison had allowed his northern employees to stay with them at the home. William Kennedy Laurie Dickson and Theodore Lehmann arrived in February in 1893. Dickson had worked for Edison in a number of capacities, including in the inventor's motion-picture division. Like many Americans, he had suffered financial losses in the Panic of 1893. A mental breakdown described as "brain exhaustion" had followed. In the warmth and isolation of Fort Myers, he began to recuperate.[26] When he was not relaxing or hunting, Dickson photographed the beautiful estate.

Symington, incensed that Dickson and Lehmann "took possession"[27] of the home, wrote long tirades to Edison. He complained that the men spent too much money and "hired a nigger cook who was not as good a cook as I was which resulted in much waste and I believe in a good deal of theft."[28] Tired of Symington's griping, Edison wrote "No ans[wer]"[29] on the bottom of his letter.

Deep into major projects in iron-ore production and experiments with motion pictures, Edison was not in a position to consider a trip to Fort Myers the following winter. Mina had the responsibility of running Glenmont and caring for their two children, who were now five and three. In 1895, Sam's doctor said he was in no condition to go South.[30] He died the following year.[31]

An Edison was in residence during the winter of 1898. Thomas Edison Jr. arrived in February. The inventor's eldest son convalesced for six weeks after being diagnosed with mental and physical exhaustion.[32] But hunting, fishing, and relaxing were not a cure for young Tom.

The 22-year-old had little education and seemingly less sense. He tried to portray himself as a younger improved version of his father. In a letter to her mother, Mina lamented, "Tom is acting disgracefully again." He had started a lamp company in the Edison name. When his father said that the lamps were no good, Tom had filed a lawsuit. "He is simply being horribly influenced by evil-minded, ignorant persons around him," Mina explained. "Everybody has tried to influence him to do right, but it is wasted."[33]

Tom granted several newspaper interviews during his visit, informing the *Fort Myers Press* that he had patented filaments for incandescent light bulbs. According to Tom, it was not his only accomplishment. He had masterminded a plan to generate electricity from ocean tides and had even invented an airship.[34] Further, he was in the midst of negotiations with his father to purchase the Fort Myers property.[35] There was no truth to any of his claims.

Over the years, it became known that Edison's estate was vacant and a number of people expressed interest in buying it. In April of 1893, he responded to an inquiry with a "no."[36] He received two more offers the following year and responded, "Don't want to sell."[37] But the failure of his iron-ore endeavors and the economic turmoil after the national financial crisis of 1893 put Edison's empire in jeopardy and his future in doubt. Late in 1896 he decided, "I will sell it if I can get my price for it."[38] The inventor received more inquiries but none that were viable. By 1899, he changed his mind again, believing that the Florida property should generate some income. "I will rent my house for $75 per month,"[39] he informed Major Evans.

Meanwhile, the townsfolk in Fort Myers had stopped waiting for Edison's return and pinned their hopes on another northerner. In late 1890, Ambrose McGregor of the Standard Oil Company arrived. He was staying at George Shultz's hotel, renamed Tarpon House, with his son, Bradford. The boy suffered from a chronic illness made worse by New York winters. In February of 1891, Ambrose and his wife, Tootie, had visited Fort Myers and decided to purchase a winter home. The following year they bought Gilliland's property for $4,000.[40]

The McGregors immediately began to update the Gilliland home. They repainted the exterior in a warm yellow with white trim and hired Nick Armeda, whom Edison had met in 1885, to serve as their caretaker. He took advantage of an irrigation system Gilliland had installed and used seaweed compost to create a lush landscape.[41] The well-kept grounds of the McGregor place were in direct contrast to the unkempt weeds at the Edison home.

The McGregors explored the Caloosahatchee on their yacht named *Whim*. All three members of their family caught enormous tarpons, repeatedly breaking the region's records for the largest that year.[42] They also made investments in the region, buying over $150,000 worth of businesses and agricultural land. On what became known as the McGregor Plantation, they planted citrus trees and experimented with rice, coffee,[43] and tobacco crops.[44]

It seemed that Fort Myers was ready to move on from the Edison era in another crucial area. In 1897, A. A. Gardner, the owner of the Seminole Canning Company, which made jellies and preserves from locally grown fruit, decided that the town had waited long enough for electricity. With the support of the local community and the owner of the new Fort Myers Hotel, he installed a 40-horsepower boiler and a 500-light dynamo at his canning factory.[45]

On January 1, 1898, the newspaper reported, "A soft, bright light suddenly appeared in all the houses and stores connected to the electric plant, and for the first time electricity was used as lighting power in Lee county."[46] Curiously,

The Fort Myers Hotel

In January 1898, the Fort Myers Hotel celebrated its grand opening. Owned by New York department store owner Hugh O'Neill, it had forty-five rooms and indoor plumbing and was the first structure in town—after the Edison and Gilliland homes—that was wired for electricity.[*] The hotel's decor was one of relaxed elegance, with pine paneling, tiled fireplaces, red carpets, and wicker rocking chairs.[**]

Meals were taken in the dining room and were served with a flourish. On tables decorated with local shells or bird feathers, an endless procession of appetizers, soups, roasts, local game, punch, desserts, and sweets appeared, each with the appropriate wine or liqueur. Children and nurses and other servants ate in a separate dining room.[***]

Although Fort Myers now had a high-class tourist hotel, the cowboy character of the town remained. The new manager's son remembered an incident that took place shortly after his father arrived:

> There was a merry-go-round in a vacant lot. . . . It was the first one that had ever come to Fort Myers, and the cowboys were deserting the saloons to ride it. It was comical to see the big hard-bitten fellows in their ten-gallon hats, chaps, and spurs, riding the little painted wooden horses round and round to the loud music. When the tired owner wanted to close up, the cowhands started shooting at the organ, so again they went again [and again], and round and round, far into the night.[****]

[*] Grismer, *The Story of Fort Myers*, 144.
[**] Braden, *The Architecture of Leisure*, 306–8.
[***] Abbott, *Open for the Season*, 55.
[****] Ibid., 53.

the front-page article neglected to mention the illumination of the Edison and Gilliland homes over a decade before. It was likely an oversight. Thomas Alva Edison had forgotten his promise to light the town and now the town had forgotten him.

As a new century approached, Fort Myers seemed again destined for

Cow Myth

There is a long-standing myth that when Edison promised to light Fort Myers with electricity, "the village officials turned down the offer because they thought the glass enclosed lights would keep the cattle and chickens awake at night."* History tells us the citizens of Fort Myers were not afraid their cows would lose sleep. They eagerly embraced the new technology and immediately raised money for the equipment. The reason Edison did not provide the service was his long absence, sparked by Gilliland's betrayal.

The myth emerged in the 1940s, when the population of Fort Myers exploded. Some of the children and grandchildren of the town's original settlers as well as newly arrived residents dismissed the region's "cracker" culture as backward. They also held great reverence for Edison. The myth emerged because the later generation learned of the inventor's offer to light the town and assumed Edison's new technology was rejected. They were more comfortable believing that their predecessors were ignorant, than learn the truth; that Edison failed to keep a promise

* Ronald Halgrim, *Edison Centennial 1947, Pageant of Light Program* booklet; Published by the Junior Chamber of Commerce Committee for the Edison Pageant of Light, EFWE.

greatness. The population was approaching 1,000 people. By February 1900 the town had telephone service. After firecrackers, guns, pistols, and even a cannon went off to celebrate the new century, the region received its best news yet. Ambrose McGregor, the county's newest and biggest booster, had replaced John D. Rockefeller as president of Standard Oil.[47] The millionaire was going to be one of the most powerful men in the world. Fort Myers would indeed be famous, and it had nothing to do with the long-absent Thomas Edison.

Fort Myers in the 1890s

In *A Yank Pioneer in Florida*, author Allen Andrews described his impressions of Fort Myers in the 1890s:

> This tropical little village of some four or five hundred inhabitants [was] so dominated by four leading families that nearly everyone belonged to one or the other or was related by marriage. If you were neither a Hendry, Henderson, Langford, or Blount you were "sorta lonesome" in Fort Myers in those days.
>
> There were shelled streets for vehicular traffic and shelled paths for pedestrians, but at night it was well to take the center of the street when strolling [to] avoid stumbling over sleeping cows in store doorways. There was no railroad, transportation being dependent on the daily steamer from Punta Gorda, main excitement of the day being to see the boat arrive and speculate as to who those strange passengers were and what was their business in town.
>
> Nearly everyone had a 'tater patch in his back yard and kept chickens. Taxes were nil. There was plenty of game in the woods, and with millions of fish in the river, if anyone went hungry, he had but himself to blame.[*]

[*] Andrews, *A Yank Pioneer in Florida*, 14.

6

The Wizard Returns

"I got a tarpon! I got a tarpon!"

—Thomas Edison

1900–1904

In Fort Myers, the giddiness of a new century was short lived. On September 30, 1900, Harvie E. Heitman received a distressing telegram at his general store. Their great champion, the man who had brought fame back to Fort Myers, was gone. Ambrose M. McGregor had died of cancer at the age of 57. The newspaper lamented, "The bereaved widow and son have the heartfelt sympathy of the people of Fort Myers."[1]

Back in New Jersey, the Edisons were enduring their own disappointments and overwhelming loss. Thomas Edison's iron-ore enterprise was a complete failure. To make things worse, his son Tom had married a "casino girl" who claimed to be playing the Edison family for "suckers." The marriage ended quickly but outlasted his father's patience. In exchange for money to start a mushroom farm, Tom temporarily relinquished the Edison name and became Burton Willard.[2]

Mina was mother to Madeleine and a son named Charles and was pregnant with her third child when she received news that her younger brother Theodore had been killed. The boy to whom she had sent an alligator in 1886 had volunteered to serve in the Spanish American War. While riding with Roosevelt's Rough Riders, he was shot by a sniper and died on July 8, 1898.[3] Mina gave birth to a baby boy three days later. He was named Theodore.

Mina and the close-knit Miller family barely had time to mourn when her sister, Jane, nicknamed Jennie, died suddenly of heart problems. With Jenny's death, Mina lost a confidant and role model. Her grief was again compounded the following February. Mina's beloved father became ill. As he was being transported to New York for a life-saving operation, his train was delayed in a blizzard. Lewis Miller died from uremic poisoning on February 17, 1899. Mina was at his side.[4]

The Edisons needed to get away. In late February of 1900, Thomas, Mina, 12-year-old Madeleine, and 10-year-old Charles packed their bags for Florida. Six-month old baby Theodore likely stayed with Mina's mother and sisters in Ohio.

The Edisons traveled by train down the East Coast to Florida and then crossed over to the west coast of the state for a trip to Tampa. Thanks to the new modern railroad system established by Henry B. Plant, the journey was a great deal faster and less arduous than before, but it still took many hours; their locomotive stopped every few miles to stock up on wood.[5]

Once in Tampa, the train halted at the porch of Plant's Tampa Bay Hotel,[6] which looked like a Moorish castle, complete with minarets, that had mistakenly been dropped on the sandy Florida soil. Rickshaws transported the family down the long hallway to the registration desk.[7]

The Tampa Bay Hotel, also owned by Plant, presented itself as an upscale tourist establishment providing an oasis of comfort and modernity on the quiet west coast. It also seemed to satisfy the Gilded Age thirst for luxury. Inside were plush reception rooms with tapestries and works of art. It had a stunning rotunda, "French Parlors," and even a great drawing room called the "Jewel Casket" that was decorated with "gems from countries far and near, from times old and new—cabinets from Spain and France, vases from India and Japan, mirrors from Venice, and bronzes from Italy and even from Peru." The hotel's advertisements boasted, "You may even sit in the throne chair of Marie Antoinette, or upon her divan, or at Napoleon's table, while you marvel at the bewilderment of the beauty before you."[8]

The hotel was surrounded by elaborate gardens and orange groves. Since golf had recently become de rigueur for the leisured classes, the Tampa Bay Hotel had its own golf course with 6,800 feet of links and an eighteen-hole course nearby. It also had its own private swimming pool and offered day trips for fishing, beach excursions, and horseback riding.[9]

Although the Tampa Bay Hotel was modern in every sense, the surrounding area was very much rural Florida. About 15,000 people lived in the town that was still run by cattle barons. The streets were mostly dusty dirt roads with an occasional wooden-platform sidewalk. But the town boasted a streetcar system with over twenty miles of track and a modern electrical plant.[10]

In an interview with the *Tampa Tribune*, the inventor declared, "I am not in Florida on business, but merely for the health of myself and family. . . . My intention . . . is merely for pleasure, and to escape the rigors of the winter at home."[11]

During the visit, Edison toured a cigar manufacturing company and the family explored Tampa. Charles and Madeleine likely took a streetcar ride to Ballast Point, which had a large open-air dancing pavilion, a theater, a bathhouse, a restaurant, and amusement attractions. Or for seventy-five cents each, the family might have taken a trip on an excursion boat that left early in the morning from the Jackson Street dock.[12] Mina would have made sure her family stayed away from the more colorful areas of the city, which included gambling houses, saloons, and a red-light district.

From Tampa, the family traveled across the bay to the Bellview Hotel, which had opened just three years before. Like the Tampa Bay Hotel, the Bellview was built by Henry Plant,[13] and to Charles's delight, the railroad was so convenient that the Edisons "got right out of the train and went right into the hotel."[14]

The family had been only there only a short while when the *Tampa Tribune* reported that the inventor was to continue on to Fort Myers. He was planning to rebuild and remodel his laboratory, continue experimenting, and spend at least a month each year in Fort Myers.[15] No one in Fort Myers was particularly surprised that the *Tribune* article was wrong. It had been many years since Edison had been to the region, and few truly expected him.

So they were all the more astounded the following winter. On February 27, 1901, the steamer *H. B. Plant* chugged up the Caloosahatchee River with all her flags flying. She docked in Fort Myers, and the great inventor Thomas Edison stepped onto the worn planks of the municipal pier. After fourteen years, the wizard had finally returned.

Accompanying Edison was Mina, Madeleine, Charles two-and-a-half-year-old Theodore and his nurse. They were joined by the inventor's cousin, Edith Edison, and Mina's sister, Grace Miller. Because the party of eight would be crowded at the Edisons' home, they planned for some of their group to lodge at the Fort Myers Hotel. But the hotel's forty-five rooms were completely booked and the Edisons failed to secure reservations. The tired travelers journeyed south of town to the Edison home. As in 1886 and 1887, they all crowded together and made do.

The group traveled about a mile along Riverside Drive, which was now paved with crushed shell but turned to dirt shortly before it reached the Edison home. The appearance of the estate had changed a great deal since the Edisons' last visits. The two-story house was no longer an earthy green and taupe combination but a somewhat faded yellow with white trim.[16] The grounds around the home in no way resembled the "piles of sand"[17] Mina had formerly described. The fruit trees—mangos, lime, lemon, orange, and grapefruit—were mature and bearing fruit.[18]

Inside, little had changed, with the exception of the addition of indoor plumbing. Short of routine cleaning, the caretakers had not touched the interior of the house. Rather than make do with the primitive kitchen, the Edisons took their meals at the Fort Myers Hotel.[19] It afforded them the opportunity to get to know many of the town's other winter visitors.

Once they had settled in, the Edison family and their guests secured carriages at Harvie Heitman's livery stable[20] and took a drive through town. There had been many changes since Edison's last visit. Of course, there was the impressive Fort Myers Hotel, where royal palm trees had recently been planted. Then, traveling north on First Street, they could see the town's first brick building, Heitman's new store. There were ten streetlights along the main street[21] as well as a number of large stately homes built by wealthy newcomers.[22]

Edison was impressed by the town's progress. "It is the prettiest place in Florida and sooner or later visitors to the East Coast will find it out," he told the *Fort Myers Press*. He also announced his intention to stay a month out of each year.[23]

The Edisons and their guests lost no time in getting acquainted with their neighbors. The manager of the Fort Myers Hotel invited Edison on a fishing expedition up the Caloosahatchee River. One of the guests described it:

Birds by countless thousands hovered over a small island—Indian curlew, lady of the lake, blue crane, egret, white ibis, and others of marvelous plumage.

We passed a picturesque old sugar mill, vast fields of sugar cane, and gleaming orange groves where the dark branches were heavy with gold. Huge alligators, lazily sunning themselves on the banks, slithered into the water and sank without a sound. . . .

Fort Thompson was simply a location. As soon as we tied up at the riverbank the men took their guns and disappeared over the side into the eerie twilight of the jungle, while the ladies took up their fishing tackle—they had no intention of being idle spectators.

As the great red sun dropped over the palms, our sportsmen came trooping aboard with their spoils. A long table stood amidships on the cargo deck and the colored cooks and waiters set out a dinner to warm the heart—venison, wild turkey, ducks, pigeons, quail, snip and fish, and a variety of other good things.

That evening we lounged on the deck listening to an impromptu concert provided by our genial Captain Menge and his crew. After the concert his men set fire to the Spanish moss hanging from the oak and cypress trees along the shore. The sheets of flame racing from tree to tree were reflected in the dark mirror of the river. The silence was broken only by our gasps of admiration and the cries of the jungle birds startled from their resting places.[24]

On another expedition, the entire Edison family went up the river on the steamer *Anah C.*, again captained by Conrad Menge. Then they took a journey down the river to the Gulf of Mexico and beautiful Sanibel Island to bathe in the sea, gather shells, and fish.[25]

Later that month, Mina and Madeleine were invited to a ladies' luncheon hosted by Elizabeth Floweree,[26] the wife of a Montana cattle magnate turned local citrus baron. The Edisons and Flowerees had known each other for years. The Flowerees had briefly stayed at the Edisons' Fort Myers home in August 1899 while their own $20,000 mansion was being built downtown.[27] The luncheon gave Mina an opportunity to connect with the wives of the new community leaders.

Another influential visitor lived only a few yards from the Edisons. Tootie McGregor and her son Bradford owned the former Gilliland house, which she called "Poinciana."[28] The two families met frequently when they were both in residence for several weeks in March of 1901. They ate their meals together at the Fort Myers Hotel,[29] and both families attended the hunting and fishing expedition up the Caloosahatchee.[30]

During the month of March, Edison largely abandoned his work to concentrate his energies on catching a tarpon. The newspaper anticipated his success: "It will be a struggle between giants and the vanquished Silver King will have the great satisfaction of realizing that it took a pretty big man to do him."[31] But the celebration was premature. Edison came back empty-handed.

The Edisons hosted their own cruise on the *Suwanee*, a steamer captained by Fred Menge, inviting many of their new friends from the Fort Myers Hotel.[32] Once at their destination on the Caloosahatchee, the guests shot at a variety of birds and an occasional alligator and hauled in eighty-three fish. Edison caught a 30-pound channel bass, some big amber jack, and one pilot fish. He had several tarpon strikes but could not land the fish.[33]

As the Edisons and their guests packed up to return north in late March, the newspaper's editor, Philip Isaacs, prevailed upon the inventor to provide him with a scoop, "anything to give out to the public[. It] would be nice to have it come from Ft. Myers." After flatly refusing, Edison reconsidered. He told the *Press* that he had invented a battery that the patent office had at refused to grant rights to because "it was said that the idea was impracticable and could not be carried out. But Edison showed that it was practicable and finally succeeded."

The new Edison battery was only half the weight of other storage batteries. He claimed that his battery could hold a charge for a week or a month. Isaacs was thrilled. After printing the information on its own pages, the *Press* telegraphed Edison's quotes to the *New York Journal*, which immediately printed the story.[34]

The Edison family attended a final dinner at the Fort Myers Hotel. The guests, indeed the whole town, now felt connected to them. The newspaper reported that "Prof. Edison and his interesting family have won the hearts of all the people who have come in contact with them." Unlike previous years, there was an assumption that they would return. They left "with regrets, but with many expressions that the acquaintance formed this season would be renewed next year."[35] On March 25, the Edisons and their guests chugged away on the steamer *St. Lucie*.

Edison Appreciated a Practical Joke

The Edisons often dined at the Fort Myers Hotel. On one of these occasions, the hotel owner's young son, Karl Abbott, found a large dead spider, tied it to a string, and went off to cause mischief. As he described it:

> Peering over the banister and down into the lobby, I was surprised to see . . . Mr. Edison [who] was in evening dress . . . his hand cupped to his ear, listening to Father. . . . I lowered the spider slowly until it reached the level of their heads. I saw Father make a pass at it, and I yanked it up a few feet, then let it down again. I heard Father cussing as he rolled up a newspaper and went after the monster in earnest. They both looked up and saw me. Mr. Edison's mild features wore a broad grin, but the look on Father's face sent me skittering down the back stairs.*

* Abbott, *Open for the Season*, 55–56.

Two months after the departure of the Edisons, a series of fires threatened Fort Myers. In the space of two weeks, two houses were burned to the ground and the Baptist Church was badly scorched. If there had been a strong wind, the entire town would have been lost. In response, the town leaders assembled a volunteer fire department and started raising money for equipment.[36] Edison pledged fifty dollars. The newspaper reported that the donation "goes to show that Mr. Edison is deeply interested in the welfare and advancement of our pretty little city."[37]

During the fall, Fred and Conrad Menge christened a new 89-foot stern-wheel boat. The magnificent steamer was named *Thomas A. Edison* in honor of their friend the inventor. It instantly became a tourist attraction. The newspaper noted, "To see the Wizard's new home, take a trip on a steamer named after him on one of Florida's most entrancing rivers, will be a treat for every visitor to this portion of the State."[38]

As the 1902 winter season approached, Mina Edison tried to convince her mother to join the family in Florida. Mary Valinda Miller, who had not seen the estate since the primitive days of 1886, was understandably reluctant. Although it now had electricity, running water, and plumbing, Mina admitted that compared to what her mother was accustomed to, "things are very crude and [accommodations have a] camping out effect."[39] In the same letter, Mina also referred to the home by its new name. It was called Seminole Lodge in homage to the Seminole Indians who lived in the region.

In late February, the family again made the journey south. Charles recounted the challenge of getting to their winter home. "There was no railroad [that] ran in there. The railroad stopped at Punta Gorda. Then you had to take an old stern-wheel riverboat and go eighty miles further around through Charlotte Harbor and then back up the Caloosahatchee to Fort Myers."

The roundabout journey did have its advantages. "It was a wonderful trip, that eighty miles, because there was just a world of bird life, and porpoises all over. Sometimes a porpoise would get right ahead of the ship, right at its bow. Then you'd see all kinds of ducks and cranes and pelicans—and I mean thousands of them!"[40]

On March 3, 1902, the steamer *H. B. Plant* arrived in Fort Myers. The local newspaper was pleased that the Edison group included one of Mina's sisters and her mother.[41] Mina had indeed convinced her mother to rough it in the wilds of Florida.

Edison went fishing a number of times that winter. Sometimes he invited friends and other times he went out alone on his new naphtha launch, a gasoline-powered boat. The inventor caught buckets of fish and was said to be as happy as "a kid playing hooky from school out a-fishing,"[42] but again he had no success with tarpon.

The Edison children loved the freedom of their southern home. Their neighbors gave them space and the family felt less scrutinized by a social elite. Madeleine remembered, "We were allowed to do more in Ft. Myers than any other place." Though her father did not approve of her riding horses, he relented in Florida. "I did ride astride, which he didn't think was so bad."[43]

That winter, the Edisons hosted a party at Seminole Lodge, inviting the manager of the Fort Myers Hotel and other area residents and tourists. Tootie McGregor did not attend, as she had left earlier in the season. Her home adjoining the Edisons' home brought back too many memories of her departed husband. She sold it and stayed at the Fort Myers Hotel.[44] She also mothballed the *Whim*.[45] Her grief was soon compounded. Her only son Bradford died in September.[46] In a period of two years, she lost her entire family.

The Edisons stayed at Seminole Lodge for about a month. Before leaving in early April, Mina and Thomas put together plans to improve and update the property. The financial difficulties Edison had suffered around the turn of the century were a thing of the past. He was out of the iron-ore business, and his sound-recording and motion-picture concerns were doing quite well. The couple was now free to make a substantial investment in the estate.

Over the next few months, Mina arranged to update nearly every room with paint and wallpaper. The plumbing was upgraded and a second bathroom was installed. The redesigned kitchen included a new lined sink and another refrigerator. Porches were widened and wicker furniture ordered. Part of the porch was screened so the Edisons could sit outside free from swarms of mosquitoes.[47]

A new well had been drilled in May of the previous year.[48] Although the water was not drinkable, it supplied a new sprinkler system.[49] The Edisons finally had a lawn. Caretaker Ewald Stulpner added flowering plants and shrubs to the "already pretty grounds."[50]

Because the steamboat channel in the Caloosahatchee River was some 1,200 feet from shore, the Edisons contracted with T. B. Campbell, owner of the Fort Myers Lumber Mill, to extend the length of their pier by 300 feet. Another firm built a boathouse to store Edison's new naphtha launch.[51]

The house and grounds were ready when the Edisons arrived on February 21, 1903. Thirteen-year-old Charles and 5-year-old Theodore accompanied their parents to Florida, but 15-year-old Madeleine stayed at her northern school.[52] Frederick Ott, one of Edison's laboratory workers from New Jersey and a trusted friend, accompanied the family.[53]

The group had barely arrived when Edison headed to his boat.[54] Over the next few weeks, he ventured out on the *Mina*, as the launch was named, almost daily and caught black bass and sea trout,[55] but still no tarpon.

On March 2, an explosion at the Edison Portland Cement Company grinding plant in Stewartsville, New Jersey, killed eight workers. A week later, W. S. Mallory, vice-president of the company, arrived in Fort Myers to give the inventor a personal report of the damage. Though the situation was in hand, Edison decided to leave two weeks earlier than planned.[56]

The next season, just before the Edisons' arrival, Southwest Florida celebrated the arrival of the one thing that could truly bring prosperity to the region. On February 20, 1904, the last railroad track was laid from the town of Punta Gorda to Fort Myers. It was a celebration unlike any other. The *Fort Myers Press* reported, "Our people practically took control of the train. . . . Mrs. J. E. Foxworthy and Misses Dot Stout and Bessie Thorp held up the engineer, M. E. Moye took charge of the bell rope and the whistle cord and kept bell and whistle going. Col. E. L. Evans was on the ground and fired a salute with his cannon."[57]

Map 6. Atlantic Coast Line Railroad, circa 1904

Ironically, passengers were not yet able to travel as far south as Fort Myers. Rails were laid on both sides of the river, but there was no railroad bridge spanning the Caloosahatchee until May 10, 1904.[58] The revelers did not care.

Three days before the big celebration, Frederick Ott arrived in Fort Myers. He had two electrical projects to complete before his boss arrived. Edison was bringing a brand-new launch that was powered by an Edison electric battery. At first, Ott intended to use the town's electric plant to charge the boat's battery, but there may not have been enough power. Instead, he fired up the 17-year-old generator in Edison's laboratory.[59]

Once this was accomplished, Ott went to work updating the wiring in the home and lighting the grounds and dock. The newspaper reported, "At night the Edison home presents a beautiful appearance with electric lights showing the fountain in place, and reflecting on the giant bamboos and other trees and shrubs. At the head of the dock is placed a one hundred candle power light, which shows for a great distance up and down the river."[60] Although the lights were beautiful, Mina's mother expressed concern: "I fear it will frighten the Birds for a while anyway. . . . They may come back when used to it."[61]

Everything was ready when the Edisons arrived aboard the steamer *St. Lucie* on February 25, 1904. Thomas and Mina and their three children arrived along with Mina's sisters and a niece. After settling in, Edison checked on his older launch, the *Mina*. Although it was gasoline powered, he had installed battery-powered lighting for night fishing the previous year. Edison claimed that even after a year of dormancy, his battery was ready for instant use.

He also checked on his new launch, the *Reliance*. It was a stunning 36-foot vessel that had cost an astounding $2,250, or the wages of the Edisons' caretaker for almost four years.[62] It had been sent to Punta Gorda by rail and then had been motored to the Edisons' dock. Edison claimed that the *Reliance*'s battery could power the boat seventy-five miles before recharging and that "all that is necessary is to touch a button to start, stop, back or go slow."[63]

Edison took the *Reliance* out for fishing trips many times during the month of March. He found the electric launch a pleasure to pilot and the perfect vessel for a quiet day of fishing. But he knew that he would never feel fully accomplished as an angler until he caught a tarpon. Finally, on March 25, 1904, the inventor achieved his goal.

That morning, he was about to start out when he realized he did not have enough mullet for bait. He gave his son Charles one fish and told him to stay behind in a little cedar rowboat to catch more. Edison and Ott traveled up the river. A few hours later, Edison got a bite. After a struggle, he landed a 40-

pound tarpon. Edison and Ott headed back to the dock with the launch's flags flying. As his son Charles remembered, "Father [was] standing on the bow and laughing at me as he shouted, 'I got a tarpon! I got a tarpon!'"

But Charles told his father to look in his own little boat. In his absence, the 14-year-old, with only one fish for bait, had landed a 100-pound tarpon. Edison was totally dejected and instructed Ott to throw his fish overboard. But Ott, usually an obedient employee, politely refused. It was his boss's first tarpon. The two fish were mounted and placed side by side on the porch of Seminole Lodge. Years later Charles remembered, "Father—in a friendly way—[was] always chagrined that I had beaten him. It was a family joke for years."[64]

7

Transformations and Torments

*"The PRESS would make a suggestion . . . that the name
of Riverside avenue be changed to Edison avenue."*

—*Fort Myers Press*

1905–1913

Thomas Edison's health declined during the winter of 1905. He underwent
a dangerous and experimental operation for mastoiditis, an infection of the
bone behind the ear. Although he recovered, the surgery worsened the inventor's already severely impaired hearing.[1] Between the illness and the pressing
responsibilities of producing large-scale batteries, a visit to Florida was out of
the question.

During the time they would have been in Florida, Thomas and Mina Edison made plans to expand Seminole Lodge. The space was far too small for
the family and guests. Architectural drawings were commissioned to double
the size of the house and add two bedrooms. But Mina was concerned that a
major addition would alter the character of Seminole Lodge. In a letter to her
brother, she wrote that it might be "better to let well enough alone." She feared
that although the addition would be fun, "it doubles everything and it might
make the place a burden instead of a comfort."[2]

In the meantime, Tootie McGregor returned to Florida. Five years after the
death of her husband and three years after her son's passing, she had again
found love. The *Fort Myers Press* reported that she had married General M.
O. Terry, a surgeon from Utica, New York. Mrs. Tootie Terry, as she was now
called, could not wait to share the wonders of the Caloosahatchee region with
her new husband. They honeymooned in Southwest Florida.[3]

The Terrys were well suited. With a new life ahead of her, Tootie took her
yacht *Whim* out of dry dock,[4] and soon she and her new husband were enjoying

day trips. They went to the islands of Sanibel and Captiva and up the Caloosa-hatchee River. Tootie also continued investing in the region, bankrolling Harvie Heitman's new hotel, called the Bradford Hotel in honor of her son. With her new husband as a partner, she also continued to oversee her agricultural plantation and made other land and commercial investments in the region.[5]

As the 1906 winter season approached, Edison was finally healthy and ready to travel. Mina, however, was reluctant to make the journey. Perhaps it was the ordeal of making logistical plans, organizing, and packing and the physical discomforts of the long trip by train. In a letter to her mother and sister, she complained, "Florida is hardly worth the trouble with such a warm winter."[6]

Fortunately, the journey to Seminole Lodge was less demanding than it had been in previous years. The Atlantic Coast Line Railroad now traveled directly to Fort Myers. The Edisons and their guests could remain in a comfortable passenger car until the train stopped across from the court house in downtown Fort Myers.[7]

Every year Mina worried about the fact that her children missed weeks of school while they wintered in Florida. Governesses could travel with them, but Madeleine was attending Oak Place School, a small girls' preparatory school run by two of her aunts at Mina's childhood home in Ohio. Mina talked with her sister Grace, who was the administrator. Grace approved a class trip to Florida for Madeleine and four other girls. Charles would attend classes with them.[8]

On February 28, the Edisons and their guests arrived in Fort Myers on the noon train.[9] Because Seminole Lodge was too small to house them all, the schoolgirls and their teachers lodged at the Fort Myers Hotel. The remainder of the Edison family stayed at Seminole Lodge.[10]

Madeleine's guests wrote glowingly about their Florida adventure. Mina's mother received letters at her home in Ohio and reported, "We get very good and cheerful words from the different ones that are with you or at the Hotel."[11] Classes were held in different locations every day. They met at the Fort Myers Hotel, at the end of the Edison dock, and even on the Menges' steamships.[12]

The Oak Place students experienced the wilds of inland Florida on a trip to Lake Okeechobee. The Edison family hosted a five-day steamship journey up the Caloosahatchee on the *Suwanee*. Captain Fred Menge steered them up the length of the river, passing the tiny towns of Olga, Alva, and LaBelle. Along the way, Mina gave the girls a birding lesson, pointing out a long-billed curlew, an everglades kite, and a turkey vulture. At Lake Flint, the girls marveled at grebes, mallard ducks, ibises, herons, and bitterns.[13]

They passed orange groves and small backwater settlements. Some stretches, canals dug by Hamilton Disston some twenty-five years before, were straight, while others twisted and turned through live oaks draped in a curtain of Spanish moss. The *Suwanee* crossed tiny Lakes Flint and Bonnet and the larger Lake Hicpochee. Finally the waters opened to Lake Okeechobee. The *Fort Myers Press* described the reaction of the students: "For once the young people seemed subdued by the indescribable feeling that comes over one, unlike that felt at sea, to find yourself out of sight of land on the Okeechobee."[14]

Captain Menge steered them across the lake to Taylor's Creek, where the steamer was surrounded by majestic cypress trees. Their boughs hung so low that the passengers on the upper deck had to duck to keep from being swept overboard. Then it was off to the mouth of the Kissimmee River and later to Fish Eating Creek.

On the return trip, the placid weather and sunshine gave way to an "ugly mood" of Mother Nature. A great storm rose up across the lake, churning its waters and tossing about the *Suwanee* and her passengers. Captain Menge kept a steady hand and guided his charges home. When they arrived safely at the Edisons' dock, the girls sang a song in honor of their captain, who blushed profusely. It was followed by three cheers for their genial hosts, Thomas and Mina Edison.[15]

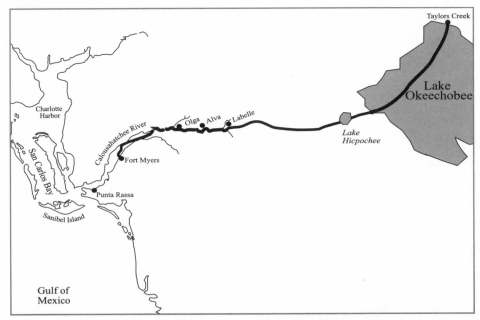

Map 7. The Edisons' journey to Lake Okeechobee, 1906

Ode to Captain Menge

Each winter the Edison family explored southwest Florida on one of
the Menge brother's vessels. Their appreciation for this service is evident in this poem penned by Madeleine

> Way down upon the Suwanee house boat,
> Far, far away,
> Right in the middle of a jungle
> Whiling the hours away
>
> Everywhere we roam
> How glad we are we're not in Akron
> Here's to the Old Folks at Home
>
> Rah! Rah! Rah
> Ma and Pa
> What's the matter with Ma and Pa
> They're allright
> Who's allright?
> Ma—Ma—Ma
> Pa—Pa—Pa
> Rah—Rah—Rah
>
> Captain Menge, Captain Menge
> You deserve a laurel wreath
> Steered us thro' the saw-grass teeth
>
> Captain Menge—Captain Menge, Captain Bonny
> Of the Suwanee
> Captain Menge
>
> We have got to say good-bye
> See it almost makes us cry.*

* Undated, unsigned poem in Madeleine Edison's handwriting. Original in the collection of the CEF; copy obtained through the Edison Papers Project.

Sadly, the pristine wilderness the Edisons and their guests experienced was changing and would be entirely altered in a few years. A new governor, Napoleon B. Broward, announced that "the Glades must be reclaimed for the people."[16] He organized a mammoth dredging and engineering project to create a cross-state waterway.

No more would live oaks, magnolias, hickories, or willows reach their branches across the river. Twists and bends in the river were ironed out, made straight and efficient. Soon even the appearance of the Caloosahatchee waters changed. Sand and humus from the interior of the state was carried down the river. The once sandy bottom and crystal-clear water became black, silty, and murky.[17]

After returning from their voyage up the Okeechobee, the Edisons and their guests took a quick trip aboard the *Suwanee* to Sanibel Island. They landed at the lighthouse, where they swam and fished from the sandy beach. On the way back they stopped at Punta Rassa. George Shultz, who had changed the name of his hotel to Tarpon House, was there to greet them. They feasted on fresh oysters in the hotel dining room. Then the satisfied and sunburned tourists journeyed happily up the river to Fort Myers.[18]

Mina hosted a 4 o'clock tea at Seminole Lodge on March 26.[19] The partygoers were friends and guests of the Fort Myers Hotel whom the Edisons had met during meals at the hotel's dining room. Tootie McGregor Terry was among them. It must have been uncomfortable for Tootie to be so close to her former home, Poinciana. R.I.O. Travers and his wife, Julia, now owned the house.

The Terrys and the Edisons shared a common vision for Fort Myers and the Caloosahatchee region. They agreed on the need for good roads, a clean waterfront, and other modern amenities but stressed that the improvements should not alter the character of the town. Their conversations at events such as Mina's tea would be the basis of mutual charity work and activism for years to come.

As the Edisons' visit was winding down and they prepared to depart, Thomas and Mina learned that the Travers, the owners of Gilliland's former home, were interested in selling. If they bought the property, they could double their space without new construction or major renovations. The second house would also provide real privacy. But if Edison showed interest, the real estate agent would be sure to tell the Travers to sell it at a high price.[20] Edison asked Harvie Heitman to arrange the deal,[21] and what a deal it was. The Edisons bought the former Gilliland estate for $4,850. Travers had purchased it for $7,000 just four years before.[22]

On April 8, after a two-month stay, the Edisons, Madeleine, Madeleine's classmates, and the family's staff began the journey northward. The *Fort Myers Press* commented, "The Edisons have taken a more lively interest in the social life of our town, and it has been a pleasure to have the famous inventor and his family with us."[23]

Spring, summer, and fall passed. As the Edisons planned for their next winter trip, sad news arrived from Southwest Florida. There had been a fire at Tarpon House on December 30. The entire hotel, including $2,000 in improvements, had been lost. George Shultz and his wife had escaped the flames with nothing but their nightclothes. The hotel, the Shultz's home, and their belongings had been insured for only $1,000.[24] But Shultz was resilient. In a matter of months, he had put together plans for a new hotel and was seeking investors. Edison was one of them.[25]

The Fort Myers Hotel, which was now called the Royal Palm, was in another kind of peril. It had changed hands twice since the turn of the century. The new owner could not support the hotel's daily operations and had closed its doors. Tootie McGregor came to the rescue. She purchased it and made a fifty-room addition.

Meanwhile, improvements were also taking place down the river at the Edison estate. As soon as Edison attained clear title to the former Gilliland house, he ordered manager Ewald Stulpner to take down the fence between the two homes. Then he had the newly purchased home's verandas widened to fourteen feet to match its twin.[26] The dock was also lengthened. Later, a large pavilion, exactly like one at the Royal Palm Hotel, was built at the end of the dock.[27]

The Edisons arrived in Fort Myers via a private railroad car in 1907[28] about two weeks after the inventor's 60th birthday. Charles and Madeleine were away at school, but 8-year-old Theodore accompanied them, along with Mina's brother Ira and his family. The Edisons and their guests went fishing and exploring in the battery-operated electric launches. Of course Edison puttered in his laboratory. Out of curiosity, he performed experiments to examine the elements in the local soil. Then he analyzed the chemical components of hyacinths, plants that clogged the riverbanks.[29]

During the winter of 1907, Mina and Thomas Edison began to take a more active role in the Fort Myers community. They invested $250 in a local country club.[30] At a meeting of the Woman's Community Club, Mina presented a check for $120 for the establishment of a town library.[31] Most significantly, on April 4, Edison wrote a letter to the town:

Chapter 7

TO THE TOWN AUTHORITIES OF FORT MYERS:

GENTLEMEN:—If it is agreeable to the town I will have royal palms planted on both sides of the road from Manuel's Branch creek to the end of Riverside avenue in the town, erect proper protection crates, furnish fertilizer and humus for one year from the time of planting, and make any necessary renewals of plants for two years; providing, the town will permit them to be located at the most favorable position along the road, a little out of the ditch toward the road, and care for the trees and crates after expiration of the periods mentioned. Should the town accept I will at once endeavor to procure the plants.

Yours respectfully,

THOMAS A. EDISON[32]

The town council immediately accepted the inventor's offer and appointed Harvie Heitman coordinator. The generosity of the gesture was not lost on the *Fort Myers Press*, which estimated the cost at about $2,500. In appreciation of what it called a "princely offer," the newspaper suggested that the name of Riverside Avenue, the road that passed through the Edison property, be changed to Edison Avenue.[33]

As the Edisons and their guests departed in late April, the family felt that they were truly contributing to the beautification of the town. Unfortunately, like Edison's offer to light the town, the palm offer became an embarrassment. Captain W. H. Towles contracted to buy the trees from Cuba, but a yellow-

Alligator Invaders!

After a visit to Fort Myers, young Theodore Edison returned home to New Jersey with five baby alligators. He kept them in a tub of water under a low-spreading tree near the house. One summer afternoon, while Mina was having a tea in the Glenmont conservatory, Theodore decided show his pets to the guests. Unfortunately, he was unable to contain all the 'wrigglers.' They slithered out of his arms and under the table. The guests were suitably alarmed!"*

* Baldwin, *Edison: Inventing the Century*, 291.

fever quarantine forced him to find trees in the Everglades and through local nurseries. The town did not adequately care for the trees as promised, and Towles had to replace those that died. Towles spent $3,993.55 but was repaid only $1,500 by Edison.

Edison felt he had fulfilled his end of the bargain. It was not his fault that the palms were so difficult to acquire or that it was so difficult for the town to keep them alive. Towles complained publicly in newspaper, which responded in his support "we heartily endorse Mr. Towles position." In order to smooth the waters, they suggested a compromise whereby the town council would pay Towles the money owed him, but "if Mr. Edison desires to reimburse the council and complete his gift to the city, that is a matter of his own consideration."[34]

The situation was embarrassing to Mina. In the end, Edison did not reimburse the city, but in 1913 the couple donated 250 young royal palms to replace the trees that had died over the years. Even after the situation was resolved, the relationship between the town and the Edisons remained somewhat strained. Riverside Avenue, which bisected the Edison property, would soon be renamed, but not after the inventor.

Tootie McGregor Terry heard about the palm ordeal while working with the Edisons on a seawall project.[35] So when she offered to fund road improvements in 1912, she had a lawyer spell out two conditions: Riverside Drive was to be renamed for her first husband, Ambrose McGregor, and cattle would no longer be allowed to roam freely on the road. The city council eagerly made motions to accept her offer but conveniently forgot about the cattle.[36] Free-roaming cows had been banned from the city limits since 1909, but enforcement was lax.[37]

From 1908 to 1910, Mina renovated and unified the former Gilliland house into the larger Edison estate. She hired the New York firm of Proctor & Company to produce design schematics for the space. She selected, ordered, and coordinated the installation of French doors, new cabinetry, wallpaper and curtains.[38]

An overwhelmed Harvie Heitman directed the actual work in Fort Myers. In addition to managing his store and hotel and sitting on the city council, it was his job to direct the Edison's caretaker, Ewald Stulpner, and labor crews. At one point, a large shipment of materials arrived from New York with no installation instructions. In a letter to Proctor & Company, Heitman tactfully requested, "If possible, won't you send us some more detailed information or specifications of this work? You[,] as architects, must know that it is

Traveling in Style

In 1908, the Edisons traveled to Florida aboard a private Pullman car called the *Pilgrim*. Thanks to prior arrangements with the Pennsylvania Railroad Company, the car carried the following supplies:

> Supply (large) of Poland Water. Chicken. Squab. Lamd [*sic*] Chops. Sirloin Steak. Pancakes. Bacon. Oranges. Grapefruit, Pineapple. Sweet and Irish Potatoes. Spinach (the spinach to be well washed) String beans. Green peas. Supply of all sorts of pies. Assorted Tarts. Bread and Rice Pudding. Green Olives. Good Chese [*sic*]. English breakfast tea. Best Mocha and Java Coffee. Two Dozen bottles ginger ale. . . . All fresh vegetables as far as possible; . . . and no canned goods.*

* Eastern Passenger Agent, Pennsylvania Railroad Company, to J. T. Rogers, Care National Phonograph Company, March 12, 1908, ENHS.

almost impossible to do this work correctly with the little information you have given us."[39]

Next, the exterior of the houses was painted a sedate gray with white trim, green shutters, and painted red roofs.[40] To unify the buildings, Mina had a wooden pergola built between them. Soon it would be covered with flowering vines, providing a breathtaking arbor. But the loveliness of the passageway was somewhat diminished on rainy days when the Edisons had to dash between the homes to avoid being drenched.

Once Seminole Lodge was in shape, the Edisons had one more major project. In 1909, the Edison children spent so much time swimming in the Royal Palm Hotel pool that Thomas Edison decided he needed one of his own.[41] The following year, he hired the firm of W. R. Wallace, which had built the hotel's pool.[42] The Edison pool was an engineering challenge. It was located so close to the river that Wallace had to perform excavation and foundation work and reinforce it with woven wire and metal.[43]

The original estimate for the pool was for $655, but with the additional work to ensure a safe infrastructure, the final bill settled out at $1,110.[44] Still smarting over the palm offer, Edison refused to pay, saying that if Wallace "thinks he has been unjustly dealt with that he can sue for it & let the court decide & I will allow $50 toward paying his lawyer."[45]

The situation was put on hold during the winter of 1911, when the entire Edison clan vacationed in Europe. When the inventor returned, he and Wallace exchanged heated letters defending their respective positions.[46] Again, Harvie Heitman found himself between warring camps. In the end, he appealed to Edison to consider the quality of the work. Surprisingly, Edison agreed to a settlement and later asked Heitman, "What did the swimming bath man say, does he still think I treated him badly[?]"[47]

During the following year, the Edison family, three of Madeleine's friends, and Fred Ott came for a visit.[48] After luxuriating at Seminole Lodge for a few days, they went on an excursion to Lake Okeechobee. The Caloosahatchee River and canals to Lake Okeechobee were in the process of being deepened and widened, as Broward had proposed. Edison, who had supported the project from the onset, was pleased that traveling on the river was becoming less difficult. Still, he lamented the loss of wildlife and birds. [49]

Madeleine's "Rules for Guests at Seminole Lodge"

Visitors to the Edisons' Fort Myers estate were expected to display a certain sense of humor and camaraderie. Madeleine provided these guidelines:

- Don't—cabbage unto yourself all the fish poles—This has been done by guests thereby incurring the grave disapproval of the entire family.

- If you perceive that we need someone with a sane understanding to manage us, look the other way. On no account try to act as a balance wheel. The family all think it's great to be crazy.

- Don't kill the black snakes under the pool. They are there for a purpose.

- Don't make the mistake of thinking you'd like to catch a tarpon. You wouldn't. Mother and father are both after one with blood in their eyes—And there are just four poles.

- If you don't think Seminole Lodge is the loveliest spot you ever wore your rubbers in—Don't let on to Father.

- Don't pick the flowers of the Century plant. We might not be there to see them bloom again.

(continued)

(continued)

- Don't fail to retire to your room during part of each day—so that the family may squabble without embarrassment.
- When going on a three days cruise don't discover when you are at the far end of the dock that you have left your tooth-brush in the house. The dock is [left blank] feet long. In a case like this— the safest thing to do is to leave your tooth-brush behind, but if you are obstinate—get Father to take a nap in the boat and then run like ---- for the shore. Above all things *don't* send one of the guides. Father's sleeping powers are fairly good but they wouldn't last *that* long!
- Don't take any conveyance to the village without making the round of the entire family to see if you can't do some errands for them.
- Don't capsize in the sailboat if you can keep it. Remember there isn't any man to rescue you in 750 miles—And besides there are the Sharks.
- However desperate you become don't flirt with the guides. We once had a guest who did this so that the entire family lost its sleep trying to chaperone her—and Mother is very tired this season.
- Don't tell us the perfume of the river hyacinths reminds you of the Jersey meadows by moon light—We're just as sorry about those hyacinths as you are but we don't like to say so.
- Don't hesitate to say you are bored.
- Don't hesitate to say you're enjoying yourself.
- Don't ask us anything about Palm Beach. We don't want to know.*

* "Rules for Guests at Seminole Lodge," unsigned but in Madeleine Edison's handwriting, no date. Original in the collection of the CEF; copy obtained through the Edison Papers Project.

The family and their guests later took a steamer to Captiva and Sanibel Islands. They found the fishing poor, probably because of changes to the nearby Caloosahatchee River.[50] Mina was gravely disappointed that the natural environment of the region was changing. Unable to control the larger issues, she chose to focus on the smaller ones. She wrote a letter to the Bureau of Fisheries asking them to stock the region with fish.[51]

The winter provided further irritations to Mina. Madeleine was engaged to a young New Jersey man named John Sloane. Under different circumstances this would have been welcome news, but Sloane was Catholic and the Edisons were Protestant. At a time when intermarriage between the two faiths was considered impossible, the Edisons chose to keep the engagement secret while they tried to work out the details. It was an agonizing process.[52]

The Edisons also felt less welcomed by their Florida neighbors. The royal palm tree fiasco was still fresh in the memories of townspeople. No doubt news about Edison's refusal to pay the full cost of his swimming pool was circulating. In letters to her son Charles, Mina vented her frustration, saying "I detest the people down here," and "This town is rank. . . . It is not so much like the early quaint town. It is too bad. Prosperity has turned their heads I fear."[53]

During the summer of 1912, Tootie McGregor Terry became gravely ill. She summoned Harvie Heitman to her bedside at her summer home in New York. In her last days, as in her life, she thought of Fort Myers. Her first concern was ensuring that the projects she had initiated would be carried out following her death. When she died on August 17, the town mourned. The following December, a statue was erected in her memory.

Although General Terry continued his wife's commitment to Fort Myers, it was not the same. Someone needed to step into her shoes and work for the benefit of the region. Thomas Edison, now in his 60s, was engaged in his own work and had no interest in becoming the town's champion. Further, it was clear he needed to win back some goodwill. In the coming decades, Mina Edison would take on the role of building good relations with the town.

Roughing It with Famous Folks

*"This is a mecca for interesting people but
it's kind of a bore having people walk in on you all the time."*

Madeleine Edison

1914–1915

As 1914 began, Fort Myers was on fire—literally. On February 4, Harvie Heitman's Lee County Packing House burst into flames. The blaze spread to a nearby dock, where a carnival was taking place. The revelers ran wildly from the merry-go-round as the flames shot from the second-story windows of the packing house then advanced down the length of a pier. The Menge brothers' steamship *Thomas A. Edison* was among a number of vessels tethered to the end of the pier. Before anyone could untie it or the fire department could reach it, the *Thomas A. Edison* was engulfed. Nothing could be done. In a matter of moments, the steamship named after the town's most famous resident was lost.[1]

The fire devastated the local economy. Insurance covered only a quarter of the estimated $165,000 in damage. But local folks were known for their persistence. Within months, Harvie Heitman erected a temporary packing company that was later replaced by an even larger plant. The Menge brothers focused their energies on the remainder of their fleet.[2] Local residents needed a distraction, and soon they learned that Edison's next visit would bring the biggest distraction yet.

Thomas Edison, the legendary inventor, would soon arrive accompanied by automobile manufacturer Henry Ford and famous naturalist John Burroughs. The town Board of Trade and Booster Club planned a big parade to celebrate the event. In honor of Henry Ford, they rounded up every Ford vehicle in the region. The newspaper's headlines read "Every Citizen Should Help Welcome Edison and His Distinguished Guests."

Henry Ford

Henry Ford was born in Dearborn, Michigan, in 1863. He loathed farm work but enjoyed tinkering with machines. By 1893, he had successfully built a gasoline engine for an automobile. A decade later he established the Ford Motor Company.

Ford's Model T, first manufactured in 1908, was an unparalleled achievement. But it was Ford's ability to streamline the manufacturing process with the first moving assembly line that assured him commercial success. For the first time, cars were priced within the reach of average consumers. By the late 1920s, about 15 million Model Ts had been sold, making the Ford Motor Company the nation's leading automobile manufacturer and Henry Ford not only a very rich man, but also something of a folk hero.*

* Peter and Horowitz, *The Fords: An American Epic*; Watts, *The People's Tycoon*.

On February 23, approximately 2,000 people waited near the Fort Myers Atlantic Coast Line railroad platform. They held banners and waited in the hot sun. Among the crowd were farmers and business owners, mothers with small children, and elderly people leaning on canes. The expected time of arrival came and went. As usual, the train was late.

More people arrived. After the courthouse lawn was packed, they lined up along Monroe Street, First and Second Streets, and Oak Street. Finally, nearly a half-hour later, the band blasted out a musical welcome. The train was finally coming. The crowd began to wave wildly as the train hissed to a stop and the Edisons, the Fords, and John Burroughs and other members of the group were escorted to waiting vehicles. The stunned tourists found themselves surrounded by spectators. In a letter to her sister, Mina wrote, "We had a comfortable train coming down but uneventful until reaching Fort Myers, where we were met by a brass band and 45 Ford cars in honor of Mr. Ford.[3] We paraded through the streets of the town and then [were] dropped at our gate."[4]

The Fords and Burroughs were certainly impressed, but 26-year-old Madeleine found the experience invasive. In a letter to her fiancé, she wrote, "All the time I was dying to get home and wash my face!"[5]

Thankfully for Madeleine as well as the other residents and guests, life at Seminole Lodge resumed its bucolic pace soon enough. There were meals in the pavilion at the end of the dock and day trips on the Caloosahatchee. The young people sailed, fished, and swam in the pool. There were sing-alongs where everyone gathered around the laboratory piano, which was horribly out of tune, and Charles Edison played his mandolin.[6]

Still, there were distractions. Another famous visitor arrived on February 26. Dr. John Harvey Kellogg, of the famed Battle Creek Sanitarium, was in the area on business when he and his wife stopped by Seminole Lodge. Kellogg was not only the inventor of the cornflake but was also the leader of a health movement. He advocated diets that emphasized consumption of grains and strict vegetarianism. Some of his other ideas, including celibacy, were well outside the mainstream.

To Madeleine, Kellogg's visit was an imposition. "This is a mecca for interesting people but it's kind of a bore having people walk in on you all the time."[7] A month after he stopped by, the Edisons received a package from Kellogg. Madeleine complained, "[He] now has sent mother pounds and pounds of some sort of medicated chocolates which we shall never get rid of."[8]

But while the atmosphere at Seminole Lodge was relaxed, its residents were always on the move. Edison, Ford, and Burroughs grew restless and decided to go on a camping expedition to the Big Cypress, an extensive wilderness area in the state's interior. Mina did not object to the trip but was angry that the

How Ford Met Edison

Thomas Edison and Henry Ford met for the first time at the Association of Edison Illuminating Companies convention in August 1896. At the time, Edison was nearly 50 and world famous. Ford was a 33-year-old anonymous employee at the Detroit Edison Company. Ford's boss introduced him to Edison as a young man who was working on designing a gas-fueled car. Edison, who himself favored electric cars, listened to Ford describe his proposed vehicle. When he was finished, Edison pounded emphatically on the table and told Ford, "Keep on with your engine. If you can get what you are after, I can see a great future."*

As it happened, Edison's encouragement came at a vital time in Ford's life, and he credited the inventor with spurring him on to success. From that time on, Ford considered himself "a planet that had adopted Edison for its sun."**

* Ford, *My Life and Work*, 234–35.
** Baldwin, *Edison: Inventing the Century*, 303–4.

women were to be excluded. She lamented, "I never can see why they think we never want to do some of the interesting things too."[9]

Even after twenty-eight years of marriage, Mina struggled with her husband's personality and the burdens of position and fame. "I am getting calmer and I hope more sensible, but it comes hard. I may learn to be more submissive and not expect so much. I suppose that is my trouble. I am longing to be first in all my husband's thoughts. It's a hard lesson to learn."[10]

When it came to the camping trip, submissiveness did not win out. Mina advocated for herself and the other women and everyone packed their bags. The group would journey to Deep Lake, about sixty miles east of Fort Myers. They left early in the morning on Saturday, February 28, traveling in five automobiles.[11]

The journey was grueling. Once beyond LaBelle, there were no paved roads. The autos bumped and jostled their riders over palmetto roots and through deep ruts and sometimes were caught in sandy spots. Once they got to the marshlands, travel became downright dangerous. Charles remembered, "We hit one pond that was, well, a small lake. The guide said, 'You got to go across this thing.'"

There was no telling how deep the water was—an inch or ten feet—and Charles was skeptical. He was driving his father, his sister, and her friend. If

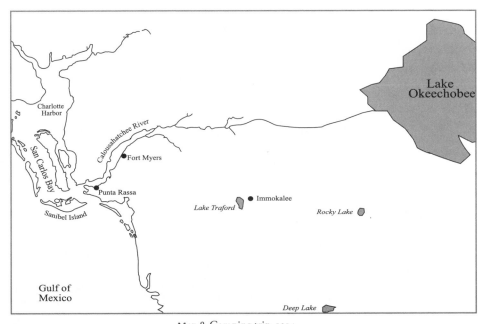

Map 8. Camping trip, 1914

they stalled, there was no way to know what would happen to them in alligator- and snake-infested water. He fought onward. "The water was almost up to the floorboards. It was about a quarter of a mile across that thing. You just had to steer by a sense of feeling the wheel." In the end, they made it through safely, as the guide knew they would.

The group's guides, Frank Carson, Len Hibble and Sam Thompson,[12] kept the Edisons and their guests safe. In addition to making sure no one got lost, they had to push the vehicles out of swamps and sand, fix flat tires, and keep radiators full. When they reached their destination, they had to clear the site, set up camp, and protect the northerners from snakes and other wildlife.

When the group settled into their campsite, the skies were clear but it was unseasonably cold. The Edisons, the Fords, John Burroughs, and their guests bundled in their winter clothes. Clara Ford was terrified of snakes, so her husband decided on a course of total snake eradication. Charles remembered, "Mr. Ford had brought his target pistol along, and incidentally he was a crack shot.... There were a lot of snakes lying up on the grass on the hyacinths alongside [the lake]. He would go ... maybe twenty-five feet—and he'd pop those snakes in the eye. He shot the heads off of about three of them."[13]

In quieter moments, campers could watch deer scamper silently through the grasslands. Rare wading birds were all around them as well wild game. Although an account in the *Fort Myers Press* assured that " no hunting was done as the season has closed,"[14] a photograph of Henry Ford holding a dead wild turkey suggested otherwise.

Henry Ford's son, Edsel, brought along a camera. He took candid as well as posed photographs of the campers. In one image, Edison had fallen asleep with his head in Mina's lap. With Edison still napping, the others in the group gathered around them for a photograph. Other images were more spontaneous, as the campers ate their meals and sat around the fire. After the trip, Edsel presented his friends with a photo album.[15]

On the first day, about the time dinner was cooking, a tremendous thunderstorm drenched the camp, followed by two or three more during the course of the evening. Most of the tents had open sides, and everything inside them was drenched after the first storm. As each new wave of the storm approached, more and more people crammed into the one enclosed tent until nearly the entire group was inside. They suffered through amicably, singing songs of sunshine and green fields until the central pole gave way and one side of the tent came loose. A torrent of rain entered, drenching those who were already soaked as well as those who were merely damp.[16]

As dawn arrived, the campers staggered from their tents. Madeleine remarked that John Burroughs's wet "red blanket [was] still clinging to him like a piece of sea weed."[17] As a group, they found humor in their misery. They made comments about how well they had slept and how lovely it was to live in the open. Burroughs suggested staying for the summer and Clara Ford said she felt selfish being entirely under water in the deluxe tent while others were only half covered. Then she said that "after a night of such liquid refreshment there was nothing she did not feel strong enough to bear, and demanded to be taken to see a snake forthwith."[18]

While Clara stared down the snakes, Henry Ford strung up a clothesline between two cabbage palms. They dried their clothes and wrung out the bedding as best they could and then gathered together to eat breakfast. Afterward, one of the guides killed a deer and the rest of the group tried to keep the news from 16-year-old Theodore, who loved animals.[19]

Another day passed with miserable conditions. Charles penned a limerick about their plight:

Consumption, pneumonia and grip[pe],
Will be the result of this trip.
We'll all die together,
From the inclement weather.
On the door-mat of Heaven we'll drip.[20]

Finally, after two days of being soaked through to their undergarments, the group gathered together. It was clear that conditions were not going to improve, and some wanted to go home. They took a vote and Madeleine remarked that "two expert swimmers among us"—Burroughs and Charles—wanted to stay.[21] They were outvoted, and the group made its way home.

Despite the challenges, the camping expedition made an impression on the Edisons' guests. They were awed by the natural landscape but were also keenly aware of the impact of human encroachment. Prior to their foray into the Big Cypress, John Burroughs had said that he wanted to "hear a panther growl."[22] Because of poaching, it is unlikely that he did. Both Mina and Thomas Edison had watched the decline in bird and wild game populations. Florida had lost 77 percent of its bird population before 1900.[23] Since then, the decimation had only escalated. Egrets, in particular, were bordering on extinction because their feathers were used to decorate ladies' hats.

Following the trip, Henry Ford allowed a rare personal interview on the subject of the connection between ladies' fashion and declining bird popula-

1914 the First of Many Camping Trips

The March 1914 camping trip in the Big Cypress was the first joint expedition by Edison, Ford, and Burroughs and their families. Although the three famous men never again camped in the wilds of Florida together, they camped in other places, including New England, New York, the Carolinas, Maryland, and Michigan.

Removed from work and the pressures of fame, the group enjoyed roughing it. Ford took brisk walks, exploring streams and nearby woods. As they had in Florida, Edison often curled up in the grass for a nap while Burroughs set off to research local birds. At night they told stories around the campfire. The expeditions were an escape, a rare opportunity for them to be themselves. The trips ended in 1924 because the press and public had become too intrusive.*

* Brauer, *There to Breathe the Beauty*.

tions with a local reporter. The automaker offered to make a donation to a fund to protect a local rookery, expressing a "strong disapproval of a fashion which creates a demand for the beautiful plumage as millinery ornament."[24]

The campers had barely unpacked their bags when they were off on other excursions. One day, Edison chartered one of Menge's steamers, the *Ada May*, for a two-day excursion up the Caloosahatchee as far as LaBelle. It was a lovely trip full of natural beauty, but a watchful one for Mina, who was keeping a keen eye Captain Menge. Though only a decade younger than her father, Menge had told Madeleine that "he would have made love to me long ago only he was afraid of mother."[25]

After just two weeks in Fort Myers, Henry and Clara Ford and John Burroughs had to go home. Edsel Ford so enjoyed the younger Edisons that he was allowed to remain. Madeleine remarked, "I think Edsel is going to stay on. He is taking to the place. I think it is good for him to be around young people as he is an only child and tracks around with extremely grown up adults most of the time."[26]

In a final interview of the season with the *Fort Myers Press*, Ford claimed that the region's climate was superior to that of California. "Mr. Edison always told me this was the best part of the state, and now I know from my own observations and experiencing that his estimate is correct. Your fruit is the finest I ever tasted, and your mild climate is something I do not believe can be surpassed anywhere."[27] Burroughs compared the region to Honolulu.[28] On March 10, Henry and Clara Ford and John Burroughs met the noon train for their journey north.

Back at Seminole Lodge, Mina reflected upon her guests. She thought there was general camaraderie among the group members but wondered about their comfort. "We enjoyed the Fords and Mr. Burroughs very much but I am afraid [that] Mrs. Ford was not very happy here. We talked snakes too much of which she is mortally afraid."[29]

Madeleine thought John Burroughs was the odd man out. "Somehow none of us seem to by duly idolatrous of Mr. Burroughs. Usually I love old men. I like to hear them talk and there is a gentleness and mellowness of character about most of them, which is very delightful—but with Uncle John something seems to be lacking."[30]

Henry Ford left behind a gift, a Model T Ford for his friend Thomas Edison. In mid-March the family took it for a spin down to Punta Rassa with Charles behind the wheel. Charles drove on the beach parallel to the shore and turned around so fast that the car got stuck and stalled. They were stranded until a group of drunken men passing by rescued them.[31]

On another excursion, Charles, Madeleine, their friend Bessie, and Edsel Ford sailed to the gulf. During the course of the day Bessie survived being stung by a scorpion and they had one car problem after another. Without any available water to fill the radiator, they resorted to leftover coffee, which all agreed smelled delightful.[32] When they ran out again, Charles and Edsel urinated into the radiator, producing a much less pleasant odor. After a third stall, a helpful farmer provided them with enough water to make it home to Seminole Lodge.[33]

John Burroughs's Impressions

Following the 1914 camping trip, John Burroughs described his companions to a friend: "I had a good time with [Ford] and Edison at Fort Myers. They are both remarkable men. Edison is a great philosopher as well as a great inventor. Mr. Ford is a real machinist & a big hearted man."*

* John Burroughs to Robert Underwood Johnson, March 29, 1914, American Academy of Arts and Letters, New York.

Also in March, the Edisons received a planned visit from the Colgate family, of Colgate soap fame. They were neighbors from New Jersey and had been great friends of the Edisons for years. Richard, Margaret and Muriel Colgate signed the Seminole Lodge guest book on March 2.[34] One night during their stay, the dinner conversation turned to the topic of mind reading. Although the meal was long over, nobody dared to move from the table. "Father gets started on the most interesting things and it is fatal to change to another room so we just stay at the table and listen," reported Madeleine.[35]

Even with all the family outings, Edison found time to work. Mitchell Mannering, a reporter from *National Magazine*, traveled to Fort Myers in mid-March to interview the famous inventor.[36] He found him at Seminole Lodge listening intently to Diamond Disc phonograph records. The New Jersey staff sent about forty records a week for Edison's approval. Due to his extreme deafness, "Mr. Edison himself sat down before the instrument, with his hand to his right ear and listened with his critical 'inner ear,' intent on detecting the least imperfection." If Edison liked the record, it went to the production department. If it was "punk," it went nowhere.[37]

The article also described the charm of Seminole Lodge and its gardens:

Across the road is a pecan grove, and almost every variety of tree indigenous to the tropics crowd the vistas and coppices, while orange, grapefruit, guavas, fig trees and almost every known variety of fruits and flowers grown in Florida are represented in this modern paradise. A long pier extends into the river, illuminated at night with electric lights, leading to a cool and shaded shelter from sun and showers, where visitors can rest in the covered chairs or swings or fish to their heart's content from rocking chairs. It is real fishing, too, with the added luxury of sitting in a swing or rattan chair while enjoying what might be called 'piazza angling.' The tarpons had begun to leap at the time of my visit. . . .

The views from the pier are delightful by day, but when night comes and the electric lights flash out of the velvety darkness, and the red, green and white lights of the motor boats flash above the phosphoric glow of the river water; while music, distance sounds and the weird "voices of the night" add to the mystic spell, the effect on the senses is almost charming beyond description.[38]

The national press was not always kind or accurate when describing Thomas Edison or his family. In April, Madeleine bristled when some newspapers claimed that Mina was keeping her husband prisoner in Florida. "We are getting sort of tired of the legend of Father as an insatiable labor machine whose only recreation is chewing tobacco. It's such a delightful dignified conception."[39]

Evidently not everyone was content to wait for magazine articles to describe Edison's projects. At the end of March, Madeleine further complained, "Father has been having lots of trouble having his mail opened by persons unknown before he gets a squint at it. About six letters have been opened with a pencil and then sealed up again on the way from here to the laboratory and this morning I found a letter in the box with the end torn right across." Her father explained that competing companies hired railroad employees to open his mail en route to the Fort Myers laboratory. Personal letters and other correspondence were not opened.[40]

On April 1, a shocking telegram arrived at Seminole Lodge. A New Jersey employee had committed suicide after discovering trouble with the account books. "Theodore and Father almost broke off their front teeth," Madeleine reported. But Mina realized that the telegram had been sent from Fort Myers. It was a somewhat cruel April Fool's Day prank orchestrated by Charles. (In 1908, John Randolf, an Edison employee who was responsible for Edison's business finances, had shot himself.)[41]

It was not the only April Fool's joke that day. Later, Fred Ott ran up to Seminole Lodge yelling that the boathouse was on fire. Mina, in on the conspiracy, raced around shouting at her children for more pails. The final prank belonged to Charles, who put a fake corpse in the ditch at the side of the road.[42] There was a sigh of relief on April 2 when the antics were finally over.

Relaxation and recreation were the only activities during the remainder of their stay. There was more fishing, sailing, and swimming as well as automobile and boat trips. Though the religious issues had still not been sorted out, Madeleine was making plans for her upcoming wedding. After years of engagement, there was finally official talk of wedding dresses and bridesmaids. She wed later that year.

At the end of each winter, Edison generally permitted an interview with the *Fort Myers Press*. In 1914, he instead allowed a conversation with Harvie Heitman to be quoted extensively in the newspaper. In it, he marveled at the beauty of the region and suggested that Fort Myers needed to promote itself more. Knowing that his witticisms made national news, Edison came up with a quote: "There is only one Fort Myers and 90,000,000 people are going to find it out."[43] (Ninety million was the population of the United States at the time.[44])

Edison offered his advice freely. He extolled the beauty of McGregor Boulevard and its royal palms but lectured how to care for them. Road improvement was absolutely essential to prove that the region was "wide awake and growing." Overall, he expressed great delight in his winter community and announced that "I have made up my mind that I will not let a year go by without coming to it."[45]

Finally in mid-April, it was time to go home. In contrast to their noisy arrival, the group departed quietly. They settled into their special train car for the long journey home and with a hiss of steam, they chugged away.

In some ways, the 1914 trip ended an era. It was the last year all the Edison children joined their parents in Florida. Charles would not return for three years. Madeleine would be absent for five. When she did return to Seminole Lodge, she would be accompanied by her husband and two (of what would eventually be four) young sons. Theodore would also not return for five years.

Despite his assertion that he would be back every year, Thomas and Mina Edison were absent in 1915. In December of 1914, the film inspection department at Edison's West Orange, New Jersey, laboratory exploded. The fire spread to the phonograph works, with eventual damage reaching millions of dollars.[46] Then the war began in Europe. In the turbulent years that followed, the Edisons, the Fords, John Burroughs, and the other guests could look back and think about their adventures in Florida.

Figure 10. The Fort Myers Hotel, later the Royal Palm Hotel, circa 1910.
FR0511. *Courtesy State Library and Archives of Florida.*

Figure 11. The Tampa Bay Hotel, where the Edisons stayed in 1900.
RC08820. *Courtesy State Library and Archives of Florida.*

Figure 12. The steamer *H. B. Plant* brought the Edisons back to Southwest Florida in 1901. NO40591. Photograph taken between 1899 and 1913. *Courtesy State Library and Archives of Florida.*

Figure 13. The Menge brothers' steamer *Thomas A. Edison*, photograph taken between 1904 and 1924. RC20043. *Courtesy State Library and Archives of Florida.*

Figure 14. Henry Ford, photograph taken in 1923. RC12325.
Courtesy State Library and Archives of Florida.

HOME OF HENRY FORD, FORT MYERS, FLORIDA

Figure 15. Henry Ford's home, the Mangoes, was located next door to
Seminole Lodge. RC01719. *Courtesy State Library and Archives of Florida.*

Figure 16. Fort Myers's Atlantic Coast Line Railroad Station became the arrival and departure point for the Edisons after 1924. NO30933. *Courtesy State Library and Archives of Florida.*

Figure 17. "Have You Seen Him?" *Fort Myers Press,* January 24, 1925.

PHONEY PHONETICS

A VERSE THAT READS WRONG BUT SOUNDS CORRECT

SEA CURE! EYE DEW KNOT BEE LEAVE YULE BEE.
AYE DUE KNOT NO-WEAL AWL BEE SEW HAP PEA
WRITE HEAR-KNOW WON URNS MEN NEE SCENTS AWL DEY.
PURR HAPS, WEE AUGHT TWO BEE AWN HOUR WEIGH
TOO YOUR UP?

W. C. SARGENT
COUNTY TREASURER —Duluth, Minn.,
HAS WORN THE
SAME COLLAR BUTTON
60 YEARS

THE STATE OF IDAHO
HAS MORE *AIRPORTS* THAN *AIRMEN*

72 Airports
51 Licensed Pilots

A SINGLE PAIL OF WATER
CAN PRODUCE ENOUGH FOG
TO COVER *105* SQUARE MILES TO A DEPTH OF **50** FT.

THE *THOMAS A. EDISON BRIDGE* – FORT MYERS, Florida
HAS NEVER HAD AN ELECTRIC LIGHT ON IT.!

4-22-35

Figure 18. Ripley's Believe it or Not!® cartoon decrying the lack of lights on the Edison Bridge, 1935. *Courtesy Ripley's Believe It or Not, © 2008, Ripley Entertainment, Inc.*

Figure 19. Thomas Edison, circa 1892. 14.914.16. *Courtesy U.S. Department of the Interior, National Park Service, Edison National Historic Site.*

Figure 20. Mina Edison, circa 1890. 14.351.12. *Courtesy U.S. Department of the Interior, National Park Service, Edison National Historic Site.*

Figure 21. Seminole Lodge, circa 1915. N030950.
Courtesy State Library and Archives of Florida.

Figure 22. Downtown Fort Myers, at the corners of Main and Hendry Streets,
circa 1910. PRO3361. *Courtesy State Library and Archives of Florida.*

Figure 23. Charles and Thomas Edison with their catch from a day on the Caloosahatchee River, circa 1901. 14.310.2. *Courtesy U.S. Department of the Interior, National Park Service, Edison National Historic Site.*

Royal Palms at Thos. A. Edison winter home.

Figure 24. "Royal Palms at Thos. A. Edison winter home," photographed by
F. W. Hunt, circa 1912. 14.400.48. *Courtesy U.S. Department of the Interior,
National Park Service, Edison National Historic Site.*

Figure 25. Theodore, Mina, and Thomas Edison in front of Seminole Lodge, 1909. *Courtesy U.S. Department of the Interior, National Park Service, Edison National Historic Site.*

Figure 26. The Edison Family, 1907. *From left to right:* Madeleine, Mina, Theodore, Charles, and Thomas Edison. *Courtesy U.S. Department of the Interior, National Park Service, Edison National Historic Site.*

Neighbors, Welcomed and Not

"Sometimes I feel that I would like to put up
a seven or eight foot high wall along the Boulevard here."

Mina Miller Edison

1916–1920

The Edisons' month-long stay at Seminole Lodge in 1916 was quiet. The usual guests, their children, Mina's sisters, and Mina's friend Lucy Bogue were visiting elsewhere. Edison decided to devote himself entirely to fishing. The results were disappointing. In April, he had a conversation with one of his neighbors:

Good morning Mr. Edison. Hope you are having a good time.

Nit.[1]

Why, what's the matter? Weather is fine and—

Yes, that's all right—but where are the FISH? Say, I remember the time when tarpon were caught opposite my home and there is nothing like that now. The tarpon have disappeared; you hardly ever hear of one being caught in the Bay.

Edison went on to say that he thought fault lay with the commercial fisheries. Mullet, feed fish for the tarpon, were being depleted and the tarpon were either dying off or going elsewhere. When the man suggested that the brand-new local golf course would replace fishing as a draw for tourists, Edison scoffed. "I tell you with all earnestness that is in me, the tourists are goin' where the fish are and if you want to stay on the map, protect the fish."[2]

Edison was a strong supporter of southwest Florida tourism and development. His quote about ninety million people finding Fort Myers ran on the front page of the *Fort Myers Press* for years. Donations to the country club and his investment in the royal palm project were designed to beautify and attract new visitors. He also endorsed canal dredging to make the Okeechobee part of an intercoastal waterway,[3] and he supported a seawall project until he realized that it would ruin his view.[4]

Like many who enjoyed the bounty of Florida's land and waters, Edison did not make a connection between his support of development and the changing environment. He complained about the lack of fish but predicted a bright future in which Fort Myers was "destined to be one of the largest and most popular cities and resorts in the state."[5]

Edison's glowing praise of Southwest Florida soon earned him a new, and very famous, neighbor. In 1916, the owner of a small bungalow neighboring Seminole Lodge wrote a letter to Henry Ford. "I have just placed my winter home, 'The Mangoes' at Fort Myers, Florida, on the market and it occurs to me that . . . you might be interested."[6] Ford's secretary wrote back a week later politely declining, saying that his employer did not visit Florida enough to warrant a winter home.[7] A month later, Ford reconsidered and requested photographs of the property.[8]

Ford had enjoyed his visit to Florida in 1914 as well as a later trip through California with Edison, Burroughs, and tire magnate Harvey Firestone.[9] There was something special about time with Edison away from business pressures and reporters' cameras. On May 26, 1916, Ford made an offer of $20,000 for the Mangoes.[10] On June 1, the front page of the *Fort Myers Press* proudly announced "Henry Ford Buys a Fort Myers Estate."[11]

Just four months before, Henry and Clara Ford had moved into Fairlane, their 1,300-acre estate in Michigan. The palatial home had cost $2.4 million to build and furnish.[12] The Mangoes was a charming bungalow that was extremely modest by comparison. At the time, the first story had a living room, a dining room, a kitchen, and a bathroom. Upstairs there were four bedrooms, bathrooms, and a sleeping porch facing the river. The grounds were considered one of the town's showplaces, with citrus trees, pawpaws, guavas, bananas, and (naturally) mangoes.[13]

Ford's first visit to his property came the following year when he arrived on his yacht *Sialia*.[14] He planned to travel up the Caloosahatchee in the 223-foot two-masted vessel, but the river was too low.[15] He and his guests disembarked at Punta Rassa and traveled to Fort Myers by land. His stay was remarkably short—only a day at his McGregor Boulevard home—before he departed aboard the *Sialia*.[16]

In July 1915, just two months after the sinking of the unarmed passenger ship *Lusitania*, Edison was approached by Secretary of the Navy Josephus Daniels. Daniels, who had read a *New York Times* interview with the inventor, asked him to serve on the United States Naval Consulting Board, which sought useful wartime technology from civilian and military sources.[17] When the group realized that the lay public knew little about submarines and sonar, they researched and developed new technologies.

Edison's Monkey Business

Thomas Edison loved animals. Over the years he and Mina had a series of cocker spaniels. The inventor also had a taste for the exotic. In 1908, he ordered two monkeys for his Fort Myers estate.* Mina described them as "a great source of amusement [to] Papa and son [Theodore] both."** They bought two marmoset monkeys next.*** All this monkey business came to an end when Edison feared that two large males might injure a child. He sent them to an ostrich farm in Jacksonville, Florida. A sign over their cage read, "These Siamese monkeys were raised on Thomas A. Edison's South Florida Monkey Farm at Fort Myers.****

The Edisons had many other pets in Florida. In 1910, Theodore wrote to his grandmother that Seminole Lodge had "chickens, 2 cats, 2 monkeys, 2 coons, 1 dog, 1 calf, 1 cow, 1 pelican, 1 pigeon, 1 gopher, 1 terpin [sic] and 2 alligators."***** Letters from 1920 mention peacocks, quail, and a raccoon that had a nasty habit of biting his master.****** When the Edisons' pets died, they remained at Seminole Lodge. Edison had them sent to a taxidermist and they were placed in the home as decoration.

* Invoices from George H. Holden, New York, March 3, April 1, 1908, ENHS.

** MME to MVM, April 4, 1909, EFWE, CEF.

*** Invoices from George H. Holden, New York, March 3, April 1, 1908, March 1, 1909, September 1, 1910, ENHS

**** "Edison Monkeys Travel," *Fort Myers Press*, April 25, 1912.

***** Theodore Edison to Mary Valinda Miller, March 5, 1910, EFWE, CEF.

****** Mina Miller Edison to Charles and Carolyn Edison, March 27, 1920, EFWE, CEF. The peacocks were confirmed by an interview of Awilda Brantly by Pam Miner, November 9, 2005, EFWE; Brantly also mentioned a resident parrot. For the raccoon, see Mina Miller Edison to Charles and Carolyn Edison, April 18, 1920, EFWE, CEF.

By the time the United States and Germany were at war, 70-year-old Edison was passionately pursuing innovations to assure an American victory. He felt it was his duty to temporarily abandon his New Jersey laboratory and devote himself entirely to the military. Though only a volunteer, Edison was soon working sixteen-hour days, just as he had in his own laboratory.

Most of the projects had to do with submarines, including improving communication equipment, improving the uses of sonar, and improving periscopes and other equipment to increase visibility.[18] Edison loved being useful and enjoyed life on the sea, but he missed Mina. He wrote her faithfully, describing himself as "your lover as ever steady, reliable and unchangeable."[19]

While Edison was working to advance the war effort, one of his children was behind enemy lines. Years before, his daughter Marion had married Oscar Oeser, a German officer. The war changed her husband. Mina explained in a letter to Charles, "Yesterday Father Dear and I received a letter from Marion and what she writes is worse than death. Oscar has been one of those awful officers whom we have seen and read about and Marion is getting a divorce."[20] Marion eventually returned to the United States.

Back in Fort Myers, Harvie Heitman, manager of the Edisons' estate, was struggling with the task of finding a caretaker. The position called for a person who was responsible, honest, a good organizer, handy, and knowledgeable about tropical horticulture. It seemed that with the exception of Ewald Stulpner, no one had done it all. An ideal candidate for the job would be a married man without children who would care for the grounds and keep the house in good repair. His wife would clean and attend to the interior of Seminole Lodge. The position paid poorly, a mere fifty dollars a month.[21]

In 1911, Heitman hired Hans Zeeman and his wife. From the start, the Zeemans were nothing but trouble. After only a few months, Heitman complained that Zeeman was "incapable of catching onto anything" and said that he had "lost all hope in him and have regretfully come to the decision that he is simply a thick-headed Dutchman who has not enough brains for the job."[22] Yet Zeeman stayed on because Heitman could not find a replacement.

Before long, Zeeman's wife had left him[23] and he was under investigation by the Secret Service for making un-American statements.[24] Mina and Charles sent R. W. Kellow, an Edison employee from New Jersey, to Fort Myers to assess the situation. He learned that Zeeman had sold the Edisons' fruit and kept the profits, maintained his horse and chickens on the Edisons' feed, and built a small house, charging the building supplies to his employers. He had also allowed friends to fish from the Edison dock and gut their catch in the Edisons' quaint pavilion.[25]

As one last test, Kellow decided to see if he could catch Zeeman in a lie. He sent him a letter asking about the success of a crop of cow peas Mina had requested.[26] Zeeman replied that they were "doing all right."[27] Kellow had him. The cow peas had not been planted.[28] Zeeman was sacked.

The next season, the Edisons visited Harvey and Idabelle Firestone at their winter home in Miami. After a pleasant stay, Mina and Thomas traveled on to Key West. At the Navy Aviation Station, Edison advised young aviators. Mina, who stayed with him in the First Officers Quarters, observed, "Father was excited to no end over everything here and the men were only too delighted to talk with him." In their free hours, they went fishing with their host or to downtown Key West to the movies.[29]

Meanwhile, less than 200 miles away in Fort Myers, the Board of Trade was putting together elaborate plans to welcome Edison with "the greatest reception he has ever received."[30] Their efforts were futile. Edison was so consumed with navy experiments that year that he never made it the southwest coast.

Mina traveled from Key West to Fort Myers and was settled in when her son Charles and his girlfriend Carolyn Hawkins came for a visit. After years of dating, Charles had decided to propose. One moonlit night as they sat at the end of the Edison dock, Charles proposed by asking the question, "Do you want a large wedding?" When she said no to the large wedding, they decided to marry there in Florida.

Once Mina heard the joyous news, she mobilized her resources, putting together plans for the ceremony. Charles telegraphed Edison in Key West, Theodore in New Jersey, and Madeleine in Washington, D.C., as well as Carolyn's family, but no one could attend the ceremony. The reasons were many: It was short notice. There was a war on. Gasoline was rationed and there was a worldwide influenza epidemic. Edison telegraphed his congratulations and the message, "If you have decided it must be, then the sooner it is done the better. It can't be worse than life in front line trenches."[31]

Carolyn bought a dress. Mina arranged for the minister and organized the ceremony. With everything arranged, Carolyn and Charles decided to attend a local dance, where one of the young men became interested in Carolyn. He was quite adamant about wanting to see her again, and indeed he did. As Charles remembered it, "When we went to get the [marriage] license, who should be the official to issue it but this same young man. . . . Flabbergasted, he counted himself out of the running right there and then."[32]

They were married at 3 p.m. on March 27, 1918. The minister from St. Luke's Episcopal Church officiated at the simple ceremony. Family friend Lucy Bogue and Mina's butler acted as witnesses. Mina guided a nervous Carolyn down a carpet on the lawn to a makeshift altar with two candles. She gave away the bride and then the two exchanged vows.[33]

With the formal ceremony over, Charles and Carolyn packed up the Model T Ford and drove to Fort Myers Beach for their honeymoon. Their plans went awry when they found themselves surrounded by swarms of hungry mosquitoe. With nowhere else to go Charles remembered that "we moseyed back to town through roads of sand. That's all they were then. I then took my bride to Hunter's Drugstore and bought her an ice-cream soda. That was our honeymoon."[34] A few days later the newlyweds and Mina left for Key West to visit Thomas Edison. Then it was home to New Jersey.[35]

In the months following caretaker Zeeman's departure, Seminole Lodge was put on a strict accounting system. For the first time, R. W. Kellow was able to anticipate maintenance costs and accurately account for them. One looming expense was the Edison dock. The structure was almost 1,500 feet long and included two boat houses, two smaller buildings, and the large pavilion at the end. Over the years, storms, wood-eating marine worms, and wear and tear had caused pilings and stringers to rot, and large sections had simply fallen away.[36]

Kellow recommended that the Edisons replace the dock entirely.[37] Heitman heartily agreed. He suggested covering pilings with concrete to increase their longevity.[38] Edison was not so sure. Replacing the dock would cost over $1,000. He may have also questioned its usefulness. Since 1906, the Edisons had arrived by train, not steamboat. The dock was now purely recreational. By the end of 1918, over $600 had been spent replacing dock pilings and stringers.[39] As far as he was concerned, a new dock would have to wait.

Another once valuable Edison asset was a concern. The laboratory was seldom used. Much of its most valuable equipment had been sent to the New Jersey laboratory. This included the direct-current dynamo that lit the estate for the first time in 1887. In April 1918, the estate was converted to alternating current and connected to the Fort Myers electrical grid.[40] Just like his neighbors, Edison now received an electric bill.

When Kellow inventoried the laboratory in 1917, it housed more recreational equipment than machinery. Over the next few years, local people purchased much of the remaining laboratory equipment. A blacksmith bought Edison's drill presses, lathes, and engines.[41] Fred Ott packed up some remaining electrical instruments, chemical supplies, and glassware for New Jersey. The east end was converted into a garage.[42] It seemed that Edison's days of experimenting in Florida were over.

Finally, in February 1919, the Fort Myers paper announced, "Arrival of Thos. A. Edison Matter of Felicitation."[43] In contrast to the headline, Edison's visit was quiet. He went fishing as often as he could and on one occasion took a trip to Sanibel Island. Daughter Madeleine visited with her sons in April.[44] Henry Ford's home was empty.

The Edisons' 1920 visit was also quiet. In a letter to Charles and Carolyn, Mina reported, "You would be gratified to see Papa and me just now. Forgetting everything but our own comfort and pleasure—Reveling in freedom and rolling in luxury."[45] Though Mina described their stay as little more than "loafing," she was hard at work with guests and community work. Harvie Heitman, his wife Florida, and Elizabeth Floweree came for visits.[46] Later, Captain Fred Menge came to spend some time with Edison.[47]

Living at Seminole Lodge may have been idyllic, but managing it was not. Following the departure of caretaker Zeeman, the Edisons' new hire lasted only a few months. Then the Edisons dropped Harvie Heitman as their agent and hired Ben E. Tinstman. Tinstman's luck was similarly poor. Though he selected a good "cracker" couple, they lasted less than a year.[48] They were replaced by yet another. Finally, Tinstman hired a couple named Smith. Because the husband was "good with the plants, honest and a neat worker,"[49] the Edisons gave the couple a raise and made improvements to the caretakers' cottage.[50]

The Edisons finally had a decent caretaker, but the manager became a challenge. Shortly after being hired, Ben Tinstman left for New York. For two years his wife, Nellie,[51] managed the estate in a frugal manner.[52] When he returned in 1920, her husband sought large expenditures for repairs and improvements. Mina Edison approved some projects but not others, complaining about the "terrific amount of money we are spending down there."[53] The issue came to a head when Tinstman threatened to quit, complaining that Mina had "no conception of the amount of work that has to be done."[54] Ben and Nellie Tinstman left the following year.

In the midst of these problems, the Edisons' neighbors were creating others. Seminole Lodge was a mile from the center of Fort Myers. Over the years, the town had grown and the commercial district had moved closer to their estate. Development brought more convenient transportation and increased tourism, but it also changed the character of the town. By 1920, there were plans for a 400-room hotel south of Seminole Lodge, near the golf course.[55] Presumably all those tourists would pass by on their way to and from the train station. More intrusive was a plan to create a pedestrian seawall. Tourists would walk along the Caloosahatchee River to the new hotel and golf course. It would pass directly in front of the Edison estate and put an end to the family's much-coveted privacy.[56]

In a letter to Charles, Mina complained about the plan, calling its originators "crazy townsmen." She and her husband had worked so hard to make "the Little Paradise of Seminole Lodge," but if something was not done, they might lose it. She grumbled, "Sometimes I feel that I would like to put up a seven or eight foot high wall along the Boulevard here."[57] Four days later she wanted a nine-foot wall.[58]

Mina was not going to give up all that they had worked so hard for. On March 23, 1920, she hosted a meeting at Seminole Lodge, inviting twenty "like-minded" men and women to form a Fort Myers "Round Table."[59] The group included influential citizens, the mayor, a county commissioner, and representatives of charity and community groups. Their chief aim was to address the "crying needs of civic reform in Fort Myers." If they lacked ideas, Mina laid out her own: a modern railroad station, city parks, the beautification of streets and homes, the elimination of noise by motorists and boats, fish conservation, and the establishment of good roads.[60] The Round Table continued to operate throughout her life.

Thanks in part to Mina's influence, neither the pedestrian seawall nor the hotel came to pass. But those threats reminded the Edisons of how important the tranquility of Seminole Lodge had become. Mina was 55. Thomas was now 73. The pressures of their lives were overwhelming, making the refuge of their "Little Paradise," essential. In coming years they would look back to the quiet of the early 1920s with nostalgia. More and more would be expected of them. The public was growing increasingly hungry to meet the wizard and his wife.

A Mind in "Cold Storage" Thaws

*"Although Mr. Edison has perfected many of his inventions here,
he comes to Fort Myers chiefly to rest."*

Fort Myers Press

1921–1924

In February 1921, Ben Tinstman, the caretaker at the estates, received word that Edison would not be coming to Florida.[1] The phonograph business was in decline due to the sluggish economy and increased competition. Though the inventor would stay in New Jersey,[2] Fort Myers was often in his thoughts. He was a baseball fan, and in April he sent a $25 donation to the Fort Myers baseball club.[3]

On October 25, the region was hit by a hurricane. Tinstman immediately sent a telegram to the Edisons. The houses survived unscathed, but the dock was almost a complete loss. "Flooring and stringers of dock gone . . . will arrange to replace flooring on dock."[4] Realizing the enormous cost and knowing that Tinstman would relish launching into the expensive project, Edison asked Mina's brother John Miller, who now acted as his assistant, to respond immediately. The dock should be repaired only to the boathouse, a mere 900 feet of its once 1,500 feet.[5]

Earlier in the year, Mina had complained that "thieving citizens" had been stealing fruit from their trees.[6] She was later shamed by the bravery of one of her neighbors. The October storm ripped the Edisons' electric launch *Reliance* from her mooring and set her adrift. One the local citizens, George Capling, went after it.[7] "At the risk of his life," he reached it just before it crashed against the downtown railroad dock.[8] The Edisons were deeply grateful.

Edison made up for the 1921 absence the following year. Although he stayed at Seminole Lodge for only a month, his days were as hectic as those spent inventing. He arrived on the afternoon train on March 22, accompanied by Mina and his cousin Edith Potter. On the way home from the station in his touring car, Edison passed the new City Hall building, which was formerly the home of his friend Edward Evans. When they arrived at Seminole Lodge, the inventor washed up and had a hearty dinner prepared by Mrs. Tina Doyle.[9]

Just a few hours later, at 11:20 p.m., the Atlantic Coast Line train arrived. The Fords' private railroad car was attached and came to a stop at the foot of First Street. Unbeknown to Henry and Clara Ford, a crowd of admirers was waiting at the station to greet them. The group remained for several minutes until they learned that the Fords were asleep. The spectators quietly found their way home in the dark night.

Very early the next morning, a crew of men was loading fruits and vegetables onto the train when they spotted Henry Ford descending from his railroad car. He took a walk around the silent streets of Fort Myers, then returned to the railcar for breakfast. Later that morning, he, Clara, and their cook and butler made their way to the Fords' little bungalow next door to the Edisons. After the couples greeted each another, Fred Ott pulled around Edison's touring car. The women were happy to stay put and talk, but Ford and Edison climbed into the back seat. They wanted to go for a drive.

They bumped along the town's shell-and-dirt roads for a while before stopping at Hill's Garage, the local Ford dealership and repair shop. The inventor and the automaker toured the small establishment, chatting with the owners and shaking hands with all the employees. "Grimy hands made no difference to these two distinguished visitors," the newspaper reported. "They clasped them warmly and had pleasant words for each workman."[10]

They also happened upon an evangelical religious service at a local auditorium. Preacher "Bob" Johnson was delivering a fiery sermon when Edison and Ford walked in. The two were invited to take a public stand by declaring their faith, but they politely declined, saying that they would rather sit quietly in the audience.[11] Their visit may have been accidental or prompted by curiosity; neither man was particularly comfortable with organized religion.

That evening the Edisons went downtown to the Arcade Theater. Built in 1915 by Harvie Heitman and his brother Gilmer,[12] the theater offered recent silent movies. That night the Edisons arrived late, but they got to see a good portion of *Forever*, a romantic movie starring Wallace Reid.[13]

When Edison and Ford first arrived in town, they made it clear to local reporters and citizens that "they [did] not wish to be bothered."[14] Nevertheless, a reporter from the *Fort Myers Press* was waiting on McGregor Boulevard early

Harvie Heitman Dies

Harvie Heitman and Edison had known each other since the turn of the century, when Heitman was a young entrepreneur opening his first store. Over the years his empire had grown to encompass many businesses.[*]

Despite his many responsibilities, Heitman acted as Edison's agent in Fort Myers, for which he was paid only $100 a year.[**] Given the amount of time he spent overseeing caretakers and renovation projects, coordinating shipments, and working to please the Edisons, it hardly seemed worth it. But Heitman genuinely respected the famous couple and wanted to ensure that they would return to the region. The appreciation was mutual. When Heitman died of stomach cancer in April 1922, Edison was an honorary pallbearer.[***]

[*] "Harvie E. Heitman Dies at 6:58 P.M.," *Fort Myers Press*, April 17, 1922.
[**] "Summary of Expenses of Seminole Lodge, March 1, 1916, to March 31, 1916," ENHS.
[***] "Harvie E. Heitman Dies at 6:58 P.M."

the next morning when Ford emerged to stretch his legs. He followed the automobile executive as he loped through town and then went for a tromp through the woods. Perhaps because the reporter kept his distance, Ford allowed a very brief interview. He told him he was "tickled to death" to get outdoors and "drink in" the beauty of the region.[15]

Edison went fishing a number of times and planned a trip to Shark River with Henry Ford to catch tarpon, but as Ford was not feeling well the trip was cancelled.[16] Ford might have wanted to stay close to home for another reason. He was in the middle of negotiating the purchase of a huge tract of land called Muscle Shoals.

Muscle Shoals was a network of rivers and dams on the Tennessee River. Ford hoped to purchase the property from the government, harness waterpower for electricity, and make fertilizer. The project, which Ford claimed would "benefit the whole world" by generating cheap electricity and fertilizer for the family farm, had wide appeal. The deal occurred at the same time as a populist movement arose calling for Ford to be elected United States president.[17] The newspaper kept abreast of each development related to Muscle Shoals and heartily endorsed it. As for the run for president, it was a logical outcome since, as the newspaper declared, "EVERYBODY wants him."[18]

A few days later, Edison and Ford were compelled to go fishing. A guest at the Bradford Hotel had caught a 75-pound tarpon on the Caloosahatchee directly across from their estates. Hoping to have similar luck, Edison and Ford set off early in the morning. Edison caught a trout, but Ford got "nuthin.'" And of course, neither captured a tarpon.[19]

The two went on a different outing on March 31, when Henry Ford and Thomas Edison accompanied their wives to the beauty shop.[20] Usually neither man was interested in such a trip. Usually it would not have been reported in the newspaper, even in bucolic Fort Myers. But this establishment was unique.

The Fort Myers Beauty Shop was owned and operated by Dr. Ella Piper. Piper was a landowner and businesswoman in a time when women were seldom either. She was educated when few women were. More miraculous still, she was a black woman operating her own business in a time when segregation and a train track literally separated white from black in Fort Myers and Jim Crow laws and social custom kept blacks "in their place." Despite all these conditions, she operated a thriving business and influenced people on both sides of the color line.[21]

What Thomas Edison and Henry Ford thought of Ella Piper and her business is not recorded. They may have thought her remarkable and inspiring or an interesting oddity. But Mina Edison and Piper became friends. In years to come, they would work together on many projects to better the region.

Just two weeks after the Fords arrived, they packed their bags, said goodbye to their McGregor Boulevard neighbors, and boarded their private railcar. There was no doubt that Ford had thoroughly enjoyed himself. He said he wanted to come back the next year for a longer visit. He was most impressed with the courtesy extended by the local people who had respected his privacy.[22]

After the Fords departed, life at Seminole Lodge was much quieter. Edison read and visited friends but declined events designed to honor him. For a time he even refused interviews.[23] By necessity, he communicated with his New Jersey laboratory, but for the most part, he relaxed for a month, claiming to have put his mind in "cold storage."[24] The *Fort Myers Press* confirmed this: "Although Mr. Edison has perfected many of his inventions here, he comes to Fort Myers chiefly to rest."[25]

On April 19, Edison went fishing with Senator C. A. Stadler, a New Yorker who had built an elegant estate just south of Ford's bungalow. They caught a string of redfish and a few mangrove snappers, but again, no tarpon. The next day Edison and Mina and their employees left for Llewellyn Park and their New Jersey home.[26]

After their departure, Charles and Carolyn Edison arrived.[27] As the sole residents at Seminole Lodge, they drank in the quiet and the solitude. Typical of an Edison, Charles got restless after two weeks of doing nothing and went fishing. In a matter of hours he accomplished what his father had tried to do for a season. He did not catch a tarpon, but he did catch what the newspaper described as "the largest sawfish ever captured in this vicinity." It was about fifteen feet long. The *Fort Myers Press* dramatically described the fight to capture the dangerous fish, which had rammed the boat and scarred its hull before Charles subdued it with a stab of his harpoon.[28] He sent his mother the newspaper article, suggesting that much of it was exaggeration: "It was some story the way it was written up."[29]

The Edisons' 1923 visit began with their very public arrival by train. Two hundred friends and admirers watched as first Mina, then a surprisingly spry 76-year-old Edison stepped from the train. Waiting in the crowd were grandsons Jack and Ted Sloane, who had arrived just days before their grandparents. They smiled pleasantly at their grandfather as he patted them on the head and whispered to each of them. Then the Edisons were off to Seminole Lodge.[30]

The famous couple devoted their time to showing their grandchildren the wilds of Florida. They took a trip to Fish Eating Creek where Captain Menge caught a sandhill crane, which he allowed the children to examine and photograph.[31] Later they went on an outing not far from the town's golf club, where they found some burrowing owls. Captain Menge uncovered the owl's clutch of glossy white eggs. Then they were off to find a gopher.[32]

On March 28, the Edisons waited at the train station for the arrival of Henry and Clara Ford. The Fords soon disembarked, accompanied by Ford's cousin Minnie and her husband. "I'm delighted to be here," Ford said to the assembled crowd at the station.[33]

The next morning, Ford took a stroll downtown. He stepped into the Pavese Barber Shop near the corner of Hendry and First Street. Owned by Rocco Pavese, an Italian immigrant, the shop was an oasis of convenience in the frontier town. It had a bathtub and two showers. A haircut was 25 cents and a shave was 15. Each day of the week, men lined up to have Rocco or one of his three brothers make them presentable. While Ford leaned back in the barber chair for his shave, he could listen to news, politics, and local gossip.[34]

That night, Edison and his family motored downtown to the Arcade Theater. The theater owner had a special surprise for his famous patron. Soon after the inventor took his seat, "Welcome Mr. Edison" flashed upon the screen. The typewritten slide brought instant applause and a smile from the inventor.

Harvey Firestone arrived the next day. The newspaper found it quite an honor to welcome Edison, Ford, and the rubber magnate. "Were John Burroughs, famous naturalist and able author living, no doubt he would be in Fort Myers at this time with his three best friends and camping 'buddies.'" The paper even made a stab at trying to convince Firestone to abandon his winter home in Miami for one on the west coast of the state, but he said he was, "jes' vistin'" for a few days.[35]

Although Fort Myers had been connected to the rest of the state by train since 1904, travel by road was nearly impossible. From Tampa to the north, there were sandy paths thick with palmettos, forests of trees, streams to ford, and rivers to cross. To the east, access from Miami was impossible. The Everglades was an impenetrable wilderness of snake-infested wetlands, alligators, and muck. The east and west coasts seemed eternally separate.

For years, town, county, and state governments legislated and floated bond issues with minimal results. Companies offered to finance road-building, but once they realized the enormity of the endeavor, they often withdrew. Finally, folks in Fort Myers decided they'd had enough of being essentially landlocked. Citizens banded together in a regional movement that demanded a route through the Everglades. To prove that such a road was feasible, they organized an expedition to cross the state and called the group the "Trailblazers."[36]

The group, which included twenty-three men, eight Model T. Fords, and one 3,000-pound vehicle called an Elcar, left Fort Myers on April 4, 1923. They expected to cross the state in three days.[37] A week later, they had not emerged. Two weeks passed. Soon the entire nation joined in the vigil. Airplanes searched overhead while worried families waited.[38]

Finally, on April 25, twenty-one days after they left, the Trailblazers reached Miami. It had been a harrowing journey. On only the second day, their automobiles had become hopelessly mired in the swamps. They had abandoned three vehicles. Despite the assistance of two Seminole guides, Assumhachee and Cornapatchee, the Trailblazers had become lost in the wilderness. Their food supplies had dwindled, then run out. The ragged explorers had survived by hunting deer and wild turkey.[39] When they finally emerged, the men were weary, but they had proved it could be done. Everyone in southwest Florida, including the Edisons, praised their efforts.[40]

While his friend Henry Ford often tried to influence government, Edison was less involved in politics. But in May, he and Ford hired lobbyists to go to the state capital in Tallahassee.[41] Their job was to convince lawmakers to oppose a plan by Barron Collier, a multimillionaire who had made his fortune in streetcar advertising.[42] Collier had bought Useppa Island in Pine Island Sound in 1911 and had continued to purchase property, eventually owning so much land that he petitioned to create a separate county.[43]

Collier's proposal might have died in the legislature were it not for his promises to guarantee financing for a safe passable road through the new county. It would become part of the new Tamiami Trail, which was named for its Tampa-to-Miami route. It was a tempting offer, one that few without direct ties to Fort Myers or Lee County government circles opposed.

Edison vehemently opposed the creation of Collier County, perhaps fearing a fiefdom in his own backyard. He made his opinion known in the newspaper and did his best to prove that the region did not need Collier or his money. Edison invited the press to tour road-building projects and offered to donate $500 for roads.[44] His proposal was meager compared to Collier's. To Edison's chagrin, Collier County was created on July 9, 1923.[45]

Although Lee County was reduced in size, the economy of the region expanded. In the months before the Edisons arrived in 1924, the Morgan Hotel opened in January on the site of a former boardinghouse. Seventy more

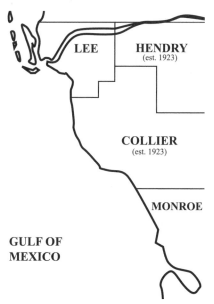

Map 9. Once part of Lee County, Collier and Hendry
become separate counties in 1923.

rooms were added to its original twenty-two the following year.[46] The first "skyscraper" in Fort Myers was an addition to the Franklin Arms Hotel. The eight-story, 84-room addition cost $300,000 and could be seen for miles. A third "skyscraper" followed with the four-story Pythian building on Hendry Street.

With an increased tax base, Fort Myers invested in its infrastructure. In 1921, streets lights were installed on First Street and a new city dock was completed.[47] A gas plant was being constructed. Sewer systems were established and paved streets extended out from the downtown.[48]

Most important for the Edisons and nearly everyone else who traveled to or from the region was the new Atlantic Coast Line Railroad station. The $48,293 mission-style stucco passenger terminal replaced the small wooden station. It had baggage rooms, a ticket office, and a telegraph office. There were separate waiting rooms and bathroom facilities for whites and blacks.[49] It was at this new facility that a large crowd waited on February 27, 1924, to welcome the Edisons.

The 77-year-old inventor looked spry and content despite a taxing journey. The Edisons had left their West Orange, New Jersey, home for Newark, where they had caught the southbound train. Harvey Firestone had accompanied them part of the way. Then the editor of the *Fort Myers Press* had boarded the train; he spent more time answering questions then asking them. Edison wanted to know about the Tamiami Trail and bridge work. He asked about his friend Fred Menge and improvements in Collier County.

In Savannah, Georgia, another reporter had boarded. When they changed trains in Jacksonville, eager crowds had surrounded the Edisons, determined to shake hands with the wizard. Along the track from Lakeland to Fort Myers, large crowds of schoolchildren and waving adults had gathered to catch a glimpse of him. By the time he arrived in Fort Myers, Edison did indeed deserve a rest.[50]

Henry Ford did not join Edison in 1924. He was still negotiating the Muscle Shoals purchase. It had passed through the House of Representatives but was bogged down by amendments.[51] Ford's lobbyists tried to convince senators that the Muscle Shoals project would bring the region and nation undreamed-of prosperity. Others thought the public resource should remain in public hands.[52]

The Edisons' guests were limited to family. Mina's sister and brother-in-law visited, as well as Edison's sister and a niece.[53] The group took it easy. They motored about in Edison's "antiquated Ford touring car." The Model T was over a decade old, but it had been equipped with four new balloon tires at the Hill & Company Garage.[54]

They took day trips to Naples, where Mina noted that they saw a green heron and six turkeys walking in a row.[55] They also motored to the inland communities of LaBelle and Moore Haven.[56] Then it was up the Caloosahatchee to Buckingham in Edison's electric launch with their friend Captain Menge. They enjoyed observing the fish, game, turtles, and shore birds.[57]

In early April, Mina received a letter from a friend who wanted to visit but was having difficulty finding a reliable route. He had wanted to take a boat from Tampa but had been told that it was out of service. There was a bus from Moore Haven, but he was not sure if it would be safe or comfortable. "The Caloosahatchee seemed . . . to be a 'river of doubt,'" he explained.[58] Mina's replied with potential routes but told him not to procrastinate. "Everything . . . is changing so rapidly that the river will be wild no longer. . . . Come to Fort Myers anyway. It is quite a place."[59]

Within days, a land route to Fort Myers was completed. On March 12, 1924, a wooden bridge spanning the Caloosahatchee River was dedicated. Though it was still a challenging journey, it was now possible to drive by automobile from Tampa to Fort Myers. The region rejoiced with a parade, a rodeo, a regatta, and a fish fry.[60] The Edisons did not feel that they were up to a public celebration but were nonetheless thrilled by the news.

Mina accepted only one speaking invitation that winter. In April, Flossie Hill, owner of a popular downtown clothing store, asked Mina to speak to the

Ninety Million Enough

In 1914, Edison predicted, "There is only one Fort Myers and 90,000,000 people are going to find it out."* The quote served as a motto for the town and appeared on the front page of every issue of the *Fort Myers Press*. By 1923, the population of the country had increased to about 100 million. So Edison revised his prediction to 100,000,000.** But the new quote never stuck. The people of southwest Florida were ambitious, but they were satisfied with only 90,000,000 finding them out.

* "There Is Only One Fort Myers and 90,000,000 People Are Going to Find It Out," *Fort Myers Press*, March 25, 1914.

** "Thomas A. Edison Has New Slogan for City," *Fort Myers Press*, May 3, 1923.

Women's Division of the Chamber of Commerce. When she accepted, the entire chamber attended.[61] Mina was a member of the National Recreation Association and spoke eloquently on the importance of city parks for community development.[62] Afterward, the newspaper declared that "the city should lose no time in taking this matter under very serious consideration."[63]

While newspaper articles and Edison's own pronouncements indicated that the inventor had put his mind in "cold storage,"[64] he and Firestone had discussed a very serious project when they traveled together at the beginning of the season. Firestone's tire empire and Henry Ford's automobile industry depended very heavily on natural rubber. Prices for that rubber were fixed by the British. In March, Firestone came to Seminole Lodge with representatives from Liberia and Singapore to discuss the prospect of growing rubber in the United States.[65]

The subject of rubber was not a new one. Edison and Firestone had discussed it during their camping trip in 1919. Firestone was surprised at the inventor's knowledge: "He told me more than I knew and more than I think our chemists knew, although to the best of my knowledge, Mr. Edison had never given any attention to rubber, except in connection with his talking machines."[66]

In January 1923, Firestone sent Edison a book called *Rubber: Its History and Development*. Edison thanked him, saying he had "lost no time in going through this book."[67] That season he began experimenting with milkweed and Mexican guayule, a short rubber-producing shrub.[68] He also sent his friend Fred Menge to New York to meet with the head scientist of a rubber company.[69] Edison was ready to tackle what he saw as a threat to American industry in 1924 when British monopolies raised rubber prices.

Before leaving Seminole Lodge, Firestone announced, "Mr. Edison feels confident that rubber trees can be grown in certain sections of Florida. He has conducted a number of experiments and thinks that rubber can be produced in large quantity and in quality equal to that shipped from the Far East right here in Lee County."[70]

Edison claimed to be resting and relaxing, as a man in his late 70s was entitled to do. Instead, he and Firestone had been experimenting and planning for over a year. Despite his apparent retirement, the wizard had one more project up his sleeve. It would consume him for the remainder of his life.

Inventor at Work and Play

"Florida will manufacture rubber yet."

—Thomas A. Edison

1925–1926

Henry Ford arrived in Fort Myers before Edison in January 1925. The auto manufacturer did not inform anyone other than the manager of his estate that he was coming. He traveled incognito and disembarked from the train without alerting anyone to his presence. Rumors that he was in town prompted the newspaper to print a photograph of Ford with the headline, "Have You Seen Him?"[1]

One reason for Ford's low profile was a lawsuit filed by Aaron Sapiro, a Chicago lawyer. Sapiro demanded that Ford's newspaper, the *Dearborn Independent*, retract numerous charges that a Jewish conspiracy was exploiting American agriculture. The issue had caused a furor and Ford was avoiding the press.[2] There were other issues he did not want to discuss. The movement to elect him president had fallen flat and there was a good deal of opposition to his attempt to purchase Muscle Shoals. Eventually he withdrew his bid for the project.[3]

A few days after his arrival, Ford and his secretary, Frank Campsall, rode in a chauffeur-driven Lincoln automobile to the small inland town of LaBelle, where Ford had purchased 8,000 acres in 1924.[4] Worried that such a large acquisition would play havoc with the local economy, Ford's employees said that there was "no truth whatever [in the rumor] . . . that their boss had purchased lands for rubber investigations in South Florida."[5] Nobody was fooled. The property was too isolated from large settlements or major transportation routes for anything else. Soon LaBelle real estate was advertised with the motto, "Henry Ford's choice. The city destined to be the center of the great RUBBER INDUSTRY OF THE UNITED STATES."[6]

Thomas Edison arrived in Fort Myers on February 5, accompanied by Mina and Theodore.[7] It was the first time the inventor had arrived before his February 11 birthday. In New Jersey, the day was celebrated with elaborate parties and reporters were allowed free access to Edison. So on his 78th birthday, Edison welcomed staff from the *Fort Myers Press*. The inventor reminisced about his earliest days in Florida, about meeting young Nick Armeda on the *Jeanette*, and about the region's cattle culture, which was changing so rapidly. He even recalled that there was only one orange tree on his property when he bought it and boasted that it was still bearing fruit.[8]

When asked about why he had selected the region for his winter home, Edison replied, "The climate was perfect and I knew that someday I would become old and useless and would mind the cold up north."[9] This comment illustrates more about his sense of humor than his sense of history. He likely was not planning for his retirement when he first saw the property at the age of 38. He also knew that, even at his advanced age, he still had a few good projects left in him—namely rubber research.

A few days earlier, the newspaper had run an editorial about Edison's place in the history of the town. It recounted his early visits and applauded his continued presence. The *Fort Myers Press* also made specific mention of the "little laboratory, still on his estate, that he did much of his early experimental work [in] with both the phonograph and the electric light."[10]

A few days later it was learned that Henry Ford had tracked down some original laboratory equipment that Edison had sold to a blacksmith in 1919. He had purchased the tools, drill presses, lathes, engines, and other machines and sent them to Dearborn, Michigan. They would be part of the Henry Ford Museum, established to preserve the nation's historic past. The *Fort Myers Press* was pleased. "Providence, it seems, intended that this primitive machinery of the great inventor should be preserved to remind the passing generations of the greatest of all inventors whose greatest work was accomplished in the little cow town on the Caloosahatchee."[11] In a few years they would regret their support.

Two days later, Henry Ford left Fort Myers as quietly as he had arrived. The newspaper commented, "It was not generally known that the automobile manufacturer was getting ready to leave the City of Palms." It lamented, "While Mr. Ford was here he successfully evaded being interviewed by newspapermen." But it made it clear that the region wanted him back. "His fig-

ure on the streets of Fort Myers has become a familiar and welcome one."[12]
For the rest of Edison's 1925 stay in Florida, he alternated between hard-nosed research and pleasure. Edison inspected the planting of two varieties of rubber on the west side of his property and tested numerous plants for rubber content. He claimed to have manufactured rubber from a tree at Seminole Lodge. To prove his point, he pulled a dark lump out of his pocket and held it up. "Florida will manufacture rubber yet,"[13] he declared.

To be successful, Edison needed to do more than produce rubber; he also needed to figure out how to minimize labor costs. He estimated labor at $3 per day in the United States, compared to a mere forty cents in Asia. He thought a vacuum process to remove the rubber from the trees would solve the problem. "Mr. Edison becomes very enthusiastic [*sic*] when talking about this method . . . and is convincing. It is easy to believe that he will successfully plan a way to do this very thing,"[14] the newspaper declared.

Harvey Firestone and M. A. Meek, a rubber expert, visited Edison in March. They inspected experimental rubber plots on McGregor Boulevard and on Ford's acreage in LaBelle and found that the plants were thriving. Meeks reported, "Well, those trees certainly look good to me. I have seen none in the Federated Malay States, Java or Sumatra that were more encouraging." He cautioned that it did not necessarily mean that the area could successfully produce rubber, but it was a start.[15]

Over the next six years, it seemed everything that touched the inventor's life had to do with his new project. Mina declared, "Everything turned to rubber in the family. We talked rubber, thought rubber, dreamed rubber. Mr. Edison refused to let us do anything else."[16] But she did pull him away from his experiments occasionally to continue to explore the region around their winter home.

On February 24, a Lincoln automobile was sent from the Hill Garage to pick up Thomas and Mina Edison and their guests for an outing. Theodore came along for the ride, as did Edison's cousin Edith Potter, Fred Ott, and Fred Menge.[17] They were driving to Naples, a trip that had formerly taken a full day of slow going over sandy roads. But now a good part of the road to Naples was newly paved with marl, a mixture of clay, sand, and limestone that was combined with crushed rock and shell. "This makes a wonderful surface," Edison declared, but he could not help himself from offering advice, suggesting that repair crews "regularly fill up the holes and smooth the surface."[18]

The town of Naples was founded in 1887 by the Naples Company, a group of ambitious investors whose grand vision of carving out a large-scale subdivision never came to fruition.[19] In April 1888, they opened a 20-room tourist hotel.[20] In the years that followed, the establishment became a private retreat for the Haldemans of Kentucky. There were so few other visitors that the locals began calling it the "Haldeman Club."

An addition containing a new inn for the hotel was built in 1915, followed by a 40-room addition in 1916.[21] Edison, who had visited during the hotel's early days, commented that it "had been changed and improved so much since his last visit that it was almost a strange place to him."[22]

After a brief stay at the hotel, the group traveled to Caxambas, where Barron Collier's yacht *Volemia* was waiting. After Collier County had been established, Barron Collier was conciliatory, saying that he did not "blame the people of Fort Myers" for their opposition to his plan.[23] His largess extended to Edison, who had vocally opposed him. The industrialist offered the inventor the use of his yacht as well as a guide. Edison gratefully accepted and took his party on a tour of the Ten Thousand Islands.

They cruised along, watching the skies while Captain Menge named each exotic bird. After stopping for lunch in Everglades,[24] the group explored the southern part of the Ten Thousand Islands. They were within three miles of Pelican Key and fifty miles of Key West when they turned around. On their return, they approached the small town of Everglades after dark. Edison admired the contrast between the charming yellow-and-white buildings of the town against the inky night. They stayed overnight.

Map 10. The Edisons and guests journey from Fort Myers to Key West, 1925.

On their way back to Fort Myers, the Edisons and their guests again looked to the skies. They saw flocks of white pelicans, white herons, egrets, and bitterns. On the road they found a wounded great blue heron. A rifle ball had severed the upper part of the bird's bill and it was slowly starving to death. The group captured it and held it down while Captain Menge trimmed the lower part of its bill so it could eat.

The Edisons and their guests were impressed by the beauty and grandeur of the region. The sunsets were breathtaking. The forests and swamps were bursting with the kinds of plant and wildlife that bring reverence and awe. But while Mina often lamented the loss of such natural resources, Edison was thinking of development. He speculated that the region could be subdivided; canals could be built and then parcels could be sold as estates.[25] The Edisons left for New Jersey in mid-April.[26]

By 1926, southwest Florida was consumed by baseball. Fort Myers was the new home of the spring training team of the Philadelphia Athletics. Beginning in 1925, national papers printed reports of the games, which were held on the north side of town at Terry Park. Manager Connie Mack and famous players like Eddie Rommel, Lefty Grove, and Al Simmons rented homes or stayed at the Bradford Hotel.[27] Their presence made Fort Myers a more interesting, more important place.

As the 1920s progressed, the state of Florida boomed. Over two and a half million new residents poured into the state. Improved transportation meant that drivers could speed along at the highest legal speed in the nation, forty-five miles per hour. No driver's license was required.[28] Among these new residents were an increasing number of extremely wealthy individuals, who benefited from the absence of income and inheritance taxes after 1924. Miami and Palm Beach exploded with subdivisions, stores, hotels, and vacation homes.[29]

The Florida boom also affected the more isolated west coast. In 1922, fees for building permits in Fort Myers amounted to $246,310. Just four years later they were a whopping $2,807,381.[30] Subdivisions with names like Rio Vista, Palmwood, San Carlos, and Russell Park taunted potential buyers with statements like, "Will you wait until all this property is sold before you investigate? If you do, you will be the loser!"[31] A new subdivision was under construction across the street from the Seminole Lodge and Mangoes. It was called Edison Park in honor of the development's famous neighbor.

Even with all the changes, the arrival of the Edisons was celebrated. Camera shutters clicked incessantly as the couple disembarked from the train in 1926, accompanied by grandsons Ted and Jack Sloane. The *Fort Myers Press* reported,

"Mr. Edison had little to say but his eyes sparkled and his handclasp was strong and vigorous as he cordially greeted his friends."[32]

A few days later, the gates of Seminole Lodge opened and Edison gave his customary birthday interview. The question-and- answer session was big news locally, and much of it was syndicated nationally with a Fort Myers byline. The *Tropical News* noted, "Last year . . . he expressed opinions on several subjects over which much controversy had raged in the last 12 months."[33] To the press, news was good, but controversy sold more papers.

Reporters focused many of their questions for Edison on the Scopes Trial, which had taken place the previous summer. John T. Scopes, a substitute biology teacher, had been arrested for teaching evolution in Dayton, Tennessee. The resulting trial pitted those who believed in creationism against those who wanted evolution taught in the schools. William Jennings Bryan argued the case for creationism; Clarence Darrow put forward the argument for evolution.

Edison, who had a collection of Darwin's books at Seminole Lodge, responded, "We have got to have truth and, in spite of all the furor over Mr. Bryan, his ideas were obsolete long ago. There is more truth to be found in nature than in the Bible, for nature never lies." Then, realizing that his comments might offend his more fundamentalist southern neighbors, he added, "There is visible evidence of an absolute Being all around us."[34]

Following the interview, Edison sent a telegraph to the Edison Pioneers in New Jersey, a group that celebrated his birthday each year. In 1926, the luncheon at the Hotel Astor was attended by five of his six children. The telegram read, "Many Thanks. Feeling Fine. Weather beautiful. Cocoanuts [*sic*] dropping all over place. Wish you all were here."[35]

Edison's advanced years did not slow his pace. When he was not busy ex-

Edison's Birthday Interview of 1926

Some questions and answers from Edison's 79th birthday interview:

On His Age

While he felt about 60, he was really 120 years old. "I've been working two shifts most of my life. Lots of other men work two shifts too, but [they] devote the other one to poker."

On Prohibition

"If it is enforced for another 20 years it will be all right. For the children of today are the important consideration, and the dry law will keep them from ever knowing whiskey. It is useless to try and change the people who are used to drinking."

On Florida

"Southwest Florida is one of the best places in the world to spend the winter and Fort Myers is the best spot in Southwest Florida. I have been coming here for 43 winters now, and hope to be here next winter too."*

On the Scopes Trial and Religion

"All this talk about fundamentalism will die out in a few years because there is nothing to it. We have got to have truth and in spite of all the furor over Mr. Bryan, his ideas were obsolete long ago. There is more truth to be found in nature than in the Bible, for nature never lies. The chief trouble with religion is that it is being exploited too much. There is visible evidence of an absolute Being all around us."

On Ford's Effort to Revive Old Time Dances

"I think it is foolish and won't succeed. People want jazz music these days. Everybody will get up and dance when a foxtrot is played, but when it's a waltz they won't."

He admitted that he didn't care for dancing and thought it an expression of the barbarian remaining in the human race. "If a champanzee had a sense of rythm he would dance himself to death."

On Education

"The biggest hope for education is through moving pictures. Use the movies for education purposes in the schools and make learning attractive."

On His Relationship with Ford

"We are both interested in the garden and in horticulture generally and other scientific fields."**

* Forty-three was an overstatement. By the winter of 1926, Edison had spent part of twenty-two winters in Florida.

** "Double Shift Makes Edison 120, Feels 50 on 79th Birthday," *Tropical News*, February 12, 1926.

perimenting with rubber, he explored and experienced the region around his southwest Florida home. At the new airport, he inspected two modern passenger airplanes named *Miss Tampa* and *Miss Miami* but made it clear he was not interested in flying. "No thank you. I wouldn't care to be up in that plane.... I am of the earth, earthy."[36]

Edison and Mina joined a throng of 5,000 people at the Lee County Fair in 1926. They toured the food, fruit, and vegetable exhibits and witnessed a fire that broke out in the inner workings of the merry-go-round. Edison spent time with the Seminole Indians and was photographed with them.

Then it was off to the baseball field, where manager Connie Mack escorted the inventor on a tour of the ballpark.[37] He was introduced to Kid Gleason, who asked, "Think you could hit one?" Edison agreed and Mack acted as catcher. As cameras clicked, Edison swung and missed. A growing crowd yelled, "Strike one." On the second pitch, to the delight of the crowd, he caught a piece of it. Though it was an easy pitch, a generous Gleason declared, "He must have invented a way to solve my curves."[38]

An accident occurred at Seminole Lodge a few days later. Grandson Jack Sloane was injured when Sidney Scarth, the Edisons' driver, accidentally backed into him when turning around in the driveway. According to the newspaper, Jack suffered only cuts and bruises and was perfectly fine when his mother Madeleine and youngest brother Peter arrived a few days later for a planned visit.[39]

The Edisons went to the movies nearly every night, but one night they chose instead to hear a local artist sing with an Edison phonograph at the Gwynne elementary school's auditorium. Unfortunately, the machine malfunctioned. Edison was not concerned, but Mina intervened, giving advice and direction. Another phonograph similarly failed. Finally, the third machine worked. After the difficulties, the newspaper speculated that next time, "perhaps Mr. and Mrs. Edison will go to the movies."[40]

Another challenge came from across the street from Seminole Lodge. A statue of a Grecian maiden was installed at the entrance to the Edison Park subdivision. Some of the women of the town peeked at it beneath a tarp and were shocked to see that she was nude. They asked Mina to intervene on their behalf. The developer, James D. Newton, a young man in his twenties, and Mina decided that a veil would solve the problem. Mina was impressed by his willingness to compromise.[41]

Harvey Firestone arrived in early March. He praised Edison's rubber experiments but expressed skepticism about the overall project. "I am afraid I am not very enthusiastic. . . . I don't believe that rubber, at least of the best grades, can be raised successfully here." Later he backtracked, saying "it will take a long time."[42]

Henry Ford joined Edison and Firestone in Fort Myers on March 8. After docking at Punta Rassa, the auto manufacturer walked the seven miles to his home on McGregor Boulevard. His wife waited for a motorboat to take her up the river.[43]

Ford had not had a chance to sit down and rest when Harvey Firestone and the Edisons came over from Seminole Lodge. Firestone brought a group of musicians from Palm Beach. They held an impromptu hour-long concert in Ford's yard featuring all the automaker's favorite fiddle tunes. Ford thanked the fiddlers and retired to his home for a well-deserved rest. Firestone then left for the east coast of Florida.[44]

While Edison and Ford were getting reacquainted, Mina gave a speech to the Fort Myers Recreation Board. She expressed enthusiasm for a local recreation plan that included new tennis courts and activities at the city hall park and but encouraged the board consider adding music instruction and performances to the recreational programming. "When we become a nation of wise players, we will have accomplished great work," she said.[45]

Later that month Mina and Thomas traveled to the inland community of LaBelle so Edison could inspect Ford's rubber plants. He found the plants developing rapidly. "Ah yes, anything will grow here," he announced. "It's a case of getting the right kind of a rubber tree or plant to make a success commercially." He spoke at length about the quality and quantities of plants and announced, "I expect to produce enough Florida rubber before long to make four Ford tires."

After a day in the hot LaBelle sun, Edison was ready for some rest and relaxation. The theater owner in LaBelle invited him to the local movie house. The small room was jammed with schoolchildren who were thrilled to see the inventor. There was a vaudeville skit, then a movie starring Hollywood cowboy star Harry Carey. Afterward the inventor said, "I enjoyed Harry Carey and the vaudeville very much. It was a good show." The Edisons spent the night at the local Everett Hotel before returning to Seminole Lodge.[46]

Back in Fort Myers, James D. Newton was preparing to officially open Edison Park. A ceremony had been planned that included a band. Pathé News would be there to film the event. A senator, the mayor, the city manager, and a slew of local dignitaries were slated to attend. Most important, the Edisons were coming.[47]

On April 7, the day of the opening ceremony, the inventor awoke with a temperature of 101. Nevertheless, Edison was fully dressed and waiting for Newton when he arrived. The experience made an impression on the young man, "He had given me his word that he would be there—and there he was, temperature and all, and close to eighty years old. I learned then what I saw on many later occasions: he was a man of integrity; he kept his word."[48]

A couple of weeks later, the Edisons were ready to return to New Jersey. It had been a busy winter. The inventor said he had enjoyed the vacation, which he had spent "sleeping as long as he likes—even as much as seven hours sometimes—and reading incessantly."[49] But he had done much more than sleep and read. He had worked exhaustively on his rubber plants and traveled throughout the region. What looked like recreation was instead preparation. The inventor was planning to launch into a full-scale campaign to provide the United States with a reliable source of source of domestic rubber. And he was doing it in Florida.

Edison Impressed by Hard Work

James D. Newton, the real estate developer of Edison Park, first met Edison in 1926. Newton recalled their first encounter:

> Sometimes, instead of sitting in the office, I'd get into overalls and work with the crews, laying streets and sidewalks and sewers. One morning I was in a ditch on McGregor Boulevard, and as I threw a shovelful of dirt over my shoulder I looked up, and there was Edison, ten feet from me, sitting in his Model T Ford with his assistant, Freddie Ott. His fine head topped by unruly gray hair, his piercing blue-gray eyes, bushy eyebrows, prominent nose and jaw, broad shoulders and chest—all made him a striking, unforgettable figure. He stared at me for a long time and then drove on without saying anything. I had met him casually a few times, but from that moment on our friendship began. I later found out he liked someone who'd spit on his hands and take a shovel. He was a worker and he admired hard work. I have a photograph that he signed for me: "All things come to him who hustles while he waits."*

* Newton, *Uncommon Friends*, 3–5.

12

Rubber Research and Road Trips

We have been talking to the uncrowned King and Queen of America.

—Dr. Emil Ludwig

1927–1928

On September 17, 1926, a powerful hurricane with wind speeds of 130 to 150 miles per hour swept across the state of Florida in the dead of night. Ninety-one people were killed in Miami and thousands of homes and businesses were flattened. The worst damage occurred around Lake Okeechobee. When the lake's shallow waters swelled to heights of more than fifteen feet, its dike crumbled and flooded Moore Haven. The wall of water extended for miles. Three hundred people in the town drowned. In the end, the region suffered $25 million in damage. Over 1,800 people died.[1]

Fort Myers survived with little storm damage, but the community was devastated in other ways. No one wanted to invest in Florida real estate. The boom was over. There would be no more new subdivisions. Existing lots and homes would sell for pennies on the dollar.[2] James D. Newton's Edison Park would stay afloat only through bartering and hard work.[3] In these difficult times as well as in the dark days to come, the Edisons' presence in Fort Myers would provide inspiration and comfort.

Much to the disappointment of his Florida neighbors, Thomas A. Edison celebrated his eightieth birthday in New Jersey. He granted the press interviews and attended an Edison Pioneers luncheon at the Robert Treat Hotel in Newark, New Jersey.[4] But the octogenarian would not be long in the north. He arrived in Fort Myers on February 19.

Edison was the first one off the train, happy to part with his heavy black overcoat and trade his flat black derby for a floppy Florida panama hat. Mina and Edith Potter accompanied him, along with his physician, Dr. John Hammond Bradshaw, who was a bit confused when the crowd cheered for him, thinking he was Harvey Firestone. The tire manufacturer had traveled with the inventor, but only as far as Jacksonville.

Ever-faithful Fred Ott was waiting at the train station with the inventor's old Model T Ford. Edison lovingly caressed it but decided instead to travel home in the more comfortable Lincoln. Frank Stout, Edison's manager, drove the group from the Atlantic Coast Line station down McGregor Boulevard to the Seminole Lodge gate.

Even before the luggage was unloaded, Edison was inspecting the grounds. Although he had been assured that his "jungle" of palms and other tropical plants had survived the hurricane largely unscathed, he was relieved. "The storm was good to us," he said. He then went in to have lunch, which included strawberries from his own garden.[5]

Although he was supposed to be resting, Edison went right to work on his rubber experiments. He showed reporters some vines from Madagascar that had survived a hurricane and three frosts. Most nights he was at his laboratory long after midnight, causing Mina to worry. She tracked him down and tried to coax him back to bed.

With so much media attention on them, Mina took an opportunity to speak directly to the press. She reminded them that Edison was aging. He had extreme difficulty hearing and did not always have time for their questions. She also complained about recent inaccuracies and misquotes.

Another topic on her mind was Edison's original 1886 laboratory, which the inventor was now using for rubber experiments. The previous year, Ford had asked Edison if he could remove the building and include it in his Dearborn museum. Without much thought, and without consulting his wife, Edison had agreed. She informed the press that the laboratory "might remain" and made it clear that she disagreed with her husband's decision.[6]

The laboratory was almost lost a few days later. A grass fire on the north side of the estate threatened Edison's laboratory and his beloved stand of bamboo. The fire department dumped eighty gallons of chemicals on the flames, with limited results. Finally they organized a bucket brigade from the river and the fire was extinguished. Edison had been at the house napping the entire time and because of his deafness had not heard the commotion. Fred Ott informed him when he awoke.[7]

On March 7, Edison was off to the Terry Park baseball field for his second annual visit to see the Philadelphia Athletics in spring training. Mina and Fred Ott accompanied him, along with a virtual army of reporters and camera crews. On the way, a reporter asked Edison if he knew who Ty Cobb was. Edison replied in the affirmative and was then asked if Cobb was a good batter. Edison gave a sly grin and teased, "Oh, I thought he was a fielder."

Once at the baseball diamond, reporters pelted him with questions. The *Fort Myers Press* described how "movie men swarmed around like bees and Mrs. Edison had trouble in keeping them away." Either his deafness or single-mindedness prevented him from responding. He picked up a bat and headed for home plate. Then he tilted his panama hat back from his face and smiled.

Ty Cobb was to pitch to the inventor, as Kid Gleason had the year before. Although he was known as the meanest man in baseball, Cobb was on his best behavior. He even tried to make it easy for the aging inventor. He stood halfway between home plate and the mound and tossed a lazy underhanded pitch. With cameras clicking furiously, Edison took a hard swing. The ball clipped Cobb on the shoulder and sent him sprawling onto his backside. Clearly the old man still had it in him.

After brushing himself off, Cobb called him "a great natural hitter." The inventor replied, "Do you think you can hit them like that when you are 80?" Cobb said he hoped so. Then, as quickly as they arrived, Thomas and Mina Edison, along with Fred Ott, climbed back into the Model T Ford. In a cloud of dust they departed for Seminole Lodge.[8]

The Edisons later invited the entire Philadelphia Athletics team to Seminole Lodge. The inventor personally conducted the players on a tour of the grounds around the homes and then crossed the street to explore his rubber experiments, educating them on the national significance of a domestic source of rubber.

Back at Seminole Lodge, Edison captivated the group with alligator stories and gave each player a cigar. He was a bit mystified when the men put them in their pockets instead of smoking them. Lefty Grove explained that he wanted to keep his as a souvenir. So Edison sent Fred Ott off to the laboratory for more. When Mina announced that punch was being served, Edison teased her, "Oh, there isn't anything in that." He and the players had a good laugh.[9]

The Edisons also took day trips. James D. Newton organized an excursion to Venice. Instead of traveling in the inventor's Model T or the Lincoln, Newton drove them in his shiny Packard roadster. After a 60-mile drive, they parked in front of the brand-new Venice Hotel.[10] Inside, Edison, who seldom gave speeches, told real estate developers about his rubber research. He explained how he hoped that a rare vine from Madagascar could produce domestic rubber, but he noted that "if America ever hopes to break up the British rubber

Joking with Edison

Thomas Edison's love of a good joke was legendary. But by the late 1920s, the inventor's deafness had made it nearly impossible for him to catch a punch line. In *Uncommon Friends*, James D. Newton described how Henry Ford found it possible to include Edison in a joke:

> One morning, when I went over to the Ford house, Frank Campsall, his secretary and assistant, was typing out jokes, each one on a separate piece of paper, as Ford dictated them. Campsall handed each to Ford, who slipped them one by one into his pocket. After he had half a dozen, we all went through the gate to see Edison. Soon enough they were swapping stories. Edison was the best storyteller I've ever heard. He was a master of timing. When he delivered the punch line he would explode with laughter and then we'd all double up. That day, Edison would tell a joke, we'd all roar, then Ford would draw out one of his slips of paper, open it up, and hand it to Edison.... Edison would read, roar at Ford's joke, and Ford would take the paper back, tear it in half, and put it in another pocket. I guess he didn't want to "tell" the same joke twice.

A typical joke:

> One day a country boy, in a moment of mischief, pushed over the family outhouse. Next day at school they read the story of young George Washington being honest with his father about chopping down the cherry tree. In a fit of remorse, the boy confessed to *his* father that he'd overturned the outhouse. His dad gave him a good beating. The boy complained that Washington's father hadn't punished his son. "Maybe not," said Dad, "but his father wasn't in the tree!"*

* Newton, *Uncommon Friends*, 15–16.

monopoly, [the rubber will have to] be harvested with a machine."[11] It was this problem that had Edison stumped.

During the day, Edison worked in his laboratory, assessing various rubber plants and hoping to revolutionize rubber production. But he believed that somewhere in the wilds of Florida a better rubber plant was waiting to be found. In early April, he ventured out in search of new specimens. He, Mina, and Edith Potter motored as far north as Tampa collecting plants and encouraging people to help him. He made the same request to everyone: "If you find any rubber trees, let me know."[12]

After a hard day of work, Edison often went to the Arcade Theater for some light entertainment. On April 13, both he and Mina were invited to a special showing of footage from a 1921 camping trip in Maryland. Harvey Firestone had sent the film of Edison, Ford, Firestone, President Harding, and others tramping through the woods. A short film about the history of the rubber tire followed. Since the inventor considered the latter an educational film, at Mina's encouragement, he invited the entire high school.[13]

As always, Mina played the role of a traditional wife of a famous man. She shooed away reporters and cared for her husband when he was suffering from stomach problems.[14] But she also struck out on her own, speaking about issues close to her heart. In March, she spoke to the Civic League, cautioning the town to reconsider a plan to place a new bridge across the Caloosahatchee near the business district. She felt it would ruin the view and hinder downtown access to the riverfront.[15] An editorial two days later commended her: "We are glad that Mrs. Edison raised the question and that she has pointed out what a loss to the city [it] would be."[16]

Closer to home she was dealing with a more challenging issue. One of the Edisons' neighbors was still pursuing the town's idea of a seawall. He wanted to fill in land near the Edisons' estate, creating a street between their home and the river. From the Edisons' perspective, the plan was a disaster. They would lose their privacy. There would be no solace at Seminole Lodge if neighbors, tourists, and reporters had easy access. Further, the waterfront would be ruined because seaweed and other materials would collect and rot and become a breeding ground for mosquitoes.[17]

The Edisons had offered to purchase rights to the property at what they felt was a reasonable price. The owner had refused to sell, holding out for more money. Mina lamented, "The property is in very bad hands and [we] feel very unhappy in dealing with them. They carry on a hold up game."[18] Clearly, Mina had to remain vigilant if she wanted to protect Seminole Lodge.

Henry Ford was absent from Fort Myers in 1927 because of the court case about his anti-Semitic newspaper. The local newspapers published several articles about the case as well as reports of a car accident that Ford blamed on sinister forces. In April, an editorial in the *Fort Myers Press* called the automaker paranoid, noting that in the future he would likely have a "regime of seclusion and mystery, of high walls and armed guards." There was also a touch of pity.

Clara Ford Wants "So Bad" to Go to Florida

During the time of the Sapiro court case, Clara Ford wrote a brief note to Charles and Carolyn Edison. She reported, "Mr. Ford is quite over his operation but has taken a cold that is hard to throw off. Expect it is on account of not being quite up to his strength, goes to business every day, working hard on a new car, and dodging sub-poena's which is so annoying, nothing but blackmail." She felt they would be less bothered in Fort Myers and declared, "I have never wanted to go to Florida so bad before."*

* Clara B. Ford to Charles and Carolyn Edison, February 3, [1928], EFWE, CEF.

"If he has indeed lost his peace of mind, he has lost that which, to any normal human being is worth more than a billion dollars any day in the week."[19]

In early May, the Edisons prepared to return north. It was the latest they had ever stayed in Fort Myers, and clearly they had enjoyed themselves. Just before they left, a high school science class toured their gardens and Edison personally guided them through the laboratory and his rubber research area. Mina explained to reporters that the laboratory would not be moved until Edison's experiments were completed. She restated her opposition to the idea of moving the laboratory and "intimated that it might never leave Fort Myers."

For his part, Edison was again asked about religion and politics. He thought an anti-evolution bill pending in the state legislature was nonsense. On the subject of the religious faith of one of the candidates in the New York governor's race, Edison declared, "What difference does it make whether he is a Catholic or a Protestant?" Lastly, he put in a plug for Florida agriculture: "We can grow anything here. We should tell the world about it."[20]

The Edisons were driven to the Atlantic Coast Line train station where a crowd of about 200 people waited. They climbed aboard the 4:30 p.m. train and bid their final farewell. They waved to friends and neighbors until the train rounded the bend and disappeared.

During their winter in New Jersey, Edison made plans for his next rubber crop, communicating with Dr. John K. Small, a botanist from the New York Botanical Garden. Small sent the inventor cuttings from many plants, including a Japanese bittersweet, and made plans to visit.[21] Edison looked forward to seeing him and offered the use of his Model T, which Small politely declined.[22] The botanist probably did not want to risk damaging the historic vehicle during his travels in the Everglades.

Small stayed with the Edisons at Seminole Lodge, arriving on January 25. The press was eagerly awaiting news about the inventor's experiments, and Small became the unexpected spokesperson. He described his plan for a month-long expedition through southern Florida and the Everglades collecting specimens for Edison. "I am hopeful of finding a plant in Florida that can be made to produce rubber in desired quantities," he said.[23]

While Edison and Small were talking rubber, Mina was coordinating plans for Edison's 81st birthday. Harvey Firestone was planning to attend but not Henry Ford. Charles Lindbergh was detained in Havana but said he would try to make it later.[24] Everyone in Fort Myers wanted to play a role in the celebration, and Mina was at her wit's end trying to plan activities that would not exhaust her husband.

On February 11, Seminole Lodge was opened and a bevy of photographers, reporters, and camera crews swarmed through the gate. For the better part of the morning, Edison answered questions and joked with his guests. His reply to a question about what advice he'd offer to young men was typical. "What's the use of giving advice to young men when they don't want it and won't take it?" By lunchtime Mina had sent the reporters away; she had her husband rest before the afternoon activities.

At 3 o'clock sharp, Edison arrived at the municipal pier in James D. Newton's Packard roadster. Mina and Harvey Firestone accompanied Edison to the speaker's platform while a large crowd cheered and a concert band played. The famous inventor waved to the crowd, which spontaneously shouted, "Happy Birthday."

The mayor made a brief speech before schoolchildren arrived. Some wore placards depicting Edison's many inventions while others formed a living flag. Finally the guests proceeded to the auditorium, where a six-foot-wide cake with 81 electric candles was unveiled. One newspaper estimated that 4,000 school children attended and said that it was definitely the biggest birthday party in the history of Fort Myers "or maybe in all Florida."[25]

Ford greatly regretted not being able to attend. He sent a long telegram commending the inventor for his work with inventions and innovations ranging from the telegraph and telephone to electric lights and the storage battery. He wrote, "I hope you may enjoy the continuation of your services to humanity for many more years."[26]

An Interview with Mina

Another reporter at the birthday interview was Marjory Stoneman Douglas, who had come to interview Mina Edison, not her famous husband. Douglas was impressed by Mina's ability to protect Edison from "a world whose attention can in a moment become a crushing burden whose favor, like a river in flood, often entirely overwhelms." Specifically, the long barrage of questions during the interview exhausted and frustrated Edison. After he made the comment about refusing to give young men advice, Mina intervened, saying, "My advice to young women is to find a man as busy as the one I found." Then she steered him away from the reporters.

Douglas published her interview in *McCall's Magazine* the following October, making the case that Mina was a social engineer. "Her work for Fort Myers ought most certainly to be recognized as one of the most outstanding civic achievements, since it is an achievement, not just in the material improvements of the city, but in the building up of a most amazing and creative community spirit."**

* Marjory Stoneman Douglas, "Mrs. Thomas A. Edison, at Home," *McCall's Magazine*, October 1929.

On February 18, word leaked that Henry Ford would arrive at the Atlantic Coast Line train depot. Once again a crowd that gathered to welcome the automaker went home disappointed. Ford arrived later that night aboard his private railcar, which was attached to the Orange Blossom Special train.[27] When he was sure that no one was around, he disembarked, declined a waiting Lincoln limousine, and walked the two miles to his home. On the way, a reporter recognized Ford and tried desperately to interview him, but he could not keep pace with the long-legged automaker.[28]

Dr. Emil Ludwig and his wife Elga also arrived that day. Ludwig, a German historian, was famous for his biographies of Napoleon and Kaiser Wilhelm II as well as a newly released book entitled *Jesus, the Son of Man*. They checked into the Royal Palm Hotel before joining the Edisons at Seminole Lodge.[29]

Over the next three days Ludwig spent nearly every waking moment with Edison. He talked with him about his early years of inventing, explored the Seminole Lodge jungle, and watched Edison dissect rubber plants as they talked about books, religion, and philosophy.[30]

Ludwig was utterly fascinated by the inventor, finding him both charming and enigmatic. In an article published three years later, he reminisced:

So I saw him in Florida stepping . . . into an old barn, overgrown with flowers. He wore a white suit, his head leaning forward a little, and was holding up a little plant in his right hand. His old features were completely overflowing with joy because it had kept its promise. The plant brought good percentages of rubber. In this tropical garden . . . he really seemed a magician, just one who was hiding at the beach in this southern gulf. . . . When, since Goethe's last years, has one seen such a fifth act?[31]

Ludwig was delighted that Henry Ford was also present for some of the interviews, but he observed in his personal diary that Mina didn't care for him. He also noted that one of Edison's greatest disappointments was that despite the fact that he had fathered six children, no one would carry on the Edison name.[32] None of his sons had become fathers and Madeleine's sons had their father's last name, Sloane.

The biographer felt that meeting both Edison and Ford was a great honor and the realization of his life's ambition. "In Germany when we think of America, we think of these two men. They are great men the world over."[33] He admired and respected Mina as well, noting her great vigilance in protecting her husband. He said to young James D. Newton that Thomas and Mina Edison were the "uncrowned King and Queen of America."[34]

While Mina certainly did not feel like a queen, her winter was filled with the responsibilities of a public figure. She gave speeches on beautification and conservation to at least eight groups, hosted numerous meetings at Seminole Lodge, and launched a campaign to ban billboards from roadways. She also founded the Valinda Literary Circle, a reading group named for her mother, Mary Valinda Miller, who had died in 1912.[35]

Mina also began to speak out about a personal subject. She wanted the word *housewife* changed to *home executive*. After all, women were not married to the home but were managers of it, just as their husbands were managers of business. She wanted women's work recognized and she wanted to "dignify the home and make men and women honor and respect us in our own field." But while she sought to create more respect for the traditional roles of mother, wife, and "home executive," she felt that wives and mothers belonged in that sphere and not outside it.[36] Her public opinions were often contradicted by her personal relationships. In Fort Myers, two of her closest friends were independent women, business owners Flossie Hill and Ella Piper.

On March 23, Henry Ford drove to LaBelle with his secretary, Frank Camp-sall, to inspect his 60-acre property. Twenty of the acres were devoted to rub-ber plants, but an additional forty had been newly planted with grapefruit and orange trees. Along the road, Ford stopped and talked with farmers. Although he had deplored farm life as a youth, he now appreciated it. He was pleased to see so much land in cultivation and announced that he was a great believer in the "back to the soil movement."[37] He returned to Fort Myers that evening and left for Michigan shortly afterward.[38]

For weeks the Edisons had planned a visit to Harvey Firestone's home in Miami Beach, but each time Mina had sent her apologies, saying "he is so engrossed in his work that I cannot get him away."[39] In early April, she finally prevailed. The Edisons crossed the state via the newly completed Tamiami Trail. They had dinner and spent the night at the Firestones' stately beach home. In the morning, the *Miami News* and *Miami Herald* arrived for inter-views.

Mina described Edison's dedication to his rubber experiments. "He thinks of nothing else now. He has no time for anything else, no recreation. Usually up at 5:30 or 6 a.m. He works all morning. A two-hour nap from 12 until 2, the only break." Edison described his research but cautioned that "there will be no announcement of results, of course, until every possible factor has been analyzed."[40]

During the winter, Ford, Firestone, and Edison formed the Edison Botanic Research Corporation, which sought to find a reliable domestic source of rub-

Map 11. Tamiami Trail, circa 1928.

ber. Edison committed his time and inventive genius, while Ford and Firestone each put up $25,000 in funding.[41] Despite the fact that they were helping Edison, it seemed that neither Ford nor Firestone truly believed Edison would succeed. In an interview, Firestone praised the inventor's hard work but described the potential outcome vaguely, saying that Edison "will do something in rubber development."[42]

Photographers descended en masse as the Edisons toured the grounds of Firestone's estate, but Edison was uncharacteristically mute. He milled around quietly while Mina requested cuttings of plants for Seminole Lodge. Firestone told the reporters that he hoped to take the Edisons in his speedboat for a trip to the Florida Keys, but Mina politely declined. They returned to Fort Myers later that evening to protect the 81-year-old Edison from overexertion.

In late April, Fort Myers was awash in plans to officially commemorate the opening of the Tamiami Trail. A motorcade would start in Tampa, stay overnight in Fort Myers, then travel on to Miami, ending at Biscayne Bay Park.

Rubber Tires

By 1927, Edison had a new favorite rubber-producer, the desert plant guayule. In October he wrote a letter to Firestone asking, in case of war, "could guayule supply Americans with shoes and inner tubes [for tires] that offered a 'fair mileage'?" Firestone immediately had his staff produce tires grown entirely with American rubber. They were sent to Fort Myers the following month for testing. One went flat before leaving the garage. Another went "all to pieces."

Edison knew that part of the problem was dirt and bark introduced during the manufacturing process and blamed Firestone's technicians. More tires were sent to Fort Myers in 1929 and 1930 with better results. One tire was placed on a plant-collecting vehicle that drove all over southwest Florida's bumpy roads. At 14,000 miles it was still in satisfactory condition. Although the tires never equaled traditional rubber tires, the staff came to the conclusion that in the case of a war, they could replace the fabric tires that had been used during World War I.[*]

[*] Rosenblum and Associates, *Edison Winter Estate: Cultural Landscape Report*, II: 21–22.

There were not enough hotel rooms to house the 3,000 people expected, so citizens of Fort Myers opened their homes to the travelers.[43]

The Edisons issued an unprecedented invitation to the visitors. For the entire day, they would open Seminole Lodge. For the first time ever, local people and visitors from all over the state could visit the gardens and see the houses. Edison's laboratory employees would act as guides, taking people around the grounds and explaining the inventor's rubber experiments. The newspaper noted, "The inventor himself may be seen at work among his plants but will not be able to find time for interviews."[44]

The excitement about the opening of the Tamiami Trail was dashed in early June. A newspaper headline decried, "Ford's Secretary Here to Superintend Taking Away of One of City's Most Historic Structures." Despite Mina's vehement opposition, Edison's 1886 laboratory was being removed. The region would lose one of its most historic landmarks.

"Dear me, I do wish he would keep out of our backyard!"[45] Mina complained of Henry Ford. For two years she had tried everything. Now, as a last resort, she ordered that none of the vines and plants entwined in the laboratory's structure be disturbed. But by mid-June, they had been cut. The 1886 laboratory was disassembled board by board and sent to Michigan.[46]

In exchange for the laboratory, Ford had a research facility constructed on the other side of McGregor Boulevard near Edison's rubber plants. The building was roughly the size of the old laboratory. But Mina would never forget the old building where the region's first electricity was generated. Later she would say, "I do not approve of disturbing historical spots. Let things [stay] put and surround historical spots with beauty."[47]

It was almost mid-June and very hot and humid when the Edisons began packing for New Jersey. They had been in Florida for five months, their longest stay ever. As they mounted the platform, Edison joked, "I don't want to leave, but she makes me," pointing to his wife. A crowd of about 150 people wished them farewell and gave them gifts of fruit and flowers.[48]

13

A President Comes to Call

"If Hoover wants to see me, he'll have to come to Fort Myers."
Thomas A. Edison

1929

The Edisons stayed so late into the summer of 1928 that only a few months passed before their return. Quick to capitalize on Thomas Edison's presence, the *Fort Myers Press* announced that Thomas Edison would soon arrive for his "46th annual visit."[1] Old-timers knew that Edison had not wintered in Florida every year. In fact, because of conflicts with his former partner Gilliland, business concerns in New Jersey, and World War I, Edison had wintered in Fort Myers only twenty-four times. Yet the number of seasons seemed inconsequential. Edison was coming, and that was all that mattered.

Two hundred spectators gathered at the Atlantic Coast Line Station on the evening of January 16 to greet the Edisons. As the snowy-haired inventor stepped down from the platform, they burst into spontaneous applause and the Fort Myers band struck up his favorite tune, "I'll Take You Home Again Kathleen." Flashbulbs illuminated the dark sky as still and moving cameras followed Edison to the Lincoln touring car. Edison waited several minutes for his wife to join him because she was talking with their neighbors about community matters. Over the course of the season she would give freely of her skills and vision.

As always, the trip from New Jersey had been exhausting. A group of reporters joined them in Jacksonville, all hoping to get an exclusive story. Edison said that he was looking forward to the arrival of Henry Ford and a visit from Harvey Firestone. Of president-elect Herbert Hoover, who was in Miami, Edison said, "If Hoover wants to see me, he'll have to come to Fort Myers."[2]

Even after the Edisons settled in at Seminole Lodge, the press intruded. On January 17, they gathered around the inventor as he worked at his new rubber laboratory on the east side of McGregor Boulevard. Dressed in a cream-colored linen suit, vest, white shirt, white bow tie, and floppy straw hat, he showed them around the new facility funded by Henry Ford. When they persisted in asking him questions, Edison declared, "Why, this isn't my birthday."

While the reporters feverishly took notes, he described his work on rubber and cheerfully tolerated a barrage of questions. Someone asked his opinion of the new small office Mina had built for him on the footprint of the 1886 laboratory recently removed by Ford. Edison replied, "Oh, I like it fine, but I like this big laboratory better."[3]

Reporters were not the only ones who wanted to see Thomas Edison in the flesh. More and more frequently, tourists parked their cars on McGregor Boulevard or walked from downtown. They lined up three deep at the white picket fence watching Edison work, pace, or sit in the Florida sun.[4] It was becoming increasingly clear that the press and public felt they were entitled to see him.

While Edison puzzled over questions of rubber production, newspaper headlines announced that Hoover would indeed come to Fort Myers to celebrate Edison's 82nd birthday. Their editorials boasted, "All this is old stuff to Fort Myers,"[5] because the city was accustomed to hosting famous folks like Edison, Ford, and Firestone. But the president-elect was no ordinary guest.

This was more than apparent to Mina's brother-in-law, who scolded, "Mr. H. is today a very different personage than the one you entertained in Glenmont. He *can't* be in Fort Myers to receive there your 'casual' invitation. That is altogether out of the question!!! Any invitation must now be vested with a formality required in the case of the Pres. Of the U.S. You may have to entertain his 'retinue,'—most certainly such secret service as his *safety* demands."[6]

Despite issues of etiquette and security, it seemed that Hoover was indeed coming. Mina did her best to ensure that the meeting was controlled. The dejected newspaper reporters complained that Edison "has made arrangements to clear away the annual birthday interview and other public incidents. . . . After that, reporters, photographers and the public will be persona non grata around Seminole Lodge."[7]

Mina was relieved, but not for long. Pressure built from the community and reporters, who complained in the newspaper about "the school children, who . . . would be grievously disappointed without understanding the reason."[8] Despite objections from the Secret Service, Edison and Hoover agreed to a short ride through the city.[9] Soon the plan had transformed into a grand parade.

Mina enlisted the help of James D. Newton to coordinate the press and oversee the interviews.[10] At 9:30 in the morning, reporters scribbled questions

Edison's 1929 Birthday Interview

Q: What are the dangers, if any, of the increasing stock speculation?

A: Ultimate panic. Loss of confidence.[*]

Q: Have you ever given any thought to the chemical development of synthetic rubber?

A: No. It has no future when rubber is quoted at 23 cents a pound.

Q: How will the success of your rubber experiments affect the future agricultural prosperity of Florida?

A: I believe those states bordering on the Gulf of Mexico can grow plant rubber with profit to the farmer in case of war prices, but it might be possible in the future to grow rubber and compete with the tropics.

Q: Is it true that you have found a plant which promises to solve the rubber production problem in the United States, and do you hope to develop it this winter?

A: I have found more than 1,200 plants to produce rubber: about 40 of them will be cultivated on a large scale.

Q: Should the United States try to have the most powerful navy in the world?

A: It should build on parity with England.

Q: Do you believe that intelligent reading and home study can take the place of the high tension college education?

A: If the boy has ambition he doesn't need to go to college.

Q: How will the approaching machine age affect the moral and physical conditions of the so-called working class?

A: Very favorably.

Q: Please give briefly your formula for a happy life.

A: I am not acquainted with anyone who is happy.

Q: With the experience of yourself, Mr. Hoover and Mr. Ford in mind, do you believe golf, tennis and other forms of physical exercise advisable for the assurance of health, usefulness and longevity?

A: No.[**]

[*] The stock market crash followed eight months later.
[**] "Edison Says Cost Bars Synthetic Rubber Making," *Tampa Tribune*, February 11, 1929.

on slips of paper. The increasingly deaf inventor read them aloud and answered them quickly, firmly, and with his typical sense of humor. Next the movie crews arrived with enormous microphones and cameras.[11]

Finally, the president-elect of the United States disembarked from his yacht *Saunterer*. He walked the length of the Edison dock and greeted the inventor with the words *Hello Fisherman*. With the initial meeting over, the press was "banished from the grounds."[12]

In the hour that followed, the Edisons and their guests relaxed in the quiet respite of the Seminole Lodge grounds. The president-elect's party included his son, Herbert Hoover Jr., who had stayed the night with the Edisons, his wife, Lou, and guests who had accompanied them from Miami Beach. Henry and Clara Ford, who had arrived quietly on February 7,[13] were present, as well as Harvey and Idabelle Firestone.[14] Next it was off to the parade.

Flanked by nervous Secret Service men, three mounted officers, and a bevy of motorcycle policemen, the Edisons, the Hoovers and their guests, the Fords, and the Firestones climbed into six automobiles. For thirty minutes they traveled five miles per hour on a circuitous route through town. They drove through Edison Park, then up and down the streets of the downtown before returning to seclusion behind Seminole Lodge's white picket fence.

People from all over southwest Florida turned out to see them. Fort Myers's population was less than 9,000,[15] but 20,000 people came out to see the celebrities. Sometimes spectators ran into the street with roses. To supplement Fort Myers's police force, officers were brought in from Tampa, Arcadia, Wauchula, and Lakeland,[16] but there were no disturbances.

The following day the *Tropical News* proclaimed, "Fort Myers yesterday achieved a distinction no city is likely to equal, much less surpass. . . . Hoover, Edison, Ford and Firestone passing in review! . . . No hour, anywhere, was ever more notable than noon-time yesterday. . . . It was truly our day of days, always to be remembered by home folks and visitors fortunate enough to be among those present."[17]

After the parade, the Edisons and their guests enjoyed a quiet luncheon, followed by birthday cake. Next on the agenda was a dance by some local schoolgirls.[18] By the time they arrived, Mina had to wake Edison, who was sleeping in a wicker chair. The inventor moaned, "Tell 'em to go away." At Mina's insistence, he roused himself and afterward shook hands with the girls.[19]

After lunch, Edison was able to resume his nap. He needed to rest up for a coast-to-coast radio broadcast that evening. He gave a brief speech thanking everyone who had honored him on his birthday. "I wish I could invite all of you to have some birthday cake," he said, "but unfortunately we can't eat by radio—just yet. I'll have to work on that problem."[20]

Two of his famous guests soon departed. President-elect Hoover had planned to spend some time fishing, but pressing matters called him back to Miami. Firestone left at about the same time.

Ford and Edison traveled to the inland community of Clewiston a few days later to see a sugar-processing mill. The inventor and automaker found the plant fascinating. Edison was curious about the machinery in the crusher and mill rolls. He declared, "It was interesting seeing how thoroughly the juice was extracted from the cane. That's my big problem with rubber experiments." Ford was interested in the heavy machinery of the large-scale operation.[21]

Finally the excitement of the birthday and frequent day trips began to catch up with the inventor. Rollins College, located in Winter Park, Florida, was planning to confer an honorary degree on Edison. Mina wrote the president of the college that "I did hope that [Edison] might be able to do it but our few hours trip to Clewiston convinces us that it would be quite out of the question." She went on to express her disappointment, "I cannot begin to tell you how much I regret it. . . . It would have been a great satisfaction to him to have received the honor from his beloved state."[22]

Though Edison was supposed to be resting, he could not resist one par-

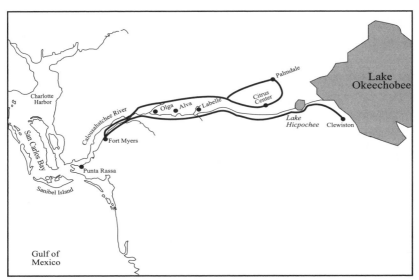

Map 12. The Edisons' visits to Clewiston, Palmdale, and Citrus Center, 1929

ticular outing, a visit to the Lee County Fair. The fair's general manager sent free passes, but Edison paid admission for himself and Mina. "This is no free lunch," he said. Edison was especially impressed by Snooky, a chimpanzee who wore clothes and smoked.[23]

Edison later declined an invitation to a Women's Community Club square dance given in honor of Henry Ford. The automaker disapproved of contemporary jazz music and current dances and wanted to revive old-time music and steps. On March 4, Henry and Clara Ford and Mina twirled to old-fashioned dances like the schottische and quadrille while the club members tried to keep up.[24] The Fords left for Michigan the next day.

Over the weeks that followed, Edison, who was feeling better, worked in his new rubber laboratory while 65-year-old Mina juggled an ambitious schedule of community work. Every day, often several times a day, she attended or hosted meetings of various garden groups, the music club, the Valinda Literary Circle, and the Fort Myers Round Table. She donated her time and money to the Boy Scouts,[25] the Girl Scouts,[26] and a group advocating flood control.[27] She worked in the black community[28] and gave multiple talks to the Young Men's Wesley Bible Class at the Methodist Church.[29]

She also dealt with a potentially explosive matter. The community was growing rapidly; the population had doubled in a decade.[30] Old and new residents clashed over their vision for the region. At one point, some new citizens had adopted the slogan "eliminate the cracker."[31] Mina, who had great respect for early settlers, stepped in and organized a party to honor the town's pioneers, asking newer residents to help organize it. The event created a new respect for old-time settlers and brought people together for a common cause.[32]

Mina also entered the world of journalism. The Woman's Community Club, at Mina's direction, published a complete edition of the *Tropical News* on April 23. Women secured advertisers and did interviews, then wrote, proofed, and printed their stories. Mina wrote numerous editorials on her pet subjects: "The Influence of the Home," "The Billboard Nuisance," and "The State Park Movement."[33] Overall, the newspaper staff was surprised by the "high degree of excellence when measured by every criterion used in judging newspapers."[34]

As the months passed, Edison regained strength and went tarpon fishing. He hooked a tarpon, but after a fifteen-minute struggle, it got away. It seemed that the inventor would never catch anything larger than that 40-pound tarpon he had caught with Charles. Mina, however, snagged a 100-pound "stingaree" after a 40-minute battle.[35]

The Edisons went on an excursion with 71-year-old Captain Fred Menge in late May. Unlike previous years when Menge had piloted steamboats up the river, this time he drove an automobile. Taking back roads, they traveled all the way to Fort Thompson, Palmdale, and Citrus Center. Along the way, they admired hoards of exotic birds, including wild pigeons, whooping cranes, and red-headed woodpeckers.[36]

In the weeks that followed, Edison puttered in his lab and Mina worked in the community. They took day trips and went to the movies in the evening. May passed. Finally, in mid-June, the summer heat became too much. After another fishing trip, during which Mina caught a 50-pound tarpon and Edison again returned empty-handed, it was time to go home.

The evening before their departure, the Edisons attended a farewell party at the Arcade Theater. A brief film debuted called *A Day with Thomas A. Edison*. In it, Edison went off to work in the morning, kissing Mina goodbye on the porch of Seminole Lodge. The next scene depicted Edison toiling in the laboratory, and the last segment observed him ascending the stairs to his quiet bedroom. The film was followed by the evening's feature presentation, Buster Keaton's *Spite Marriage*.[37] The next day the Edisons left for New Jersey.

During their absence, Fort Myers was much in the minds of the Edisons, especially Mina, who tried to discourage a local effort to create a monumental Temple of Light to honor her husband. Her refusal was largely due to concern

Edison and the Talkies

Thomas Edison loved going to the movies. During the winter season, his 1914 Model T Ford was regularly parked in front of the Arcade Theater in downtown Fort Myers. He could follow all the action on the screen, and though he could not always hear accompanying music, he could feel the vibrations of a piano. In 1927, The *Jazz Singer* opened up the world of talking movies and left the inventor behind. In a 1930 interview Edison complained, "The talkies have spoiled everything for me. There isn't any more good acting on the screen. My, my, how I should like to see Mary Pickford or Clara Bow in one of those good old fashioned pictures. They concentrate on the voice now; they've forgotten how to act. I can sense it more than you because I am deaf. It is astounding how much more a deaf person can see."

for her neighbors. The real estate decline had hit the economy hard and the Edisons did not want people fund-raising on their behalf. Mina explained, "[Mr. Edison] feels. . . that just now on account of the hardships in Florida that the people are taxed so heavily it is hard for them to meet their expenses and believes it would be better to wait until later before carrying out this project."[38]

The Edisons did agree to another project. Rosamond Chadwick, one of Mina's community friends, asked for permission to erect a bronze plaque to commemorate the anniversary of Edison's light bulb. Unlike previous monuments, this one was to be dedicated to both the inventor and his wife. Profiles of both Thomas and Mina Edison would remind citizens and visitors of Edison's scientific contributions and Mina's community work. The Edisons agreed to attend the unveiling.[39]

All plans were put on hold in August when Edison caught a cold. It quickly developed into pneumonia and his physicians feared for the worse. But the inventor rallied. By early September the 82-year-old was sitting up and in good spirits. His doctor credited the recovery to the inventor's "natural vigor and unusual powers of resistance."[40]

The following month, stories of Edison's health were eclipsed by the stock-market crash. Overnight, many millionaires had become penniless. Family fortunes disappeared and the nation's future seemed bleak. The frugal Edisons would find the times difficult but not unbearable. The same could not be said of many of their South Florida neighbors. The real estate bust had already dashed hopes and made life challenging, but the days ahead would be worse. The townspeople would be thankful for the Edisons, who would bring them publicity and hope.

14

Honors and Exhaustion

"Stay Right Here, Sir."

—Fort Myers Press

December 1929–1930

Southwest Florida's economy collapsed when the real estate market went bust, and the Great Depression put an end to any hope of a quick recovery. New construction came to a virtual standstill, and the many thousands who worked in the building industry lost their jobs. In coming years, tourism dollars would dry up. Few in the struggling nation could afford oranges or grapefruit, so the citrus industry was crippled. Local farmers let their fruit rot on the vine.[1] The one bright spot was Edison, who returned to Florida year after year despite his advanced age. But he was turning 83, which was twenty-three years older than average life expectancy.[2] How long could Edison endure?

Edison was still weak following a summer bout of pneumonia when he and Mina made plans to go south in 1929. For the first time ever, they arrived in Florida in early December. Mindful of the hoopla that usually greeted their arrival, Mina informed the press that there should be no crowds at the station and that there would be no interviews. The local press honored their privacy, but other reporters accosted him on the train along the way. Edison explained that he was "just fair" and "hadn't been feeling so well."[3]

The *Tropical News* shared Mina's concern for her husband's health and printed an editorial the day of their arrival. Entitled, "Stay Right Here, Sir," it declared that in the interests of the inventor's health, the famous couple should not return to New Jersey. After all, "Last year he remained until June and for all that went back and caught a case of pneumonia. That should be a lesson to teach him that the climate up there is not to be trusted and to convince him that the only place a person is safe . . . is here in Fort Myers."

In addition to the northern weather, the newspaper cautioned about "the mischief Henry Ford will be getting him into."[4] The comment was a reference to the Golden Jubilee of Light, which the automaker had hosted in October. The Edisons attended the event which took place at Ford's Greenfield Village in Michigan. Celebrating the opening of Edison's reconstructed Menlo Park, New Jersey, laboratory the celebration included days of activities. After enduring endless ceremonies and honors, Thomas Edison had collapsed and had been bedridden for days. At the end of the Jubilee, he had said weakly, "I am tired of all the glory. I want to go back to work."[5]

There were other reasons for editors to disdain Ford's efforts. Greenfield Village was also the location of Edison's 1886 Fort Myers laboratory. They also resented millionaire Ford's unwillingness to contribute to the community. A September 1929 editorial had complained, "What he will do about sparing a little small change for Fort Myers, we do not know." The editorial went on to detail Ford's plan to transform Detroit's garbage into industrial grease. It implied that Ford was not interested in the Michigan community either. He only wanted the grease to "yield a profit."[6]

In contrast, Mina mobilized her charitable Fort Myers Round Table to meet at Seminole Lodge just after she arrived. Representatives of the local welfare board reported on the hardships local families were facing in the approaching holiday season. Mina and the group announced a campaign to create Christmas food baskets. She and her husband each donated ten dollars to the cause, which was matched by others.[7] Over the next few weeks, at Mina's direction, food and money were collected to ensure that no one went hungry on Christmas Day.

The Edisons' first Christmas in Florida was quiet, without children or grandchildren. Mina presided over the annual lighting of the town's Christmas tree and attended Christmas Eve services at St. Luke's Episcopal Church. Edison was showered with gifts from friends as well as publishers and clothing makers, who hoped for endorsements. He passed up a traditional Christmas dinner for plain milk, which had become the staple of his diet. Finally, in the afternoon he crossed McGregor Boulevard. Even on Christmas, he wanted to be in his laboratory.

The new year brought Edison notice in *National Geographic Magazine*. The inventor was featured prominently in an article entitled "Florida—The Fountain of Youth." It described his rubber research and featured a photograph of Edison in his laboratory and an aerial image of Fort Myers.

An air circus arrived in town a few days later. In honor of the great inventor, the circus staged a performance directly over Seminole Lodge. From their yard, the Edisons watched planes fly in formation and saw "Daredevil Burns" perform his famous knee hang. As a special thank you, the Edisons invited the performers to dine with them.[8]

Mina devoted much of January to community work. She took a well-earned day off at the end of the month to go golfing with her sister Grace and James D. Newton's mother. Sixty-five-year-old Mina had never played before and was surprised when she drove a ball ninety yards. Her efforts won the admiration of her son Theodore. An avid golfer himself, he congratulated her, "[I] see you made your first nine holes of golf in 99! . . . I hope you get a lot of fun out of it."[9] Mina intended to. She took out a membership at the Fort Myers Country Club and bought a full set of clubs.[10]

Henry Ford arrived in town on February 7. As always, he avoided a public reception by slipping off his private railcar before the train reached the downtown depot. He walked the long distance to his McGregor Boulevard home, but before he entered the bungalow, he crossed the street to Edison's rubber laboratory, and he and the inventor exchanged warm greetings.[11]

The next two weeks were entirely consumed with plans for Edison's birthday. A local committee had taken over much of the organization. This was a relief to Mina but was also a concern because she worried that too much activity would cause her husband to relapse. President Hoover and former president Coolidge declined invitations. Hamilton Holt, president of Rollins College, would address the crowd. Harvey Firestone, the Fords, and Fred Ott would be there to see the unveiling of the plaque dedicated to the Edisons.

On the day of his 83rd birthday, Edison was exhausted. The annual birthday interview was held at the small office on the former site of Edison's 1886 laboratory. Edison carried a cane but claimed it was only an ornament. About twenty-five reporters presented written questions. He answered many questions with a simple "yes" or "no." A report that Edison fainted after the press conference was denied, but Mina's birthday present said it all. She bought him a yellow wheelchair.[12]

Edison was a half-hour late to the plaque dedication. When he arrived, the crowd cheered wildly and the Fort Myers Concert Band launched into Edison's favorite song, "I'll Take You Home Again Kathleen," interrupting Dr. Hamilton Holt's speech. After things quieted down, Holt resumed his address, calling the inventor "the greatest living American" and a "living immortal." Holt's speech was so eloquent and heartfelt that he could be forgiven one inaccuracy. He said that Edison was turning 97, not 83.[13]

Edison's 1930 Interview

Q: Do you think that absolute prohibition will ever be accomplished in the United States?

A: Yes.

Q: What is the greatest education force operative today?

A: Young men's desire for a technical education.

Q: How old do you feel?

A: Generally 50 years but lately some microbes have spotted me and done some experimenting with my internal machinery so I feel about 85 years.

Q: In your opinion when will television be practical for home entertainment?

A: Some day.

Q: What is the biggest thing the American people can accomplish during the next year?

A: Pay more attention to engineers than politicians.

Q: When and where do you expect to start large scale planting of Solidago Levanworthii (the species of goldenrod Mr. Edison has found to have the largest rubber content)?

A: I expect to have the first single unit perfected in two or three years. Will probably erect it at Mr. Ford's place near Savannah.

Q: Can you tell us of the greatest disappointment you encountered in your work?

A: I am always disappointed until a problem is solved. Not more than one out of 20 of the details work at first.

Q: What will become of common labor when the full automatic machine eliminates hand work?

A: He will own a home and a lot of new things[,] providing alcohol doesn't intervene.

Q: What field offers the greatest opportunity for invention today?

A: Chemistry and physics.

Q: Do you think there is life on other planets. . .

A: I could guess, but I won't.[*]

[*] "Edison on Birthday Feels More Than 83," *Tropical News*, February 12, 1930.

When the speech was over, the band exploded into a fanfare of trumpets so loud that even the nearly deaf inventor was startled. A Girl Scout and a Boy Scout pulled back a cloth to reveal a bronze plaque with the likenesses of both Thomas and Mina Edison. Carved in the rock below the plaque were the words *Erected by the Citizens of Fort Myers*.[14]

Those who feared that Edison's extreme age and exhaustion would keep him home were pleasantly surprised when he attended the Lee County Fair the next day. Accompanied by Mina, Harvey and Idabelle Firestone, and Mina's sister and brother-in-law, Edison inspected agricultural exhibits before heading to the midway. At a game concession, Mina won a stuffed rabbit. When asked what color she wanted, her husband answered "Yellow," because it was her favorite color. For the remainder of the evening, Edison, the famed inventor, walked around the midway with the yellow rabbit comically tucked under his arm.[15]

The next day Edison rested at home, but Mina invited a group forty-six people, including the Fords, to the fair. She encouraged everyone to forget their troubles and "just be boys and girls again." Mina took a spin on a ride called Leaping Lena, sharing the car with a local minister. Henry Ford was content to view the exhibits until he was badgered into riding the carousel. As he bobbed up and down on his painted pony, the millionaire seemed more interested in the ride's machinery than in the experience. At the end of the evening, Mina treated everyone to peanuts and lemonade.[16] In the bleakness of the Depression, the night was a very pleasant diversion.

On March 5, Henry Ford allowed a rare personal newspaper interview, answering questions from a pre-approved list. Ford supported developing the Everglades into agricultural land. He also opined that Florida's bank closures were caused mainly by high railroad rates.

Ford said little about Edison's domestic rubber experiments. His actions spoke for themselves. He had invested in a plantation of 3 million acres in South America, announcing, "We may go into the manufacturing of rubber to increase production."[17] His investment in Edison's rubber research was sentiment, not a belief in the project's feasibility.

A couple of weeks after the birthday celebration, Thomas Edison was well enough to travel to Winter Park, Florida. There he would receive an honorary degree at the Rollins College Founder's Day celebration. Attired in a cap and gown and smiling broadly, the inventor marched in, supported on the arm of Dr. Hamilton Holt.

"No words can add to your name or fame by any title or honor it can bestow," Holt told the inventor. "Rollins College, therefore, must rest content with honoring itself by conferring upon you the degree of Doctor of Science."[18] Edison, who had had little formal education, smiled and sat down. Then, holding the sheepskin in both hands, he nodded and chucked audibly.[19] Photographs and accounts of the event were published in newspapers worldwide.

Mina continued her community work. In March, she organized elaborate events to benefit local projects. Of all the activities planned, the most popular were the two-dollar rides in an airplane loaned by Harvey Firestone. The next day, a newspaper editorial referred to Mina as the "First Lady of Fort Myers," noting that "Mrs. Thomas A. Edison and her Flower Guild have done more this winter to banish gloomy pessimism than any one factor."[20]

Shortly afterward, Mina sponsored another charity event. Local society women were invited to take the place of working women at her friend Flossie Hill's store.[21] Like earlier efforts that brought together old and new residents, the event allowed women with seemingly conflicting lifestyles to learn from each other. In addition to her other qualities, Mina had a keen sense for ways to bring people together.

At about the same time, Joe Chappel, a famous writer who was then editor and owner of *The National Magazine*, stopped by Edison's experimental goldenrod plots. Chappel, who was only a decade younger than Edison, had a long relationship with the inventor. "I have chewed tobacco off and on with Mr. Edison for 40 years," he claimed. "I have interviewed eight kings, known the most famous men of the century—but to me Mr. Edison is the greatest and most lovable man of all."[22]

Botanist Dr. John K. Small, a repeat visitor who had corresponded with Edison for years, soon followed. The famous botanist had been one of the first in the scientific community to praise the inventor's rubber research. Small had helped Edison identify specimens and sent him plant and seed samples.[23]

The inventor's precarious health kept him at home during much of February, but in March the Edisons took car trips to the Everglades.[24] Later he felt well enough to visit Harvey and Idabelle Firestone in Miami. Edison inspected experimental rubber plants on the grounds of Firestone's stables. Firestone reported that "Mr. Edison told me my rubber plants were 'old-fashioned.' He is going to give me some 'modern' ones to replace some of them."[25]

Firestone took the Edisons on a tour of the city's new waterfront aquarium.

The inventor found it fascinating, but when the *Miami Herald* interviewed him, the topic was rubber. "I feel very much encouraged over results of recent experiments. Of course, we have a long way to go but we are getting there." When asked to name the one thing above all else he would wish for, Edison said, "Good health."[26] He was probably thinking in terms of the years of research good health would allow him to do.

In April, Edison's daughter Marion arrived at Seminole Lodge for the first time since 1887.[27] Marion had settled in Connecticut after her return from Germany and reunited with her estranged family. Four decades after her last visit to Fort Myers, Marion learned that the community had changed from a small cattle town to a burgeoning city. Seminole Lodge was a beautiful showplace.

As the winter progressed, Edison's health improved and he worked longer and longer hours in his rubber laboratory. His favorite plant, a tall species of goldenrod, turned out to be a little too tall to easily process. In April, he announced that he planned to cross it with a smaller-growing variety.

Soon a new machine that Fred Ott had designed to extract rubber from pulverized leaves and stems[28] was ready for testing. "I have just made a great discovery . . . [that will] produce an emergency rubber supply for the United States which farmers can grow and harvest in six months," Edison announced. "I would like to see 25,000 acres of this new plant growing. . . . The beauty of this goldenrod is that it grows fast. We can mow it down and it will grow right up again."[29]

Edison's hopes were premature. In coming months, he struggled with his rubber mill. It had been made with copper and brass pipes, which somehow neutralized some of the chemicals necessary for rubber extraction. He planned to replace the pipes with iron, but the apparatus would not be ready again for months.[30]

Over the season, the Edisons frequently donated to local charities.[31] It might be assumed that the Edisons were so financially well off that such generosity came easily. But like the rest of the nation, the famous couple was hard hit by the Depression. Edison had stayed in the phonograph business too long, producing old-fashioned products and music. Charles and Theodore had spent years trying to convince their father to break into radio manufacturing. When he finally agreed, it was too late.[32] The Edisons were better off than most, but the donations still represented a sacrifice.

The inventor's winter visit, which had begun in early December, extended into the first week of June, making it the Edisons' longest visit ever. Mina filled her days with community work, attending or hosting several meetings a day. She also made a speech to the all-male Rotary Club.[33] Edison fussed over his goldenrod plots, fought with his rubber mill, and tested samples in the laboratory, hoping desperately to make one last contribution to his nation.

They also made time for day trips. As Edison's health improved, they cruised to Useppa Island on one of Baron Collier's yachts.[34] Later they attended a barbecue with a local Bible class[35] and a Girl Scout[36] rally at Fort Myers Beach. Another outing took them by automobile to Collier City and Marco.[37] On yet another trip they went in the opposite direction and explored Venice.[38]

By June it was time for the Edisons to return to New Jersey. Edison looked a great deal healthier than he had when he arrived and swung his cane around to demonstrate its uselessness. At the train station, he greeted well-wishers and patted babies. Mina, loaded down with bundles of flowers given by friends, kept a watchful eye on her husband. She was surprised when a group of women surrounded her and launched into an impromptu serenade in her honor.

The Edisons finally boarded the passenger car and went to the platform at the end of the train. Standing side by side, they waved and said their goodbyes. As the newspaper described it, Thomas and Mina Edison, "held their positions waving in return to the farewell of several hundred persons until their figures faded from sight into the evening mist."[39]

During the remainder of the summer of 1930, Mina kept contact with her Florida neighbors, ensuring that the members of a Chautauqua reading group she had founded received their diplomas.[40] She also corresponded with the Fort Myers Chamber of Commerce about plans to dedicate a bridge to her husband the following year.[41] Mina agreed that she and Edison would attend the event but insisted that he not be asked to speak. She also requested the scheduling to be such that "he will not have to sit through the speeches. . . . It is hard on him because he cannot hear."

She also recommended that the town preserve the "old fort." The garrison had been built in the 1850s as a defense against the Seminole Indians. During the Civil War, it had been occupied by Union soldiers. By 1930, it was falling apart. Mina suggested that it be repaired and cleaned up: "It could be made into a charming little rest place with . . . exhibits or something of that sort."[42] Sadly, her suggestion was ignored and the fort was lost forever.

After a slight illness in October, the inventor's health improved.[43] In December, Mina wrote to young friend, Sidney Davis, that "I am glad that now

I can talk with you instead of writing as we shall very soon be traveling south-ward."[44] After spending Christmas in New Jersey, they planned to arrive in mid-January. As in previous years, Mina's plans were fraught with worry. She hoped that her husband would remain healthy enough to travel. Once in Florida there would be new concerns. Everyone would want to see him, interview him, honor him. Mina wondered just how much longer she could protect her husband.

Figure 27. Thomas Edison at Seminole Lodge, circa 1929. *Courtesy U.S. Department of the Interior, National Park Service, Edison National Historic Site.*

Figure 28. Thomas Edison at the Key West Naval Base, World War I.
RCO5160. *Courtesy State Library and Archives of Florida.*

Figure 29. "Hello Fisherman!" Edison greets President-elect Herbert Hoover, 1929 (Mina Edison and secret serviceman in the background). RC19386. *Courtesy State Library and Archives of Florida.*

Figure 30. President-elect Hoover, Henry Ford, Thomas Edison, and Harvey Firestone, 1929. RC13467. *Courtesy State Library and Archives of Florida.*

Figure 31. Edison, Hoover, and entourage tour Fort Myers, 1929. RC03550. *Courtesy State Library and Archives of Florida.*

Figure 32. Edison at the bat and Connie Mack catching, 1927. *Courtesy U.S. Department of the Interior, National Park Service, Edison National Historic Site.*

Figure 33. Ty Cobb, Thomas Edison, and Connie Mack at Terry Park, 1927. *Courtesy U.S. Department of the Interior, National Park Service, Edison National Historic Site.*

Figure 34. Thomas Edison with his beloved Model T, c. 1920s. RC11236.
Courtesy State Library and Archives of Florida.

Figure 35. Unveiling of the Edison plaque, February 11, 1930. *Left to right:* boy scout, Henry Ford, Thomas Edison, Harvey Firestone, girl scout. *Courtesy U.S. Department of the Interior, National Park Service, Edison National Historic Site.*

Figure 36. (*top left*) Henry Ford and Thomas Edison in front of Edison's electrical laboratory before it was disassembled, 1928. 14.400.120. *Courtesy U.S. Department of the Interior, National Park Service, Edison National Historic Site.*

Figure 37. (*bottom left*) The disassembly of Edison's electrical laboratory, June 19, 1928. 12.240.9. *Courtesy U.S. Department of the Interior, National Park Service, Edison National Historic Site.*

Figure 38. (*above*) Roger Firestone, Harvey Firestone, and Thomas Edison in Edison's rubber laboratory, 1931. 14.400.71. *Courtesy U.S. Department of the Interior, National Park Service, Edison National Historic Site.*

Figure 39. Thomas and Mina Edison, February 11, 1931. 14.400.114. *Courtesy U.S. Department of the Interior, National Park Service, Edison National Historic Site.*

Figure 40. Edison with a goldenrod sample from his rubber research, circa 1930. 14.400.75. *Courtesy U.S. Department of the Interior, National Park Service, Edison National Historic Site.*

15

The Last Hurrah

"Be as brave as your fathers before you. Have faith. Go forward."
—Thomas Edison

1931

The Edisons were ready to travel to Fort Myers after Christmas, but they waited until mid-January. Madeleine, at 43, was about to give birth to her fourth child, and Mina wanted to be with her for the birth. On January 8, 1931, Madeleine safely delivered her son Michael. Like his brothers before him, Michael's middle name was Edison.

In the meantime, Fred Ott and six assistants organized the Florida laboratory. Every year the inventor went to the laboratory within hours—sometimes minutes—of his arrival. The men readied Edison's rubber equipment and Fred Ott shined up the brass radiator on the old Model T.[1] Everything was prepared by the time Edison traveled south in Harvey Firestone's private railroad car.

Despite Mina's request that their arrival be a quiet one, the newspaper announced that "they will get a reception at the station."[2] So, taking a lesson from Henry Ford, the couple slipped into town, arriving hours ahead of schedule at the town's alternate station. Disappointed reporters were appeased when Edison's agent, Frank M. Stout, relayed a quote from the great inventor. "Yes, we're glad to be back. It feels like living again to be back home in Fort Myers."[3]

The next morning, Edison's laboratory staff eagerly awaited the arrival of their boss, but he did not come. They finished setting up a miniature distilling machine he had sent from New Jersey to replace the rubber mill with the pipe problem. Finally they tested the new machine, assuming that Edison would cross McGregor Boulevard to evaluate their progress. He did not.[4]

Days passed. The inventor did not leave Seminole Lodge. No visitors were allowed and Mina restricted contact with the laboratory staff. Edison's birthday and all the expected activities were fast approaching with little hope that the inventor would be healthy enough to participate. Finally, Mina called John Harvey Kellogg. The doctor had recently established a branch of his Battle Creek, Michigan, sanitarium outside Miami. Kellogg arrived the first week of February and examined Edison. Mina wrote him, "Thank you many times for the interest you take in Mr. Edison. Your visit helped him and me very much and he seems to be resting much better."[5]

Though Edison had improved, he was by no means healthy. For years he had suffered from Bright's disease, which was slowly causing his kidneys to fail. At nearly 84, he also had diabetes and gastric ulcers.[6] These conditions brought a number of discomforts, including extreme fatigue, difficulty walking and dressing, frequent trips to the bathroom, and itching all over his body.[7] Even on his best day, basic tasks challenged the inventor.

As a city committee planned Edison's birthday, Mina repeatedly stressed that the event should be no longer than an hour. Reluctantly they agreed.[8] This birthday would be more historically significant than others. Something in Fort Myers was finally being named for the inventor. The new $500,000 bridge spanning the Caloosahatchee was to be called the Edison Bridge.[9]

As February 11 neared, Mina juggled care of her husband, houseguests, plans for the celebration, and fund-raising for the American Red Cross. The local chapter was struggling to raise $1,400 to help farmers in the dust bowl. She organized the Valinda Literary Circle to advertise a sale of oranges for the Red Cross on a local radio station. While his wife was fund-raising, Edison sat quietly nearby in his car. He could not hear what was going on. When newspaper reporters asked his opinion, he said, "I'm sick of the whole radio business, and I guess you fellows are pretty sick of it too."[10]

Finally, Edison's 84th birthday arrived. The gates of Seminole Lodge opened and reporters arrived at his small office. They waited fifteen minutes past the appointed time while Edison had a breakfast of milk and received a shave from local barber Mike Pavese. Finally, leaning on a cane and wearing a blue suit with a sunflower in the lapel, Edison walked to the small office and sat down. The reporters handed him typewritten questions. He responded in writing, speaking only when the Paramount News team insisted on sound footage. Outside the Edisons' white picket fence, a crowd of about a hundred people jockeyed for position, trying to catch a glimpse of the venerated inventor.[11]

The day after the interview, a newspaper editorial sought to downplay some of the inventor's more controversial statements. In reference to his comment

Edison's 1931 Birthday Interviews

Q: Do you think prohibition is succeeding or failing?

A: Succeeding.

Q: What is the best way to relieve the unemployment problem in America?

A: This question is several sizes too large for me.

Q: If an honest, sincere, hard-working man cannot obtain a job and his family is in privation, what do you think he should do?

A: That's a sticker. Turn himself over to the Red Cross who represents us all.

Q: Are we living at too fast a pace?

A: No.

Q: Whom do you regard as the five outstanding men in the world today?

A: (Mr. Edison gave no answer.)

Q: What achievement in your great career gave you the biggest thrill and most satisfaction?

A: The phonograph.

Q: What's the chief ingredient for success of a man's career?

A: Ambition and the will to work.

Q: Do you regard Mr. Hoover's administration to date as a failure or success, and why?

A: A success.

Q: Are you in favor of the "dole" system of helping the jobless?

A: Am not in favor of any kind of dole.

Q Can America combat the steady growth of racketeering?

A: Yes.

Q: What is the condition of your health?

A: Pretty good.

Q: What is the outstanding development of the last ten years from a scientific standpoint?

A: Too numerous to mention. Science is moving rapidly.

Q: What are your present aims other than rubber research?

A: Perfecting some old inventions.

Q: Do you agree with former Secretary of Agriculture Jardine that rubber production in the United States is only a matter of mechanical perfection?

A: Both mechanical and chemical.

Q: Do you expect to do any work here this Winter in regard to an anti-fog device for aviation and what are your ideas as to the best method to overcome the fog danger?

A: Yes.

Q: Have you obtained any actual rubber yet from your new distilling machine?

A: Yes.

Q: We understand you have definitely decided that Solidago Leaven-worthii is the best plant for rubber and that now your problem is to perfect an extracting process. What are the difficulties still to be overcome in this?

A: Not yet decided. Have found in Central Florida andother Solidago much better than Leavenworthii. It grows twelve feet high.

Q: Have aviation developments of the past year altered your previous attitude that flying is still unsafe?

A: Somewhat changed by the advent of the autogiro, which is a great advance.

Q: Do you expect Ford this Winter, and, if so, when?

A: Yes. Can't say when.

Q: Do you favor municipally owned public utilities?

A: Decidedly no.

Edison was asked a number of other questions including his opinion of Premier Mussolini of Italy. He replied, "Man of great executive ability, probably a good man for the Italians."

that Benito Mussolini was a "man of great executive ability, probably a good man for the Italians,"[12] it said: "The implication no doubt is that a dictator would not be a good man for Americans." The editor was less sympathetic regarding Edison's support for the increasingly unpopular President Hoover: "There will be considerable dissent from the opinion that Hoover is a success as president and that prohibition is succeeding." In the end, the editor said, "But all in all Mr. Edison's answers are about what the average sensible American would write."[13]

Following the interview, Edison was conducted to a group of children from the Dunbar School Glee Club. The black high school students sang a series of

Stephen Foster songs. Helen Stebbins, who was 14 at the time, remembered, "He had a funny looking horn [that he held up to his ear so he could hear]. Mrs. Edison was telling him the titles of the songs. He looked very tired."[14] Finally, after the performance, Edison was allowed to rest.

The afternoon festivities began when twenty young women dressed in white arrived at Seminole Lodge to walk alongside the inventor's car from McGregor Boulevard to the corner of Fowler Street, where the dedication would be held.[15] Florida governor Doyle E. Carlton gave a speech praising the inventor. Fort Myers mayor Josiah H. Fitch spoke briefly but sincerely: "Today we are touching a high spot in the history of Fort Myers. Whatever efforts we make here today to honor Mr. Edison will fall short of his honor to us."[16]

After the speeches, the Edisons made their way to the bridge, stopping when they reached a great green-and-orange ribbon. With still cameras clicking and film cameras rolling, Thomas Edison untied the ribbon, gave a whoop, and waved his hands above his head. The Thomas A. Edison bridge was officially opened.

Queenie Adams, the Edison's cook, baked a large coconut "sunshine cake" with two layers of white icing to celebrate her employer's birthday. The Fires-

The Edison Bridge

Four years after the inventor dedicated the Edison Bridge, an image of the structure appeared in *Ripley's Believe It or Not!* with the caption, "The Thomas A. Edison Bridge—Fort Myers, Florida Has Never Had an Electric Light on It!"[*] The illustration was printed after an anonymous postcard was sent to Ripley's. Embarrassed, the town immediately began raising funds to illuminate the bridge. Fifty-four streetlights were added to the span in 1937.[**] The Edison Bridge was a local landmark until it was demolished in 1992 to make way for a larger bridge.[***]

[*] "'The Thomas A. Edison Bridge' cartoon (19350423) Ripley's Believe It or Not!, Orlando, Florida, 1935.

[**] "Thousands Here Brave Rain for Edison Bridge Lighting," *Fort Myers News-Press*, November 26, 1937; "Edison Bridge Is Now Lighted," Untitled, published source, likely *The Floridian*, November 27, 1937, "Edison Bridge" subject file, Southwest Florida Museum of History.

[***] Pamphlet, "The Edison Bridge, 1931–1992," Southwest Florida Museum of History, 1992.

tones and other guests at Seminole Lodge enjoyed it, but Edison stuck to his milk diet. A great deal of cake was left over and a friend of Mina's suggested that it be sold for charity. What better charity than the Red Cross's effort to feed people in drought-stricken areas?[17] Mina staffed a booth at Heitman's Arcade the following day. The slices netted the Red Cross $107.[18]

Henry Ford arrived almost two weeks later. As usual, he slipped into town quietly and reunited privately with Edison.[19] A few days later, Ford took the ferry from Punta Rassa to Sanibel Island to go to a local fair. Ford enjoyed the exhibits and had a barbecued-pork sandwich for lunch. When he asked for a drink, he was offered liquor. A supporter of prohibition, Ford replied, "I'd dig a well first."[20]

The Edisons celebrated their forty-fifth anniversary a few days later.[21] The next day Mina invited sixty guests from local garden groups to attend a movie at the Arcade Theater. Edison stayed home because he was conserving his strength for a radio broadcast to take place on February 28. Using two microphones set up in the small office, Edison spoke to a group in Chicago honoring utilities mogul Samuel Insull. After immigrating to the United States, Insull had become a private secretary to Edison. Now he was said to be worth $3 million. After the broadcast, Edison returned to Seminole Lodge to rest.[22]

Edison, traveling with Mina, her sister Grace, and Lucy Bogue, crossed the Tamiami Trail in early March to visit Harvey Firestone in Miami. The local reporters who hoped to interview the inventor were sorely disappointed. Edison avoided the press. There were no rubber plantation tours or aquarium visits. The photographers only got one picture of the inventor, sitting on an automobile running board looking away from the camera.[23] They instead took a picture of Mina at the reins of a horse and buggy from Firestone's stables.[24]

The trio of famous men was brought together the next weekend when Firestone joined Edison and Ford back in Fort Myers. They were talking among themselves outside Edison's rubber laboratory when 67-year-old Ford jumped up and went over to a eucalyptus tree. After chinning himself over a branch six times, he challenged 63-year-old Firestone to do the same. The tire manufacturer attempted the feat but could not do it until Ford assisted.

Firestone was saved from further embarrassment when Edison's old Model T rolled into the yard. "There she is," said Edison. "She still runs." Ford replied, "Yes, and there are still about six million of them on the roads." Firestone, who manufactured tires for the Model T, thought the number was about right.[25]

The next day, as Ford prepared to return north, he allowed an interview with a local reporter. The automaker said that the Great Depression had been caused by dishonesty. "People inflate stocks—that's dishonest. People buy inflated stocks with the hope of getting rich at the expense of someone else. That's also dishonest."

In his opinion, the Depression was not as serious as it was made out to be. "These really are good times but only a few know it." Laziness was at the heart of the nation's problems. "The average man, however, won't really do a day's work unless he is caught and cannot get out of it," Ford said. "There's plenty of work to do if people would do it."[26] Henry Ford's words were offensive to those who were unemployed and struggling.

As the Depression deepened, jobs that had seemed solid disappeared. The Bank of Fort Myers and Trust closed its doors on April 16. It would take eight years for the bank's assets to be liquidated. Those who could document their accounts received fifty-nine cents on the dollar. By the summer, one of the town's newspapers, the *Tropical News*, was ready to fold, but instead it merged with the *Fort Myers Press* to become the *Fort Myers News-Press*. The consolidation drove more people to the unemployment lines.[27]

Despite the bleakness of the times, the region still had baseball. For the seventh year, the Philadelphia Athletics held their spring training in Fort Myers. Edison loved the team, and nothing could keep him away from Terry Field. On March 23, in the middle of the third inning, the great inventor arrived to take his place in a box seat. Instantly, the crowd jumped to its feet in thunderous applause. The players on both sides briefly stopped the game to honor the inventor.[28]

A commemoration of the eighth anniversary of the wilderness trek of the Trailblazers to Miami occurred in early April. Though Edison was scheduled to attend the event with Mina, he sent his regrets. Mina spoke and planted the first of what would be 200 cajeput trees[29] to beautify the automobile corridor.[30]

The inventor rallied a few days later when he was invited to attend the Florida meeting of the National Congress of Parents and Teachers. The group awarded Edison a silver cup, membership, and the distinction of being the organization's only male member. Mina spoke briefly in place of her husband, thanking the group for the cup and commending them for their custom of planting a tree in the host city.[31]

Thomas Edison also made a brief appearance at a Seminole Lodge picnic. Mina invited twenty-six schoolgirls from the Open Air School in Sarasota.

The girls, whose ages ranged from 6 to 16, were allowed to explore the grounds of the expansive Edison estate and were given a tour of the inventor's rubber laboratory.[32]

A few days later, the Edisons hosted a movie party for the young women who had accompanied them to the bridge dedication on his birthday. George Eastman, a friend from the Kodak Company, sent a film for the Edisons' home projector.[33] Mina served cake and ice cream, and Edison told the young women stories and jokes.[34]

As April passed into May and May to June, Mina's name was mentioned in the local newspapers far more often than that of her husband. She attended meetings, luncheons, and tree-planting ceremonies. She gave radio addresses and public talks on women's work in the home, birds, road beautification, and cooperation among charities.

For a second year she spoke to the Rotary Club on the importance of parenting.[35] Stressing the paternal role in the family, she asked, "Are you fathers taking the responsibility necessary with your girls to make the woman that some man can refer to as a mother and be proud of? Are you training your boys to want the girl of character rather than one who simply looks pretty?" In her opinion, fathers had a clear responsibility: "Mothers cannot do it all alone."[36]

The newspaper praised Mina Edison for her dedication to local issues in an editorial. "Wives of great men usually are content to bask in the reflected glory that hovers about their husbands. An outstanding exception to that general rule is found in Fort Myers where many beneficial community activities receive an invaluable impetus from the leadership and active participation of Mrs. Thomas A. Edison."[37]

In the meantime, inventor Edison was trying desperately to make progress in his rubber research. To him, it was not just a scientific battle but a national one as well. For over a year, newspapers in the Soviet Union had claimed to have successfully extracted rubber from crude oil. John K. Small had investigated and found the reports to be inaccurate, but the stories persisted.[38]

On May 7, Edison discussed the issue with a reporter, saying, "I don't think the Moscow report is true. I don't believe you can get good rubber from oil. I would even go so far as to say that oil rubber is a fake." He went on to say that he felt that communism would fail because "property in common has never been successful. . . . The Russian plan would never work out in this country. To begin with, you never could get the American people under control to the extent that the Russians have been controlled. It is impossible."[39]

Edison felt his rubber experiments were ready to pass from the preliminary stage. Most of his plants excreted between 6 and 8 percent of rubber. If he could standardize the amount of rubber extracted, he would be well on the way to commercial success.[40] But Edison knew it would be a long shot for domestic rubber to compete with imported supplies. "I would not say that it was impossible. Time will tell the tale."

On the subject of synthetic rubber, Edison was adamant. "The ingredients cost more than the rubber which makes the experiments impractical. The great German dye trust has experimented with synthetic rubber and has taken out many patents but none of them is practical."[41]

Charles arrived in Fort Myers on June 9 with his wife Carolyn for a brief vacation before accompanying his parents north. Edison was thrilled to see his son, teasing him at the train station, "What did you bring that overcoat down here for?"

Despite his infirmities, Edison insisted he join his son tarpon fishing. As usual, the younger Edison caught a number of tarpon during his forays on the Caloosahatchee. His father caught nothing.[42] A few weeks later, the Fort Myers Chamber of Commerce began issuing medals to anglers who had caught a tarpon of 100 pounds or more. In spite of Edison's poor record, they called it the Edison Medal and issued him the first one.[43]

Edison was interviewed on a nationwide broadcast from his rubber laboratory shortly after Charles arrived. His address was brief but inspiring. "My message to you is to be courageous. I have lived a long time. I have seen history repeat itself again and again. I have seen many depressions in business. Always America has come back stronger and more prosperous. Be as brave as your fathers before you. Have faith. Go forward."[44]

Finally on June 15, 1931, Thomas and Mina Edison were escorted to the town's second train station, the Seaboard Air Line station, for the 9:15 a.m. train. While waiting, Edison talked with Fred Ott and Captain Fred Menge and Mina said her goodbyes to Flossie Hill and the local community women. Finally, the Edisons climbed aboard the passenger car. As the train pulled away from the platform, the Edisons began waving to their friends with handkerchiefs. Slowly they disappeared from sight.[45]

The couple remained on the train until they reached Jacksonville, where they switched trains.[46] Thirty-two hours later, they arrived at the Market Street station in Newark, where an entourage was waiting. Sons Theodore and Tom Jr. and daughter Madeleine were there with their spouses. Mina wrapped a blanket around her husband's shoulders as they shuttled him through the pouring rain to the waiting automobile.[47] Edison was exhausted.

A Walk of Friendship

Dr. Hamilton Holt from Rollins College in Winter Park, Florida, once asked Mina if she would be willing to give him a stone from the estates for the college's Walk of Fame. Holt remembered, "Mrs. Edison was so impressed by the Walk of Fame that she asked if I had any objection to her following our example, but she did not want a Walk of Fame in her place but a Friendship Walk composed of stones from friends and family. She asked me to give the first one."*

By April 1931, the Edisons' Friendship Walk had eight stones, including ones from Samuel Insull, Harvey Firestone, Henry Ford, and the Valinda Literary Society. Miss Josephine Stadler, a Fort Myers neighbor, gave them a stone made of native coquina shell. Eight more were expected before the Edisons returned north.**

* Personal notes of Hamilton Holt describing the stones on the Rollins College Walk of Fame, Rollins College Archives and Special Collections.

** "Gift Stones Are Building Edisons' 'Friendship Walk,'" *Tropical News*, April 29, 1931.

Two weeks after arriving home, Mina wrote to her brother-in-law, "Mr. Edison is not feeling very well and has not gone to the laboratory as yet since returning home."[48] A month later, she took him to a sanitarium in Morristown for tests. Mina's mood was reflected in a letter to Fort Myers friend Sidney Davis: "I do hope the weather is comfortable in Fort Myers. It is far from being so here, very hot and humid. Everywhere business dull and many unemployed." She rallied, "I am sure that things will change however and all will be well again."[49]

Edison's condition did not improve. On August 1, he collapsed at his New Jersey home. His physician rushed to his side. After making him as comfortable as possible, he released a public statement conveying the seriousness of his condition.[50] Over the next few weeks Edison rallied and relapsed repeatedly. Ford visited him at Glenmont, informing the press that reports that Edison was retiring were "all bosh."[51] Optimistic reports circulated over the next few weeks, but those around him knew. His body was deteriorating. Even the Wizard of Menlo Park could not avoid death.

From all over the nation, letters poured into Glenmont. Fort Myers declared a citywide day of prayer for the inventor on October 4.[52] A neighbor wrote, "My family and I joined with Fort Myers yesterday in prayer for Mr. Edison."[53] Men, women, and children sent letters saying how much they admired Edison, how he had inspired them, and how much they appreciated his contributions.

There were also desperate letters from people who wished to save him. A woman from Kinsley, Kansas, offered her own blood for a transfusion.[54] Some suggested home remedies or recommended physicians and healers. Others were crass opportunists, like two New Yorkers who separately offered to make death masks of the inventor as soon as he died.[55]

Edison was in and out of consciousness and recognized no one but Mina. A package arrived from Fort Myers. The staff there had finally succeeded in

Goldenrod Rubber Research Continues

The Edison Botanic Research Corporation resumed Edison's quest for a domestic source of rubber after his death. The company's shareholders, mainly Ford, Firestone, and Mina Edison, provided financing, and experimentation continued until Charles Edison convinced the U.S. Department of Agriculture take over the project in 1934.[*]

When the venture was relocated to Savannah, Georgia, Mina immediately complained that the rubber research had "been taken away from us."[**] Her resolve deepened in 1935, when she visited the Georgia research station and was incensed by its small scale. She informed Harvey Firestone, and within a week, Firestone, Ford and Thomas A. Edison Inc. had funded the Fort Myers staff for the remainder of the season. The scenario was repeated in 1935 and 1936.[***]

Finally, Mina bowed to the inevitable and permanently closed the Fort Myers facility in 1936. It was a painful decision, one she considered a personal failure. She had hoped to continue Edison's research and make "the garden an educational point of interest at Fort Myers."[****]

[*] Rosenblum and Associates, *Edison Winter Estate: Cultural Landscape Report*, II: 40–41.
[**] MME to CE, March 8, 1935, EFWE, CEF.
[***] Rosenblum and Associates, *Edison Winter Estate: Cultural Landscape Report*, II: 42–43.
[****] Rosenblum and Associates, *Edison Winter Estate: Cultural Landscape Report*, II: 41, 44.

vulcanizing some small pieces of goldenrod rubber. Mina pressed them into her husband's hand and told him the good news. A lucid moment followed. He was happy. He had finally achieved his dream. The wizard had again done the impossible.[56]

Thomas A. Edison sank into a coma on October 14. He emerged briefly and uttered his last words, "It is very beautiful over there."[57] He died at 3:24 a.m. on October 18, 1931. Before sunrise, Mina dispatched a telegram to the mayor of Fort Myers. "Mister Edison passed away peacefully. . . . Kindly notify the civic and religious organizations."[58] Even in her grief, Mina ensured that their friends in Fort Myers learned about Edison's death from her, not the newspapers.

A Widow at Seminole Lodge

*"I am almost afraid to come to Fort Myers.
I cannot bear to cast a shadow upon them there."*

—Mina Miller Edison

October 1931–1947

Mina Edison had stood by her husband through countless illnesses, dangerous operations, and periods of decline. That he lived to be 84 was a miracle in itself and a credit to her loving care. Still, his passing was something of a shock. In some ways she wished she could go with him like John Ott, Fred Ott's brother and a faithful Edison employee, who had died just hours after his boss.[1]

The day after her husband's death, Mina had his bronze casket placed in the West Orange, New Jersey, laboratory. Edison company employees and their families filed passed the open casket for an hour before the general public arrived. In all, more than 50,000 people paid their respects.[2] Henry Ford was not one of them. He could not bear to look into the casket and said, "I want to remember him the way he was."[3]

On October 21, Mina, dressed in mourning black, went downstairs to the conservatory of Glenmont, where her husband's body lay for the private funeral. She entered and closed the doors behind her, spending an hour with her husband of forty-five years. It was her last goodbye to "Dearie," as she privately called him.

The ceremony had not yet begun before Edison's sons and daughters began fighting over who would sit in the front row. Mina gathered her resolve and diffused the situation before they made a spectacle of themselves. Perhaps fearing she'd break down in front of the 400 assembled guests, she arranged to listen to the service through speakers in an upstairs room. Some of her family members, the Fords, the Firestones, and First Lady Lou Hoover were with her.[4]

After a eulogy and the playing of "I'll Take You Home Again Kathleen," the mourners praised the great inventor. When the service was over, most of the guests departed. Those who remained in the upstairs room formed a procession to nearby Rosedale Cemetery.[5] Mina, family members, the Fords, and the Firestones watched as Edison was laid to rest. Several hours later, as a national tribute, President Hoover asked the citizens of the nation to dim their lights for one minute at 10:00 p.m. in honor of Thomas Edison.[6]

With the funeral over, Mina hoped to rest, but she found herself surrounded by her enraged children and stepchildren. In the will, her own daughter, Madeleine, and the children of Edison's first marriage, Thomas Jr., William, and Marion, received only trust funds from the Edison Portland Cement Company. Sons Charles and Theodore inherited the bulk of the estate. Their siblings felt the division unfair, and the issue created rancor among them for years to come.[7]

As the fall progressed, Mina received hundreds of letters of condolence. Her friends in Fort Myers were free with their concern, but a depressed Mina felt ill equipped to face them. Rather than endure a Christmas alone, she visited members of the Miller family in Puerto Rico. She hoped to spend part of the winter in Fort Myers, but in a letter to Sidney Davis, she confessed, "I am almost afraid to come to Fort Myers. I cannot bear to cast a shadow upon them there . . . but when one is lonely it is difficult not to show it. I try to keep busy for one goes to pieces otherwise."[8]

Fort Myers was in Mina's thoughts on her husband's birthday. In remembrance of him, she sent flowers to every patient at the local hospital as well as those who were ill in their homes.[9] Meanwhile, the citizens of Fort Myers sought to remember the inventor on a grander scale. Six hundred people attended an Evans Park memorial service at the site of the plaque dedicated to Thomas and Mina Edison in 1930.[10] The Council of Spanish War Veterans also wanted to honor Edison but was divided between those who wanted a large-scale monument and others who thought a memorial library a more fitting tribute to the inventor.[11]

On February 25, 1932, still dressed in black, Mina Edison arrived in Fort Myers with her sister Grace and Edison's cousin Edith Potter.[12] Despite her apprehensions, after a few days she found herself comfortable again at Seminole Lodge. A little over a week after her arrival, she sponsored a meeting of the Fort Myers branch of the National Plant, Flower and Fruit Guild at her home. Among the topics discussed were Mina's project to rid the region of billboards, the scarcity of local birds, and educational programs to encourage

The Edison Children

Following the reading of Edison's will, William Leslie Edison threatened to sue. He changed his mind when Charles informed him that the cement stock he had inherited was worth about $50,000 a year.

Tom Jr. and his wife Beatrice wrote to Mina on a regular basis and visited her in Fort Myers in 1934. He died on August 25, 1935, while registered under a fictitious name at a hotel. William died two years later after a long battle with cancer.*

Following her return from Germany in 1917, Marion Edison Oser settled in Connecticut and tried to reunite with her siblings. She resumed a relationship with Mina, calling her "Dearest Mother," and received a watch in Mina's will. She died in Norwalk, Connecticut, in 1965 at the age of 92.**

Madeleine was estranged from the Edison family following her father's death. She maintained a relationship with her mother and helped establish the Edison Birthplace Museum in Milan, Ohio. Madeleine had four boys, Thomas, John, Peter, and Michael, and seven grandchildren when she died in 1979.*** Her grandson, David E. E. Sloan, has written a book about her life called *Edison's Daughter*.

Charles served as president of Thomas A. Edison, Inc. until it merged with the McGraw Company in 1957. He became assistant secretary, then secretary, of the U.S. Navy and was elected New Jersey governor in 1941. Like his father, he suffered from profound hearing loss. He died on June 30, 1969, at the age of 78.****

Theodore Edison was an inventor like his father, achieving his first patent in 1932 for a device used to reduce vibration in machinery. By the 1930s, Theodore had started his own firm called Calibron. Theodore supported the preservation of southwest Florida's environment. He died on January 28, 1993.*****

* Baldwin, *Edison: Inventing the Century*, 412–413.

** "Last Will and Testament of Mina M. Edison, December 20, 1946, copy courtesy of David Sloane; "Mrs. Oser, 92 Dies; Daughter of Edison," *New York Times*, April 17, 1965.

*** "Sloane," The *New York Times*, February 15, 1979.

**** "Charles Edison, 78, Ex-Governor of Jersey and U.S. Aide, Is Dead," *New York Times*, August 1, 1969.

***** Baldwin, *Edison: Inventing the Century*, 415; "Theodore M. Edison: An Illustrious Father Guided Inventor, 94," *New York Times*, November 26, 1992.

love of nature. Mina also advocated for the protection of Seminole Indians lands in Everglades National Park.[13]

Over the next few years, Mina devoted herself entirely to her community. During her winters in Fort Myers, she maintained a grueling schedule, which included leadership in the National Plant, Flower and Fruit Guild; the Valinda Literary Circle; and the local music club. She also continued to act as class mother for the Young Men's Wesley Bible Class, at one point bringing Harvey Firestone to visit the class.[14] She gave speeches on local issues such as beautification and education to the Girl Scouts, the Rotary Club, the Fort Myers Woman's Club, and the local Woman's Christian Temperance Union.[15]

Mina was keenly aware that the Depression made life difficult for her friends in Florida. "Fort Myers too is having its struggle and I am hearing from many," she confessed. "It is very heartbreaking not to be able to meet everybody's call, not only those whom you know and are dear to you but distress from all over the world."[16]

The hard times did not end. By 1935, only 35 percent of people could pay their taxes. The rest risked foreclosure and homelessness. Building projects organized through Roosevelt's New Deal helped, but not everyone benefited.[17]

Mina used her famous name and position to help many groups, but her frequent work within the black community was potentially dangerous. In the South, Jim Crow laws and customs limited interaction between the races. In segregated Fort Myers, blacks were permitted to live only in the Safety Hill neighborhood. Local police and the local Ku Klux Klan chapter, called the Klan of the Palms, maintained the status quo.[18] Defying segregation could get a black person killed. A white person who was perceived as being too involved in the black community could be run out of town or worse. Even for Mina, circumventing segregation was dangerous.

From experience, Mina knew that the best way to improve relations between the blacks and whites was through face-to-face interaction. She chose to become president of the Safety Hill Garden Group and organized beautification and cleanup programs where black and white women worked together. In May 1933, Mina took part in a ceremony to plant trees at the black Dunbar High School. Because of her standing in the community, few complained publicly. Some of the women who met each other due to Mina's influence formed lifelong relationships.[19]

Mina also began to look at Seminole Lodge differently. On one hand, it was her home. On the other, it was part of Edison's legacy. For years she had allowed outsiders limited access. Now she opened the estate to the public

Queenie Adams Dies

During the cold New Jersey winter of 1937, Queenie Adams, Mina's cook, learned that she was dying of heart disease and had about a month to live. She had spent eleven years working in the inventor's kitchens, leaving her family in Florida each year and traveling north to work for the Edisons in New Jersey during the winter. She was famous for her fried chicken and homemade ice cream as well as her sense of humor and sweet demeanor.* She told Mina that she wanted to be back in her own bed surrounded by her loved ones.

Mina immediately arranged for her to be transported from the hospital by ambulance to an Atlantic Seaboard train. She was carried by stretcher to a private car and accompanied by two nurses. Queenie Adams arrived safely in Fort Myers and the arms of her husband and children.** She died on January 11, 1937. Her funeral was attended by 250 people, and the Newark, New Jersey, newspaper announced, "Queenie Adams Mourned; 'Wizard' of Edison Kitchen."

* Interview with Lynn Given and Kristin Herron, ENHS.

** *Fort Myers News-Press*, January 12 and 13, 1937; *Newark Star-Eagle*, January 18, 1937.

*** Queen Adams's death certificate, January 16, 1937, Office of Vital Statistics, State of Florida; "Requiescat J. Pace," Southwest Floridian, January 18, 1937; Mina Miller Edison's Clipping Book, EFWE; "Queenie Adams Mourned; 'Wizard' of Edison Kitchen, *Newark Star-Eagle*, January 18, 1937.

more frequently through events such as programs to educate children about birds.[20]

She became fiercely protective when she thought the estate was in jeopardy. In 1934, a local man petitioned the city to waive building restrictions so he could erect a gas station across from the Edison estate. The Community Congregational Church opposed it, but it was a telegram from Mina Edison read just before the city council voted that turned the tide. She said that the station would be a "catastrophy [*sic*]," and the council voted it down.[21]

After four years of widowhood, Mina remarried. The groom was Edward Everett Hughes, a retired steel manufacturer who had been one of Mina's childhood playmates at Chautauqua.[22] The marriage was a happy one. When they traveled separately, they wrote often, referring to each other as "Precious Edward"[23] and "Dearest Sweetheart."[24] Their respective children seemed pleased with the match. Mina's children referred to their new stepfather affectionately as "Daden."[25] The Hughes children adored "Mother Mina."[26]

The winter following their marriage, the couple visited Fort Myers. It was only moments before a reporter slipped and called Mina "Mrs. Edison" instead of "Mrs. Hughes."[27] Edward Hughes seemed to take the slight in stride. Edison, though dead, was ever-present. Mina continued her involvement in the Edison companies and organizations dedicated to his memory. She and Edward Hughes lived together at Glenmont and Seminole Lodge, though he spent some time on his own at Beacon-on-Hudson, New York,[28] and the College Arms Hotel in Deland, Florida.[29]

After only five years of marriage, Hughes died on January 17, 1940. Almost immediately, people began to again refer to Mina as "Mrs. Edison."[30] Before a full year of mourning was over, she too began to sign her name "Mina Edison."[31] In later years, Mina was quoted as saying, "Mr. Edison was the only husband I ever had."[32] To an extent, that was true. Hughes was a friend and a companion. Edison was her husband.

At 75, Mina Edison was again on her own, but not without purpose. In February 1941, She was barely off the train at the Atlantic Coastline Railroad station in Fort Myers when she made an announcement. She was going to build an Edison memorial library and museum.[33] Such a structure would honor her late husband's memory and offer a valuable resource to the town.

Although Fort Myers had technically had a library since 1903, it was a small reading room that was open only to paying subscribers. The reading room's location had been moved many times,[34] and it did not adequately serve the town of 10,000.[35] The new library would not only be a memorial to her husband but also a living institution.

Mina hired a New York architect to draw up specifications[36] and a Palm Beach landscape company to design the grounds.[37] Architectural designs were proposed that ranged from a Spanish-influenced stucco building to more traditional classical designs.[38] In April 1941, she selected the contractors. The site would contain a library, an art gallery, music rooms, and cloisters and would be located across the street from Seminole Lodge, where Edison's goldenrod research laboratory had been located. She wanted it started within months, "unless we get into a war." She explained, "I am apprehensive of the world situation and if the United States should be drawn into war . . . the memorial library would be out of the question."[39]

Mina's foresight was accurate. The next December, Pearl Harbor was

An Awe-Inspiring Experience with Mina Edison

During the late 1930s and 1940s, Bernese Davis, the wife of Sidney Davis, was a frequent guest at Seminole Lodge. She greatly admired Mina Edison for her knowledge, wit, and ability to make people feel at ease. One day she took an automobile trip with Mina and Mona and Jetty Burroughs, Mina's Fort Myers neighbors. At Highland Hammock in Sebring, they walked on the boardwalk through the forest. Bernese wrote:

> We heard a bird and Mrs. Edison said, "Let's all be quiet and see if I can call the bird." She called the bird and the bird came. Others came. She made other sounds. I don't think I've ever had a moment when I've felt any nearer to God and creation. All those birds were around us and Mrs. Edison was having the time of her life making all those birdcalls.[*]

[*] Bernese Davis, interview with the author.

bombed and war was declared. Young men volunteered or were drafted into the armed services. Women took over the home front and aided the war effort. Everything was rationed, from sugar and flour to gasoline. Fort Myers became host to two military bases, a gunnery school in Buckingham, and an Air Corps headquartered at Page Field. Between 1942 and the war's end, some 16,000 men were stationed there.[40]

Shortly after her arrival in Florida in April 1942, Mina was sitting at the local Walgreens drug store when she noticed some young servicemen. She went over and introduced herself and said, "I love you young people and I'm very interested in the lives of you soldiers, even more so since you've come into my town." Private Leon Teger offered Mina his seat. She asked the servicemen about their homes, how they were treated at the base and in town, and if they were lonely.[41]

A few days later, Teger received permission for Mina, her friend Mrs. Colgate, and her sister Grace Hitchcock to visit the 98th bombardment group on base. Dressed in a blue suit with an orchid corsage, she walked across the runways, entered soldiers' tents, and inspected the kitchens. Later she joined the enlisted men for a dinner of creamed spaghetti with veal, boiled sweet potatoes, cole slaw, and baked beans.[42] On another visit, she donned earplugs and shot a machine gun.[43]

Mina began to plan activities for the enlisted men because she felt that they did not have some of the advantages of the officers.[44] She set aside seats at the movie theater and invited them to Seminole Lodge for dinner. Encouraged by her social secretary, Jeanette Perry, she abandoned the traditional formal dinners served by her British butler for casual buffets on the wide verandahs. The enlisted men sat on the porch floors, laughing and singing and telling stories.[45] For men who desperately missed home and family, it was a wonderful time. Mina even wrote letters home to some of their parents.[46]

Mina also made time to honor Fort Myers's black soldiers. She joined the mayor in dedicating a "colored veterans home" in April 1942. In her remarks, she remembered back to a time when Safety Hill "was almost unlivable," but now, thanks to hard work from the black community and the city, the neighborhood was much improved. She also urged local black families to open their homes to black soldiers serving at the Fort Myers air base.[47] Hosting the men herself would have been a flagrant violation of segregation. Even Mrs. Edison could not step that far over the color line.

Mina kept up her work with the garden group, although no longer in a leadership position. She also had frequent speaking engagements, but she had begun to feel that her message of the woman as home executive did not appeal to the new generation, whose role model was Rosie the Riveter. In a letter to a Fort Myers friend, she lamented, "You know I want to help in any way I can, but I feel that I am an old story."[48]

Her friends and family were dying off one by one. Fred Ott died in 1936. Fred Menge died in 1937. Harvey Firestone died a year later. In 1940, she lost her brothers Lewis and John. In November 1946, her beloved sister Mary died.[49] Henry Ford died in 1947.[50]

Plans for the Edison library were stymied. The war was the primary reason, but financial constraints also played a role.[51] Mina maintained Glenmont and Seminole Lodge with all the associated expenses, including the cost of maintenance, taxes, and a support staff for each site. Though she had set aside money, building a large-scale library was quickly becoming beyond her means.[52]

In March 1945, Mina was approached by members of a Fort Myers foundation that sought to use the Edison estate as the site of a memorial university.[53] Her son Charles and her attorney approved. Mina was interested, but it never came to pass.

Mina Edison's arrival in 1947 was timed to coincide with festivities for an

Edison Parades and Pageants

Memorial services were held for Edison each year following his death until 1937. In 1938, the townsfolk decided they would rather honor the inventor's life by celebrating his birthday. The Woman's Community Club, the Junior Chamber of Commerce, and the Jaycees created an elaborate program with an evening pageant and a parade.*

In years to come, coronation dances, balls, regattas, and jalopy races were added to the program. The events were suspended during World War II. In 1947, the celebration was bigger and better than ever with everything from sports matches to fireworks and a gopher derby.** Fifteen thousand people attended, and Mina Miller Edison not only rode in the parade but crowned the king and queen of "Edisonia."***

* Grismer, *The Story of Fort Myers*, 268–69; "Visitors Jam City as Plans Progress for Edison Pageant," *Fort Myers News-Press*, February 4, 1947.

** "Pageant of Light Opens," *Fort Myers News-Press*, February 8, 1947.

*** Grismer, *The Story of Fort Myers*, 269; "Mrs. Edison Here; Gopher Derby Is Delayed to Today," February 14, 1947.

Edison Pageant. The weekend of events came to a standstill when her train was five hours late. When she finally arrived, the events resumed. In the space of about forty-eight hours, the 82-year-old widow was whisked to a gopher derby, a baby parade, and a coronation ball.[54] The next day she rode in the lead car of the Edison Pageant parade, which was seen by 25,000 spectators.[55]

Not everyone was pleased with Mina's schedule. Her friend Ella Piper complained, "I don't like them putting to[o] much upon you when you are here. They don't seem to realize you can't go along with them as they go—Once and a while is alright, but every day & night—It is too much."[56] Another Fort Myers friend chastised, "I am very much afraid you are not resting as the Dr. told you to. Remember you promised me you would."[57]

Mina's long dedication to Fort Myers and the greater regions was appreciated. A *News-Press* editorial honored her, declaring her the reigning First Lady. But in a stunning lack of tact, the paper suggested that her reign would last only "until she is reunited with her 'wonderful man' to whose success her love and devotion contributed so much."[58]

Whether it was due to the editorial or the reality of her advanced age and failing health, Mina made a decision about the disposition of Seminole Lodge. On February 18, 1947, she deeded her estate to the city of Fort Myers for the sum of one dollar. Two days later, the newspaper headline declared, "City Gets Edison Place."[59] After nearly sixty-two years of ownership, the homestead on the Caloosahatchee River no longer belonged to an Edison.

A month later at the public ceremony transferring Seminole Lodge, Mina made a brief speech. "My faith and belief in the sincerity of the people of Fort Myers prompts me to make this sacred spot a gift to you and posterity as a Sanctuary and Botanical Park in the memory of my honored and revered husband, Thomas A. Edison, who so thoroughly believed in the future of Fort Myers."[60]

The last few weeks of Mina's stay were a whirlwind of dinners, visits with friends, and remembrances of years past. Charles and his wife Carolyn came down from New Jersey to say goodbye to Seminole Lodge. Madeleine joined them later, reflecting, "We did enjoy the lazy days at Fort Myers. I couldn't have borne it not to see the place again as it always was."[61] On April 9, 1947, Mina said goodbye to her beloved Seminole Lodge and to Fort Myers. She and her sister Grace traveled one last time along royal palm-lined McGregor Boulevard before climbing aboard their northbound train. In her private railroad car, Mina watched as the town she first visited in 1886 receded into the distance. It was the end of an era.

Mina Miller Edison died on August 24, 1947. Like her beloved husband, she died at Glenmont surrounded by her family. News reached Fort Myers the next day. The front page of the *News-Press* announced, "Mrs. Mina Edison Dies; Fort Myers Grieves Loss of City's 'First Citizen.'"

Figure 41. Rubber research devotees. *Left to right*: Russell Firestone, Henry Ford, Mina
Edison, Harvey Firestone, J. V. Miller, and Harry Ukkelberg, May 1, 1934. 14.352.35.
Courtesy U.S. Department of the Interior, National Park Service, Edison National Historic Site.

Figure 42. Mina Edison, Thomas Edison Jr., and his wife, Beatrice, 1934. 14.354.3. *Courtesy U.S. Department of the Interior, National Park Service, Edison National Historic Site.*

Figure 43. Mina with her second husband, Edward Hughes, 1940. 14.352.65.
*Courtesy U.S. Department of the Interior, National Park Service,
Edison National Historic Site.*

Figure 44. Mina Edison crowns the king of Edisonia, 1947. C003191.
Courtesy State Library and Archives of Florida.

Epilogue

"Mina Edison had willed Seminole Lodge to the City of Fort Myers,
wanting to memorialize her husband with a museum, and indeed there appeared
to be a community-wide feeling that the estate belonged to the people. . ."

All This Belongs to Me (fiction) by Ad Hudler, Ballantine Books, 2006.

Historic sites can mean a great deal to a community. They offer a source of pride, prestige, a sense of history, and sometimes even a revenue stream. Since it became a museum in 1947, Seminole Lodge has offered all of these things and more to southwest Florida. In return, the Edisons—both Thomas and Mina—have become virtual deities.

During his lifetime, Edison's relationship with his winter neighbors was often fraught with difficulty, as evidenced by his unfulfilled promise to electrify Fort Myers, the palm ordeal, and the payment dispute over the installation of his pool. Opinions changed in the decades following his death. In the 1940s residents easily believed the story of insomniac cows over a broken promise by the inventor.

Today, reverence for Edison borders on hagiography, or the worship of the saints. A stroll through the region shows that there is very little not named for the inventor. Edison Avenue was christened during his lifetime. There is also a bank, an elementary school, a community college, an auto mechanic, a cab company, an apartment complex, and a blood bank named for Edison. To those who know about the inventor's ambivalence toward organized religion, the Thomas A. Edison Congregational Church is an interesting contradiction. Crowning it all is the quintessential American tribute, the Edison [shopping] Mall located a few miles from Seminole Lodge.

While it may be tempting to write off these tributes as kitsch or consumerism, the truth is that even today, many decades after the inventor's death, Edison is a hero in the region. He is regaled for what he accomplished during his long life and what he gave to a world longing for light. And he should be honored. But, Edison should also be remembered as a practical joker, a frustrated fisherman, and an ambitious explorer, because that is part of the inventor's legacy as well. It is the complexities of Thomas and Mina Edison's lives in Florida that make them interesting and inspiring to the local community, but also to the larger nation and indeed, the world.

Notes

Chapter 1. A Florida Adventure

1. *New York Sun*: "The Magician of Science," March 31, 1878; "The Napoleon of Science," March 10, 1878; "The Inventor of the Age," April 29, 1878.

2. Josephson, *Edison: A Biography*, 20.

3. "Edison's U.S. Patents, 1883–1889," available at http://edison.rutgers.edu/patente3.htm.

4. Israel, *Edison: A Life of Invention*, 147.

5. Josephson, 99.

6. Baldwin, *Edison: Inventing the Century*, 147.

7. Marion Edison Oser, oral history A-518, March 1956, ENHS.

8. Israel, *Edison: A Life of Invention*, 237.

9. Baldwin, *Edison: Inventing the Century*, 146–47; Israel, *Edison: A Life of Invention*, 237.

10. Tebeau, *A History of Florida*, 271.

11. Mary Stilwell Edison to Samuel Insull, February 27, 1884, D8414B, TAEM 71:605.

12. "Florida: The State of Orange-Groves," *Blackwood's Magazine*, September 1885, 325.

13. TAE to Samuel Insull, telegram, February 28, 1885, D8503T, TAEM 77:60.

14. TAE to Samuel Insull, [February] 11, 1885, D8503J1, TAEM 77:45.

15. Mary Stilwell Edison to Samuel Insull, February 27, 1884, D8414B, TAEM 71:605.

16. Barbour, *Florida for Tourists, Invalids, and Settlers*, 289.

17. Interview with TAE, n.d. (ca. 1917), ENHS.

18. Barbour, *Florida for Tourists, Invalids, and Settlers*, 309.

19. Interview with TAE, n.d. (ca. 1917).

20. Ibid.

21. Untitled article, *Fort Myers Press*, March 14, 1885; interview with TAE, n.d (ca. 1917).

22. Israel, *Edison: A Life of Invention*, 237.

23. Barbour, *Florida for Tourists, Invalids, and Settlers*, 149; Rosenblum and Associates, *Edison Winter Estate: Cultural Landscape Report*, I-25–34.

24. Interview with TAE, n.d. (ca. 1917); Grismer, *The Story of Fort Myers*, 114; "Armeda Family Came from Spain," *Fort Myers News-Press*, July 5, 1969.

25. Gonzalez, *The Caloosahatchee*, 15–16.

26. Fritz, *Bamboo and Sailing Ships*, 6–7; Ste. Claire, *Cracker: The Cracker Culture in Florida History*, 175.

27. Stuart McIver, "Tarpon House," *Florida Sportsman*, March 1985, 37.

28. Grismer, *The Story of Fort Myers*, 136–39.

29. Abbott, *Open for the Season*, 52.

30. Fritz, *Bamboo and Sailing Ships*, 5; McIver, "Tarpon House," 37–38; Grismer, *The Story of Fort Myers*, 136–39.

31. "Florida: The State of Orange-Groves," *Blackwoods Magazine*, September 1885, 325; "Press Five Months Old When It Ran First Edison Story," *Fort Myers News-Press*, November 22, 1934.

32. Grismer, *The Story of Fort Myers*, 116–17.

33. Interview with TAE, n.d. (ca. 1917).

34. Rosenblum, *Edison Winter Estate: Cultural Landscape Report*, I-25–31.

35. "Distinguished Arrivals," *Fort Myers Press*, March 28, 1885.

36. "Edison Recalls Early Days in City of Palms," *Fort Myers Press*, February 11, 1925.

37. Grismer, *The Story of Fort Myers*, 117.

38. Ibid., 117–20.

39. *Cracker* was a term for Florida cattlemen that likely derived from the crack of their whips. For more information about the etymology of *cracker*, see Ste. Claire, *Cracker: The Cracker Culture in Florida History*, 27–37.

40. Grismer, *The Story of Fort Myers*, 113–14, 116–19.

41. Gonzalez, *The Caloosahatchee*, 92–99.

42. Ibid., 86–87.

43. "Distinguished Arrivals," *Fort Myers Press*, March 14, 1885.

44. Gonzalez, *The Caloosahatchee*, 68–72; Grismer, *The Story of Fort Myers*, 111–13.

45. Grismer, *The Story of Fort Myers*, 108.

46. "Inventor Now Enjoying His 45th Season Here," *Tropical News*, April 25, 1928.

47. Advertisement, *Fort Myers Press*, March 14, 1885; Grismer, *The Story of Fort Myers*, 112, 114.

48. Fritz, *Bamboo and Sailing Ships*, 7.

49. Grismer, *The Story of Fort Myers*, 112; Advertisement, *Fort Myers Press*, March 20, 1886.

50. "Florida: The State of Orange-Groves," 325.

51. McKay, *Pioneer Florida*, 2: 325–28; Wynne and Horgan, eds., *Florida Pathfinders*.

52. Akerman, *Florida Cowman*, 85, 114.

53. Rosenblum, *Edison Winter Estate: Cultural Landscape Report*, I: 1–27, 28.

54. Contract between TAE and Huelsenkamp & Cranford, March 21, 1885, D8539A, TAEM 78:325.

55. Grismer, *The Story of Fort Myers*, 114–115.

56. "Distinguished Arrivals," *Fort Myers Press*, March 28, 1885.

57. Ibid.

Chapter 2. The Edison and Gilliland Estates Rise

1. Nolan, *Fifty Feet in Paradise*, 74–78.

2. Grismer, *The Story of Fort Myers*, 103, 129.

3. Peter O. Knight, County Clerk, Monroe County, Key West, Florida, July 25, 1885, abstract and letter to TAE, D8539E, TAEM 78:328–29.

4. Huelsenkamp & Cranford, telegram to TAE, September 18, 1885, D8539H, TAEM 78:339.

5. Untitled article, *Fort Myers Press*, August 1, 1885; Rosenblum, *Edison Winter Estate: Historic Structures Report*, I-2–4.

6. Ancient laws thought to be unchangeable.

7. "Florida: The State of Orange-Groves," *Blackwoods Magazine*, September 1885, 326.

8. Letter to TAE from Huelsenkamp & Cranford, September 26, 1885, D8539I, TAEM 78:340.

9. Gonzalez, *The Caloosahatchee*, 88–91.

10. Ezra Gilliland to TAE, September 17, 1885, D8503ZCQ, TAEM 77:16.

11. Huelsenkamp & Cranford to TAE, March 31, 1885, D8539B, TAEM 78:326. Marginalia by TAE.

12. Josephson, *Edison: A Biography*, 302.

13. "Edison First Met Wife in Winthrop," *The Winthrop Review* (Winthrop, Mass.), October 23, 1931.

14. Ibid.

15. Edison, *The Diary and Sundry Observations of Thomas Alva Edison*, 20.

16. Lillian Warren, transcript of interview with Kathleen McKirk, n.d., 41–42, ENHS.

17. Marion Edison Oser, interview A-518, March 1956, 6, ENHS.

18. See *Steiger's Educational Directory for 1878*, 24, and Israel, *Edison, A Life of Invention*, 244.

19. Baldwin, *Edison: Inventing the Century*, 152–53; Josephson, *Edison: A Biography*, 304–6.

20. Edison, *The Diary and Sundry Observations of Thomas Alva Edison*, 30.

21. Invoice to TAE from Alden Frink, September 23, 1885, ENHS.

22. Invoice to TAE from the Kennebec Framing Co., November 25, 1885, ENHS.

23. Rosenblum, *Edison Winter Estate: Historic Structures Report*, I-5.

24. Invoice to TAE from Francis Cobb & Co., November 23, 1885, ENHS.

25. Invoices to TAE from Read Nichols, November 23, December 1, 1885, ENHS.

26. Invoice to TAE from J. F. Hayden Coal, November 24, 1885, ENHS.

27. Invoices to TAE from Baumann Brothers, January 6, February 15, 1886, ENHS.

28. Invoices to TAE from James McCutcheon & Co., February 13, 1886, ENHS.

29. Invoice to TAE from Lewis & Conger, December 21, February 1886, ENHS.

30. Rosenblum, *Edison Winter Estate: Historic Structures* Report, I-5.

31. "Pay Role [*sic*] Edison & Gilliland, Myers Fla., April 5 to 10 [1886]," ENHS.

32. Rosenblum, *Edison Winter Estate: Historic Structures Report*, I-5.

33. "To Eimer and Amend" (a listing of the chemicals that went down on the schooner *Fannie A. Millikin* and were to be reimbursed in the amount of $1341.70), February 11, 1886, ENHS.

34. Invoice to TAE from Arthur & Bonnell, December 31, 1885, ENHS.

35. Invoice to TAE from Bergmann & Co., December 18, 1885, ENHS.

36. Invoice to TAE from Bergmann & Co. for "municipal dynamo," December 18, 1885, ENHS.

37. Untitled article, *Fort Myers Press*, February 13, 1886.

38. Invoice to E. T. Gilliland from Ambrose Martin, November 20, 1885; invoice to TAE from E. Stearns, November 24, December 21, 1885, ENHS. ("Gill" is written at the bottom of the November 24 and December 21 invoices to denote that these purchases were for Gilliland, not Edison.) Invoice to E. T. Gilliland from C. & R. Poillon, November 30, 1885.

39. Invoice to E. T. Gilliland from Abbey & Imbrie, November 28, 1885, ENHS.

40. Invoice to TAE from Hartley & Graham, November 27, 1885, ENHS. ("Gill" is written at the bottom to denote a Gilliland purchase.)

41. Invoice to TAE from Peck & Snyder, December 7, 1885; invoice to TAE from Kennebec Framing Co., November 25, 1885, ENHS. ("Gill" is written at the bottom of both invoices denoting Gilliland's purchases.)

42. Nerney, *Thomas A. Edison: A Modern Olympian*, 272–223; Baldwin, *Edison: Inventing the Century*, 169–71.

43. "Edison's Preparations," *Fort Myers Press*, November 21, 1885; "Summary of Expenses Paid by Eli Thompson, December 5, 1885 to February 27, 1886," ENHS. November 17, 1885 to April 27, 1886, ENHS.

44. Untitled article, *Fort Myers Press,* December 5, 1885.

45. Bill paid to Joseph Vivas by TAE and Gilliland, December 5, 1885, ENHS; "Summary of Expenses Paid by Eli Thompson, December 5, 1885, to February 27, 1886"; Grismer, *The Story of Fort Myers*, 276.

46. Since Bassler made only $1.50 per day, it is unlikely that he was a professional landscape gardener. Invoice Edison and Gilliland to Bassler, February 27, 1886, ENHS.

47. "What Edison Is Doing," *Fort Myers Press*, March 20, 1885.

48. "What Do You Think about It?" *Fort Myers Press*, January 16, 1886.

Chapter 3. Honeymoon in Florida

1. MME to MVM, February 28, 1886, EFWE.

2. S. Paul Brown, *The Book of Jacksonville*, 113–14; T. Frederick Davis, *History of Jacksonville*, 487–88; Frisbie, *Florida's Fabled Inns*, 15–16.

3. Advertisement in the 1886 Jacksonville, Florida, City Directory, Jacksonville Public Library.

4. Jane E. Miller (Jennie) to MME, February 28, 1886, FM001AAH; TAEM 161:849.

5. Gilliland's reply does not exist, but in a letter to Sam Edison, he outlined his response to Edison. March 7, 1886, TAEM, 79:86.

6. MME to MVM, February 28, 1886, FM001AAH, TAEM 161:849.

7. Edison's technical notes and drawings, February 28, 1886, NM020AAS, TAEM 44:712. Sent to Richard Dyer.

8. TAE, telegram to Samuel Insull, March 3, 1886, D8603ZAI, TAEM 79:84.

9. Barbour, *Florida for Tourists, Invalids, and Settlers*, 105–6.

10. Ibid., 113–14.

11. Information courtesy Janice S. Mahaffey, Reference Services, Putnam County Library, Palatka, Florida.

12. "About the Putnam," *The Daily News* (Palatka, Fla.), March 7, 1886.

13. Barbour, *Florida for Tourists, Invalids, and Settlers*, 134.

14. Edward King, "Pictures from Florida," *Scribner's Monthly Magazine*, November 1874, 3.

15. Rowe, *The Ideal of Florida in the American Literary Imagination*, 59–60.

16. Barbour, *Florida for Tourists, Invalids, and Settlers*, 127.

17. Ibid., 130.

18. Ibid., 134.

19. Jane Miller to MME, March 10, 1886, EFWE.

20. TAE, telegram to Samuel Insull, March 8, 1886, D8639A, TAEM 79:1127; Samuel Insull, telegram to TAE, March 10, 1886, TAEM 79:89.

21. Geo. H. Adams & Son, Map of Florida, 1884, Historical Map Collection, P. K. Younge Library of Florida History, University of Florida, Gainesville. There is no correspondence from Sanford, but TAE's telegrams and Jane Miller's letters both refer to plans for a trip to the town. From Sanford, the train traveled to Tampa, where the steamer *Manatee* made a regular run to Fort Myers.

22. "Personal," *Tampa Guardian*, March 17, 1886; information from Rodney Kite-Powell, curator of the Tampa Bay History Center.

23. Untitled article, *Fort Myers Press*, February 27, 1886.

24. Untitled article, *Fort Myers Press*, March 20, 1886.

25. Invoice to TAE and Gilliland from Jeffcott & Bowman, proprietors of the Keystone Hotel, Fort Myers, March 23, 1886, ENHS.

26. Grismer, *The Story of Fort Myers*, 108.

27. Speech by MME given at the dedication of Seminole Lodge to the city of Fort Myers, March 6, 1947, EFWE.

28. "Mrs. Hughes Recalls Early History Here," *Fort Myers News-Press*, May 13, 1937.

29. "Pay Role [*sic*] Edison, Gilliland," March 15–20, 1886, 155, ENHS.

30. Ibid.

31. TAE refers to her as "the girl" in the telegram (February 18, 1886, EFWE, CEF). A letter from Jane Miller to MME (February 28, 1886) mentions Louise, who may have

been Louise Rittesbaugh, a longtime Miller family domestic servant; see Hendrick, *Lewis Miller: A Biographical Essay*, 83.

32. Untitled article, *Fort Myers Press*, May 1, 1886 refers to Misses Lena and Nora McCarthy.

33. Speech by MME given at the dedication of Seminole Lodge to the city of Fort Myers, March 6, 1947.

34. "Mrs. Hughes Recalls Early History Here, *Fort Myers News-Press*, May 13, 1937.

35. "Early Recollections of Mrs. Marion Edison Oser," 8, March 1956, LB012, ENHS.

36. "Fort Myers Notebook," March 18, 1886, N314003, TAEM 42:815.

37. Simonds, *Edison: His Life, His Work, His Genius*, 224–25.

38. "Mrs. Hughes Recalls Early History Here," *Fort Myers News-Press*, May 13, 1937.

39. "Story by Mrs. Edison Tells of Early Days in Fort Myers," *Fort Myers News-Press*, August 25, 1947.

40. Untitled article, *Fort Myers Press*, April 3, 1886.

41. Rosenblum and Associates, *Edison Winter Estate: Cultural Landscape Report*, I-46.

42. "Fort Myers Notebook," N-86-04-05, ENHS.

43. Grismer, *The Story of Fort Myers*, 120.

44. Theodore Westwood Miller to MME, May 16, 1886, FS001AAA, TAEM 161:1034.

45. Untitled article, *Fort Myers Press*, May 1, 1886.

46. Hendrick, *Lewis Miller: A Biographical Essay*, 117–18.

Chapter 4. Waiting for the Light

1. Grismer, *The Story of Fort Myers*, 122.

2. Untitled article, *Fort Myers Press*, March 17, 1887.

3. Baldwin, *Edison: Inventing the Century*, 182.

4. "An Interview with Thomas A. Edison," *New York World*, March 28, 1887, in Gonzalez, *The Caloosahatchee*, 105–13.

5. Jane Miller (Jennie) to MME, March 8, 1887, FM001AAW, TAEM 161:907.

6. Marion Edison Oser, interview A-518, March 1956, 6, ENHS.

7. Ibid., 8.

8. Ibid., 8.

9. Israel, *Edison: A Life of Invention*, 257.

10. *Fort Myers Press*, February 19, 1887.

11. Marion Edison to TAE, April 24, 1887, FB001AAA, TAEM 161:5.

12. Gonzalez, *The Caloosahatchee*, 109–10.

13. Ibid., 111.

14. Grismer, *The Story of Fort Myers*, 115. The newspaper account of the lighting of the Edison home is currently missing from Fort Myers Press microfilm, but Grismer likely had access to it.

15. Untitled article, *Fort Myers Press*, March 10, 1887.

16. Israel, *Edison: A Life of Invention*, 257.

17. Technical drawings by TAE: March 1, 1887 (NA007005, TAEM 98:405), March 2, 1887 (NA008005, TAEM 98:464), and March 3, 1887, (NA008015, TAEM 98:468). Thanks to Paul Israel for specifying the type of magnets.

18. Baldwin, *Edison: Inventing the Century*, 182.

19. William Halsey Wood to TAE, D8704SGH, TAEM 119:316; Grismer, *The Story of Fort Myers*, 138; Gonzalez, *The Caloosahatchee*, 10–13.

20. William Edison to MME, March 27, 1887, FD001 AAC, TAEM 11:318.

21. Baldwin, *Edison: Inventing the Century*, 182.

22. Israel, *Edison: A Life of Invention*, 257.

23. TAE to Charles Batchelor, April 6, 1887, D8704AAP, TAEM 119:121.

24. MME to LM, April 26, 1887, FH001AAA, TAEM 161:486.

25. LM to MME, April 26, 1887, FH001AAA, TAEM 161:486.

26. Marion Edison to TAE, April 24, 1887, FB001AAA, TAEM 161:5.

27. MME to LM, April 26, 1887, FH001AAA, TAEM 161:486.

28. "Wizard Edison in Florida," *Fort Myers Press*, April 21, 1887.

Chapter 5. Waiting for the Inventor

1. Untitled article, *Fort Myers Press*, February 16, 1888.

2. William Halsey Wood to TAE, December 1, 1887, D8603U, TAEM 79:62.

3. MVM to MME, F100ABK, TAEM 161:582.

4. TAE to George B. Prescott, March 10, 1888, D8818AGF, TAEM 122:189.

5. L. C. Washburn to TAE, January 14, 1889, D8947AAE, TAEM 126:938.

6. Untitled article, *Fort Myers Press*, June 14, 1888.

7. Detailed information on the Edison and Gilliland breakup is in Rosenblum and Associates, *Edison Winter Estate: Cultural Landscape Report* I-63–65; Rosenblum, *Edison Winter Estate: Historic Structures Report*, I-12; Josephson, *Edison: A Biography*, 328–30; and Baldwin, *Edison: Inventing the Century*, 185–91.

8. Untitled article, *Fort Myers Press*, January 17, 1889.

9. William Hibble to TAE, January 12, 1889, D8947AAD, TAEM 126:935.

10. William Hibble to TAE, December 3, 1889, D8947ABA, TAEM 126:964.

11. Alfred Tate to William Hibble, December 20, 1889, LB035292, TAEM 140:75.

12. William Hibble to Alfred Tate, December 26, 1889, D8947ABB, TAEM 126:965.

13. William Hibble to Alfred Tate, January 11, 1890, 9041AAB, TAEM 129:589; Alfred Tate to William Hibble, January 20, 1890, LB036170, TAEM 140:253.

14. MME to Alfred Tate, February 24, 1890, D9041AAE, TAEM 129:593.

15. William Hibble to Alfred Tate, November 22, 1890, D9041AAO, TAEM 129:605.

16. Postcard from C. E. Robbins to TAE, March 13, 1890, D9041AAG, TAEM 129:596. The list of delinquent taxpayers was in the March 13, 1890, issue of the *Fort Myers Press*.

17. Marginal note in William Hibble to Alfred Tate, March 14, 1890, D9041AAH, TAEM 129:597.

18. William Hibble to Alfred Tate, November 22, 1890, D9041AAO, TAEM 129:605.

19. William Hibble to Alfred Tate, December 6, 1890, D9041, TAEM 129:607.

20. James Symington to TAE, March 19, 1891, EFWE.

21. James Symington to TAE, April 15, 1891, D9112AAL, TAEM 130:995.

22. James Symington to TAE, April 15, 1891.

23. Alfred Tate to Major James Evans, June 13, 1891, LB0494, TAEM 142:32.

24. Rosenblum and Associates, *Edison Winter Estate: Cultural Landscape Report*, I-53.

25. Major James Evans to TAE, June 22, 1891, D9132AAK, TAEM 131:364.

26. Baldwin, *Edison: Inventing the Century*, 232; personal communication from Paul C. Spehr.

27. James Symington to TAE, March 20, 1893, D930AAE, TAEM 133:933.

28. James Symington to TAE, April 24, 1893, D9308AAJ, TAEM 133:940.

29. James Symington to TAE, April 24, 1893.

30. B. H. Welton to TAE, January 2, 1895, D9506AAA, TAEM 135:709.

31. "Samuel Edison," *Fort Myers Press*, March 5, 1896.

32. Baldwin, *Edison: Inventing the Century*, 261.

33. MME to MVM, January 7, 1898, microfilm, book 22, reels 9, 10, CEF.

34. "The Young Wizard Here," *Fort Myers Press*, February 10, 1898; Israel, *Edison: A Life of Invention*, 389–90.

35. Untitled article, *Fort Myers Press*, March 24, 1898.

36. W. D. Collins to TAE, April 13, 1893, D932AAA, TAEM 134:303.

37. E. Fitzhebert to TAE, March 28, 1894, D9412AAB; TAEM 135:128; Mrs. H. D. Baldwin to TAE, March 20, 1894, D9412AAA, TAEM 135:128.

38. TAE to W. C. Battey, December 15, 1896, LB059245, TAEM 143:518.

39. TAE to Major James Evans, July 26, 1899, LB06353, TAEM 143:1043.

40. Grismer, *The Story of Fort Myers*, 139; Untitled article, *Fort Myers Press*, April 28, 1892.

41. Rosenblum and Associates, *Edison Winter Estate: Cultural Landscape Report*, I-67.

42. Untitled article, *Fort Myers Press*, December 8, 1892; "The Second Largest Tarpon," *Fort Myers Press*, May 11, 1893.

43. Grismer, *The Story of Fort Myers*, 139.

44. Untitled article, *Fort Myers Press*, July 19, 1894.

45. Grismer, *The Story of Fort Myers*, 145–46.

46. Untitled article, *Fort Myers Press*, January 6, 1898.

47. "A. M. McGregor, President of the Standard Oil Company," *Fort Myers Press*, February 15, 1900.

Chapter 6. The Wizard Returns

1. "Death of A. M. McGregor," *Fort Myers Press*, November 1, 1900.

2. Israel, *Edison: A Life of Invention*, 390–392; Baldwin, *Edison: Inventing the Century*, 269–70, 293–95.

3. "Joy and Grief in Edison's Home," *Newark [?]* [likely *Newark News*], July 12, 1898, CEF microfilm; Vincent, *Theodore W. Miller: Rough Rider*.

4. "Hon. Lewis Miller Laid to Rest," *The Cleveland Press*, February 21, 1899; obituary for Lewis Miller, *New York Tribune*, February 18, 1899; obituary for Lewis Miller, *New York Sun*, February 18, 1899; Baldwin, *Edison: Inventing the Century*, 270.

5. Charles Edison, oral history with Wendell Link, April 14, 1953, 72, ENHS.

6. "Great Wizard; The Wonderful Inventor Stops Here on His Way to His Winter Home at Fort Myers," quoted from the *Tampa Tribune*, *Fort Myers Press*, March 8, 1900.

7. Nolan, *Fifty Feet in Paradise*, 114.

8. *Tampa Bay Hotel*, pamphlet, 1900, Henry B. Plant Museum, Tampa, Florida.

9. *Tampa Bay Hotel*.

10. Grismer, *Tampa: A History of the City of Tampa and the Tampa Bay Region of Florida*, 212–30.

11. "Great Wizard; The Wonderful Inventor Stops Here on His Way to His Winter Home at Fort Myers."

12. Grismer, *Tampa, A History of the City of Tampa and the Tampa Bay Region of Florida*, 212–30.

13. Braden, *The Architecture of Leisure*, 281–90.

14. Charles Edison, oral history with Wendell Link, April 14, 1953, 72, CEF.

15. "Great Wizard; The Wonderful Inventor Stops Here on His Way to His Winter Home at Fort Myers."

16. Rosenblum and Associates, *Edison Winter Estate: Cultural Landscape Report*, I-41; Rosenblum, *Edison Winter Estate: Historic Structures Report*, I-15.

17. "Mrs. Hughes Recalls Early History Here," *Fort Myers News-Press*, May 13, 1937.

18. Rosenblum and Associates, *Edison Winter Estate: Cultural Landscape Report*, I-54.

19. "Thomas A. Edison; The Great Inventor Arrived at the Fort Myers with His Family Yesterday," *Fort Myers Press*, February 28, 1901.

20. Grismer, *The Story of Fort Myers*, 140–41.

21. Ibid., 146.

22. Ibid., 148.

23. "Thomas A. Edison; The Great Inventor Arrived at the Fort Myers with His Family Yesterday."

24. Abbott, *Open for the Season*, 61–62.

25. "Mr. Edison Having a Big Time," *Fort Myers Press*, March 14, 1901.

26. All documents and newspaper articles refer to Elizabeth Floweree as "Mrs. D.A.G. Floweree." Her first name is provided in A. W. Bowen and Co., *The Progressive Men of the State of Montana.*

27. Untitled article, *Fort Myers Press*, August 31, 1899; and Grismer, *The Story of Fort Myers*, 148.

28. Rosenblum and Associates, *Edison Winter Estate: Cultural Landscape Report*, I-67.

29. Untitled article, *Fort Myers Press*, March 21, 1901.

30. Abbott, *Open for the Season*, 61.

31. "Prof. Edison Fishing for Tarpon," *Fort Myers Press*, March 28, 1901.

32. "Fort Myers Hotel Notes," *Fort Myers Press*, March 28, 1901.

33. "The Wizard Gone North," *Fort Myers Press*, April 4, 1901.

34. "The World Waiting to Hear from Edison," *Fort Myers Press*, April 4, 1901.

35. "The Wizard Gone North," *Fort Myers Press*, April 4, 1901.

36. Grismer, *The Story of Fort Myers*, 169–70. Grismer said that Edison donated $100, but the *Fort Myers Press* listed a $50 contribution.

37. "Thos. A. Edison Subscribes to Fire Fund," *Fort Myers Press*, June 6, 1901.

38. "The New Steamer Thos. A. Edison, *Fort Myers Press*, August 29, 1901; "Launch of the Thomas A. Edison," *Fort Myers Press*, October 10, 1901.

39. MME to MVM, January 27, 1902, CEF, EFWE.

40. Charles Edison, oral history with Wendell Link, April 14, 1953, ENHS.

41. "Edison at His Winter Home," *Fort Myers Press*, March 6, 1902.

42. Untitled article, *Fort Myers Press*, March 20, 1902.

43. Madeleine Edison Sloane, interview with Kenneth K. Goldstein, March 3, 1973, 65 ENHS.

44. "Big Real Estate Deals," *Fort Myers Press*, February 20, 1902.

45. Untitled article, *Fort Myers Press*, January 16, 1902.

46. Grismer, *The Story of Fort Myers*, 140; Rosenblum, *Edison Winter Estate: Historic Structures Report*, I-20–21.

47. "Thomas A Edison Arrives with His Family on Saturday," *Fort Myers Press*, February 26, 1903; Rosenblum and Associates, *Edison Winter Estate: Cultural Landscape Report*, I-75–76.

48. Untitled article, *Fort Myers Press*, May 15, 1902.

49. Rosenblum, *Edison Winter Estate: Historic Structures Report*, I-20.

50. "Improving the Edison Place," *Fort Myers Press*, May 22, 1902.

51. Rosenblum, *Edison Winter Estate: Historic Structures Report*, I-20.

52. "Thomas A Edison Arrives with His Family on Saturday," *Fort Myers Press*, February 26, 1903.

53. "Edisons Leave for Home," *Fort Myers Press*, April 2, 1903.

54. "Thomas A Edison Arrives with His Family on Saturday."

55. "'Lucky Jones' Lands a Seven Foot Silver King," *Fort Myers Press*, March 19, 1903; "Thomas A Edison Arrives with His Family on Saturday."

56. "Edisons Leave for Home," *Fort Myers Press*, April 2, 1903.

57. "Fort Myers Celebrates!" *Fort Myers Press*, February 25, 1904; Grismer, *The Story of Fort Myers*,163–66.

58. Turner, *A Short History of Florida Railroads*, 97.

59. "Electric Launch Coming for Edison," *Fort Myers Press*, January 28, 1904; "Edisons to Arrive Next Week," *Fort Myers Press*, February 18, 1904; "Edison Electric Plant Started Up," *Fort Myers Press*, February 25, 1904.

60. "Edisons at Their Winter Home," *Fort Myers Press*, March 3, 1904.

61. MVM to MME, March 18, 1906, EFWE.

62. General Manager of the Electric Launch Company to TAE, January 9, 1904, D0420, TAEM 189:254. Ewald Stulpner's wages are documented in Stulpner to TAE, February 3, 1904, D0420, TAEM 189:258.

63. "Edisons at Their Winter Home."

64. Venable, *Out of the Shadow*, 257–58; Charles Edison, oral history with Wendell Link, April 14, 1953, 76–77, ENHS.

Chapter 7. Transformations and Torments

1. Josephson, *Edison: A Biography*, 417.

2. Rosenblum, *Edison Winter Estate: Historic Structures Report*, I-26

3. Grismer, *The Story of Fort Myers*, 180.

4. "Gen. Terry and Mrs. McGregor Married," *New York Times*, December 12, 1905, quoted in the *Fort Myers Press*, December 21, 1905.

5. Grismer, *The Story of Fort Myers*, 180, 185, 196, 207.

6. MME to "My Darlings," Akron, Ohio, February 13, 1906, EFWE.

7. Grismer, *The Story of Fort Myers*, 164–67.

8. Charles Edison, oral history with Wendell Link, April 14, 1953, 75, ENHS. See also multiple letters from Madeleine Edison to the Edison Family, undated but on stationery from Oak Place School, Akron, Ohio, CEF microfilm.

9. "Edison Arrived Yesterday, The Wizard and His Family Here for Six Weeks' Stay," *Fort Myers Press*, March 1, 1906.

10. "Hotel Notes," *Fort Myers Press*, March 1, 1906.

11. MVM to MME, March 15, 1906, EFWE.

12. *Fort Myers Press*, March 22, 1906; Charles Edison, oral history with Wendell Link, April 14, 1953, 75, ENHS.

13. MME's marginal notes in Blanchan, *Birds That Hunt and Are Hunted*, CEF, EFWE.

14. Untitled article, *Fort Myers Press*, March 29, 1906.

15. Ibid.

16. Grismer, *The Story of Fort Myers*, 192.

17. Ibid., 192–93.

18. "Edison Visits Okeechobee Region," *Fort Myers Press*, March 29, 1906.

19. Untitled article, *Fort Myers Press*, March 29, 1906.

20. H. E. Heitman to TAE, May 8, 1906, D0619, TAEM 190:612.

21. H. E. Heitman to TAE, May 12, 1906, LB074, TAEM 197:586; and H. E. Heitman to TAE, August 13, 1906, X104C, TAEM 622:486.

22. Abstract, Land in Section 23, produced by the Lee County Abstract Company and witnessed by W. M. Hendry, Clerk Circuit Court, May 24, 1906, EFWE.

23. "Edisons Return North," *Fort Myers Press*, April 12, 1906.

24. "Famous Hotel at Punta Rassa Burned," *Fort Myers Press*, January 3, 1907.

25. George Shultz to TAE, August 3, 1907, D0723, TAEM 191:493.

26. Rosenblum, *Edison Winter Estate: Historic Structures Report*, I-26–27.

27. "A Large Pavilion for Mr. Edison," *Fort Myers Press*, March 7, 1907; Rosenblum, *Edison Winter Estate: Historic Structures Report*, I-34.

28. Pennsylvania Railroad Company to TAE, January 26, 1907, D0723, TAEM 191:479.

29. "Edison Makes Interesting Analysis," *Fort Myers Press*, March 14, 1907.

30. "Edison Subscribes $250 for the Country Club," *Fort Myers Press*, March 14, 1907.

31. Untitled article, *Fort Myers Press*, April 18, 1907.

32. "Edison's Offer Is Accepted with Thanks," *Fort Myers Press*, April 4, 1907.

33. Ibid.

34. "Another Side to the Palm Matter," *Fort Myers Press*, September 7, 1911.

35. "Seawall Proposition Was Ably Discussed," *Fort Myers Press*, February 27, 1908.

36. "McGregor Boulevard," *Fort Myers Press*, February 22, 1912.

37. Grismer, *The Story of Fort Myers*, 183.

38. Multiple invoices from Proctor & Company, including invoice to H. E. Heitman, January 20, 1910, ENHS.

39. Harvie Heitman to Proctor & Company, November 13, 1909, ENHS.

40. Proctor & Company to Harvie Heitman, November 27, 1909, ENHS.

41. MME to MVM, April 7, 1909, EFWE, CEF. (Citations with both EFWE and CEF indicate that at the time of publication, the CEF items were located at the EFWE.)

42. W. R. Wallace & Co. to H. E. Heitman, May 13, 1910, ENHS.

43. W. R. Wallace & Co. to H. E. Heitman, June 24, 1910, ENHS.

44. W. R. Wallace & Co. to TAE, December 8, 1910, and February 2, 1911, ENHS.

45. TAE to H. E. Heitman, May 10, 1911, ENHS.

46. W. R. Wallace to TAE, April 4, 1911; TAE to W. R. Wallace, April 19, 1911, ENHS.

47. Marginal notes in TAE to H. E. Heitman, May 7, 1911, CEF microfilm.

48. Untitled article, *Fort Myers Press*, March 7, 1912; "Edisons Have Arrived," *Fort Myers Press*, March 14, 1912.

49. Untitled article, *Fort Myers Press*, April 4, 1912.

50. "Inventor Enjoyed Trip," *Fort Myers Press*, April 11, 1912.

51. MME to the U.S. Department of Fisheries, November 15, 1912, EFWE.

52. Multiple letters between Madeleine Edison and John Sloane, winter of 1912, collection of David E. E. Sloane.

53. Smoot, *The Edisons of Fort Myers*, 103.

Chapter 8. Roughing It with Famous Folk

1. "President Heitman of the Packing House Company Estimates the Total Damage," *Fort Myers Press*, February 5, 1914; Grismer, *The Story of Fort Myers*, 195–96.

2. Grismer, *The Story of Fort Myers*, 195–96.

3. "Thos. A. Edison and Family, John Burroughs and Henry Ford Extended Royal Welcome," The *Fort Myers Press* reported that there were thirty-one cars, February 23, 1914.

4. MME to Grace Miller Hitchcock, February 27, 1914, EFWE, CEF.

5. Madeleine Edison to John Sloane, n.d., collection of David E. E. Sloane.

6. Madeleine Edison to John Sloane, March 7, 1914, collection of David E. E. Sloane.

7. Madeleine Edison to John Sloane, February 26, 1914, collection of David E. E. Sloane.

8. Madeleine Edison to John Sloane, March 31, 1914, collection of David E. E. Sloane.

9. MME to Grace Miller Hitchcock, February 27, 1914, EFWE, CEF.

10. MME to Grace Miller Hitchcock, February 27, 1914, EFWE, CEF.

11. Charles Edison, oral history with Wendell Link, April 14, 1953, ENHS; "Sixty Miles into the Woods," *Fort Myers Press*, March 2, 1914. Charles Edison said that the destination was Deep Lake, but the *Fort Myers Press* reported that the destination was Rocky Lake.

12. "Sixty Miles into the Woods," *Fort Myers Press*, March 2, 1914.

13. Charles Edison, oral history with Wendell Link, April 14, 1953, 79, ENHS.

14. "Sixty Miles into the Woods," *Fort Myers Press*, March 2, 1914.

15. Madeleine Edison to John Sloane, April 5, 1914, collection of David E. E. Sloane.

16. Smoot, *The Edisons of Fort Myers*, 121.

17. Ibid., 123.

18. Ibid., 124.

19. Ibid., 124.

20. Ibid., 125.

21. Ibid., 124.

22. "John Burroughs Says Fort Myers Reminds Him of Honolulu," *Fort Myers Press*, March 5, 1914.

23. Davis and Arsenault, *Paradise Lost? The Environmental History of Florida*, 246.

24. "Henry Ford Contributes to Fund for Rookeries in Alligator Bay," *Fort Myers Press*, March 5, 1914.

25. Madeleine Edison to John Sloane, February 24, 1914, collection of David E. E. Sloane.

26. Madeleine Edison to John Sloane, March 10, 1914, collection of David E. E. Sloane.

27. "Edison Guests Leave Today," *Fort Myers Press*, March 10, 1914.

28. "John Burroughs Says Fort Myers Reminds Him of Honolulu," *Fort Myers Press*, March 5, 1914.

29. MME to Grace Miller Hitchcock, March 31, 1914, EFWE, CEF.

30. Madeleine Edison to John Sloane, March 10, 1914, collection of David E. E. Sloane.

31. Madeleine Edison to John Sloane, March 14, 1914, collection of David E. E. Sloane.

32. Madeleine Edison to John Sloane, March 18, 1914, collection of David E. E. Sloane.

33. Venable, *Out of the Shadow*, 255.

34. Seminole Lodge Guest Book, March 2, 1914, EFWE.

35. Madeleine Edison to John Sloane, March 25, 1914, collection of David E. E. Sloane.

36. Madeleine Edison to John Sloane, March 19, 1914, collection of David E. E. Sloane.

37. Mannering, "Thomas A. Edison and His Triumphs," *National Magazine*, December.

38. Ibid.

39. Madeleine Edison to John Sloane, April 12, 1914, collection of David E. E. Sloane.

40. Madeleine Edison to John Sloane, March 28, 1914, collection of David E. E. Sloane.

41. Israel, *Edison: A Life of Invention*, 422. Thanks to Leonard DeGraaf, archivist of ENHS, for placing the incident in context.

42. Madeleine Edison to John Sloane, April 1, 1914, collection of David E. E. Sloane.

43. "There Is Only One Fort Myers and 90,000,000 People Are Going to Find It Out," *Fort Myers Press*, March 25, 1914.

44. Decennial Census of the Untied States, U.S. Bureau of the Censusm, www.census.gov.

45. "There Is Only One Fort Myers and 90,000,000 People Are Going to Find It Out."

46. Baldwin, *Edison: Inventing the Century*, 335–36.

Chapter 9. Neighbors, Welcomed and Not

1. Lousy. Presumably from the term for a young louse.

2. "Thos. A. Edison Gives Warning Against Nets," *Fort Myers Press*, April 11, 1916.

3. "Edison Party Enjoying Outing," *Fort Myers Press*, April 4, 1912.

4. "Thomas A. Edison Rapidly Improving," *Fort Myers Press*, March 2, 1908.

5. "Bright Future Is Predicted," *Fort Myers Press*, April 24, 1916.

6. Robert W. Smith to Henry Ford, March 7, 1916, HFMGV.

7. Letter to Robert W. Smith from Henry Ford via his Assistant Secretary, S. Anderson, March 13, 1916, HFMGV.

8. James Hutton to Henry Ford, April 20, 1916, HFMGV. Letter marked "Personal."

9. Brauer, *There to Breathe the Beauty.*

10. Telegram from James Hutton to Otis Anderson(?), May 26, 1916, HFMGV.

11. "Henry Ford Buys a Fort Myers Estate," *Fort Myers Press,* June 1, 1916.

12. Henry Ford Estate, Dearborn, Michigan, Henryfordestate.org/fairlanestory.htm.

13. "Henry Ford Buys a Fort Myers Estate," *Fort Myers Press,* June 1, 1916.

14. The newspapers erroneously referred to the *Sialia* as the *Stella.* According to Carol Whittaker, reference archivist at the Benson Ford Research Center, Ford did not own a yacht called *Stella.*

15. Baldwin, *Henry Ford and the Jews,* 43.

16. "Henry Ford Is in the City," *Fort Myers Press,* March 13, 1917.

17. Israel, *Edison: A Life of Invention,* 446–47.

18. Ibid., 447–50.

19. Baldwin, *Edison, Inventing the Century,* 343–46.

20. MME to CE, April 6, 1920, EFWE, CEF.

21. "Summary of Expenses for Seminole Lodge, March 1, 1916 to March 31, 1916," ENHS.

22. Harvie Heitman to TAE, November 7, 1911, ENHS.

23. Harvie Heitman to MME, May 13, 1915, CEF microfilm.

24. "Report on Fort Myers, Fla. Estate of Thomas Alva Edison, June 11, 1917," 4, EFWE.

25. Ibid., 2–4.

26. Marginal note by TAE on Harvie Heitman to R. W. Kellow, June 19, 1917, ENHS.

27. R. W. Kellow to Harvie Heitman, July 12, 1917, ENHS.

28. Harvie Heitman to R. W. Kellow, July 19, 1917, ENHS.

29. MME to Madeleine Edison Sloane, February 8, 1918, B037CE, TAEM 0:0.

30. "Board of Trade Plans Fine Reception for Thomas A. Edison," *Fort Myers Press,* January 29, 1918.

31. Note from TAE to CE, EFWE, CEF. CE's note on reverse: "Message sent by Father from USS Sachem off Key West about March 25, 1918 in response to my telegram asking his blessing on my marriage to Carolyn Hawkins. Original in his handwriting as given to an aide to send."

32. Venable, *Out of the Shadow,* 64–67.

33. "At Seminole Lodge Today Miss Carolyn Hawkins and Charles Edison Married," *Fort Myers Press,* March 27, 1918.

34. Venable, *Out of the Shadow,* 67.

35. "Edison Family Enroute to New Jersey Home," *Fort Myers Press,* April 2, 1918.

36. Rosenblum, *Edison Winter Estate: Historic Structures Report,* I-52. "Torredos" were described as having eaten away the dock.

37. "Report on Fort Myers, Fla. Estate of Thomas A. Edison, June 11, 1917," EFWE.

38. Harvie Heitman to TAE, May 28, 1917, ENHS.

39. "Summary of Expenses for Seminole Lodge January 1, to December 31, 1918," ENHS.

40. Rosenblum, *Edison Winter Estate: Historic Structures Report*, I-47.

41. "Great Inventor's Workshop Is Shorn of Tools," *Fort Myers Press*, April 9, 1919.

42. Rosenblum, *Edison Winter Estate: Historic Structures Report*, I-47.

43. "Arrival of Thos. A. Edison Matter of Felicitation," *Fort Myers Press*, February 14, 1919.

44. "Thos. A. Edison Concludes His Winter Vacation," *Fort Myers Press*, April 11, 1919.

45. MME to Charles and Carolyn Edison, March 27, 1920, EFWE, CEF.

46. MME to Charles and Carolyn Edison, March 15, 1920, EFWE, CEF.

47. Photostat of a postcard from MME to TE, March 20, 1920, EFWE.

48. Rosenblum, *Edison Winter Estate: Historic Structures Report*, I-48.

49. Mrs. Tinstman to R. W. Kellow, August 16, 1919, ENHS.

50. Letters from Mrs. Tinstman to R. W. Kellow, July 26, August 16, and October 31, 1919, and May 26, 1920, ENHS.

51. In correspondence, she was referred to as Mrs. Tinstman. According to the 1927 Fort Myers Directory, her first name was Nellie. *Fort Myers Directory*, 1927, Southwest Florida Historical Museum.

52. Letters from Mrs. Tinstman to R. W. Kellow, July 26, August 16, and October 31, 1919, and May 26, 1920, ENHS.

53. Marginal notes by MME on R. W. Kellow to MME, November 2, 1920, ENHS.

54. Ben Tinstman to R. W. Kellow, December 3, 1920, ENHS.

55. MME to Charles and Carolyn Edison, March 30, 1920, EFWE, CEF.

56. "Thomas A. Edison Rapidly Improving," *Fort Myers Press*, March 2, 1908; MME to CE, March 27, 1920, EFWE, CEF.

57. MME to Charles and Carolyn Edison, March 23, 1920, EFWE, CEF.

58. MME to Charles and Carolyn Edison, March 27, 1920, EFWE, CEF.

59. MME to Charles and Carolyn Edison, March 23, 1920.

60. "New Civic Organization Is Formed at the Home of Mr. and Mrs. Edison," *Fort Myers Press*, March 24, 1920.

Chapter 10. A Mind in "Cold Storage" Thaws

1. "Edison Not Coming," *Fort Myers Press*, February 22, 1921.

2. Israel, *Edison: A Life of Invention*, 455–57.

3. "Thomas A. Edison Is Booster for Base Ball Team of City," *Fort Myers Press*, April 26, 1921.

4. B. E. Tinstman, telegram to John V. Miller, October 26, 1921, ENHS.

5. John V. Miller to B. E. Tinstman, November 9, 1921, ENHS.

6. R. W. Kellow to B. E. Tinstman, February 25, 1921, ENHS; Carlisle Sherois, interview with the author, June 20, 1995.

7. The article describes a "Mr. Capling." George is listed in the *Fort Myers Directory* for 1927, Southwest Florida Historical Museum.

8. B. E. Tinstman to John Miller, October 26, 1921, ENHS.

9. "Thomas A. Edison Arrives," *Fort Myers Press*, March 22, 1922.

10. "Edison and Ford Visit Business Section of City," *Fort Myers Press*, March 23, 1922.

11. "Public Stand for Christ Is Taken by Many," *Fort Myers Press*, March 25, 1922.

12. Board and Colcord, *Historic Fort Myers*, 22.

13. "Mr. Edison and Party See Film," *Fort Myers Press*, March 24, 1922; Independent Movie Database entry for *Forever*, available at http://www.imdb.com/title/tt0012188.

14. "Edison and Ford Visit Business Section of City," *Fort Myers Press*, March 23, 1922.

15. "Henry Ford Takes a Walk; His Wife and Mrs. T. A. Edison Shop," *Fort Myers Press*, March 25, 1922.

16. "Sister of Mrs. Edison Arrives for Visit Here," *Fort Myers Press*, March 28; "Henry Ford Is Fasting for a Day or Two So He Will Feel Fit Once More," *Fort Myers Press*, March 29, 1922.

17. Lacey, *Ford, the Men and the Machine*, 211–14.

18. "Henry Ford Is Fasting for a Day or Two So He Will Feel Fit Once More."

19. "Edison and Ford Go Fishin' and Land Some Trout," *Fort Myers Press*, March 30, 1922.

20. "The Edisons and Guests Visit Beauty Parlor," *Fort Myers Press*, April 1, 1922.

21. For more information on Ella Piper, see Prudy Taylor Board, "Thoroughly Modern Ella," *Fort Myers News-Press*, June 10, 1984; and author's interviews with Linda Holdsclaw, Estalina Gill, Vivian Hill, Jacob Johnson, and Marie Harrell, all in March 2001.

22. "Henry Ford and Mrs. Ford Wind Up Visit Here," *Fort Myers Press*, April 5, 1922.

23. "Thos. A. Edison and Family Leave Fort Myers Today," *Fort Myers Press*, April 20, 1922.

24. "Thomas A. Edison to Remain Here Another Week," *Fort Myers Press*, April 17, 1922.

25. "Mrs. Edison Spends the Morning in Up to Date Stores Here," *Fort Myers Press*, April 14, 1922.

26. "Thos. A. Edison and Family Leave Fort Myers Today."

27. "Charles Edison and Wife Are Here for Rest," *Fort Myers Press*, April 30, 1922.

28. "Charley Edison Has Exciting Time Fishing," *Fort Myers Press*, May 16, 1922.

29. CE to MME, May 29, 1922, EFWE, CEF.

30. "Thomas A. Edison and Mrs. Edison Arrive at Winter Home Here," *Fort Myers Press*, March 15, 1923.

31. Mina Edison's marginal notes dated March 19, 1923, in Blanchan, *Birds That Hunt and Are Hunted*, CEF, EFWE.

32. "Mr. Edison Calls upon Owl Family," *Fort Myers Press*, March 29, 1923.

33. "Detroit Manufacturer Arrives with Party for Fortnight's Stay," *Fort Myers Press*, March 29, 1923.

34. "Detroit Manufacturer Arrives with Party for Fortnight's Stay"; "Uncle's Success Lures Pavese to States," *Fort Myers Press*, January 30, 1971, 8A.

35. "Our Three Distinguished Visitors," *Fort Myers Press*, March 29, 1923.

36. Grismer, *The Story of Fort Myers*, 234–35.

37. Davis and Arsenault, *Paradise Lost? The Environmental History of Florida*, 267.

38. Grismer, *The Story of Fort Myers*, 235.

39. Grismer, *The Story of Fort Myers*, 234–35.

40. Multiple articles, *Fort Myers Press*, April 25, 26. Undated *Tropical News* article from same period.

41. "Edison and Ford Are Opposed to Creation of County for Collier," *Fort Myers Press*, May 1, 1923.

42. Board and Colcord, *Pages from the Past*, 149.

43. Davis and Arsenault, *Paradise Lost? The Environmental History of Florida*, 268.

44. "Thomas A. Edison Has New Slogan for City," *Fort Myers Press*, May 3, 1923.

45. Board and Colcord, *Pages from the Past*, 150.

46. Board and Colcord, *Historic Fort Myers*, 27; Grismer, *The Story of Fort Meyers*, 218–19.

47. Grismer, *The Story of Fort Myers*, 217.

48. Ibid., 218.

49. Board and Colcord, *Lee County*, 86; Board and Colcord, *Historic Fort Myers*, 16.

50. "Fort Myers' Foremost Citizen Arrives for a Rest and--to Fish," *Fort Myers Press*, February 27, 1924.

51. "Henry Ford Is Expected to Arrive," *Fort Myers Press*, March 12, 1924.

52. Lacey, *Ford, the Men and the Machine*, 218.

53. "Fort Myers' Foremost Citizen Arrives for a Rest and--to Fish"; "The Edisons and Guests on a Picnic," *Fort Myers Press*, March 27, 1924; "Edisons to Leave on Friday," *Fort Myers Press*, April 7, 1924.

54. "Edison's 'Fliv' Has New Tires," *Fort Myers Press*, February 21, 1924.

55. MME's marginal notes in Blanchan, *Birds That Hunt and Are Hunted*, 164, 288, CEF, EFWE.

56. "Edison to Leave on Friday," *Fort Myers Press*, April 7, 1924.

57. "The Edisons and Guests on a Picnic."

58. Richard Rogers Bowker to MME, March 3, 1924, Richard Rogers Bowker Papers, New York Public Library.

59. MME to Richard Rogers Bowker, [March 1924], Richard Rogers Bowker Papers, New York Public Library.

60. Grismer, *The Story of Fort Myers*, 215.

61. "Mrs. Edison to Speak," *Fort Myers Press*, April 10, 1924.

62. Venable, *Mina Miller Edison: Daughter, Wife, and Mother of Inventors*, 19.

63. Editorial, *Fort Myers Press*, April 12, 1924.

64. "Thomas A. Edison to Remain Here Another Week," *Fort Myers Press*, April 17, 1922.

65. "Mr. Firestone and His Experts Confer with Thos. A. Edison," *Tropical News*, March 14, 1924.

66. Vanderbilt, *Thomas Edison: Chemist*, 282.

67. Rosenblum and Associates, *Edison Winter Estate: Cultural Landscape Report*, II-11.

68. Vanderbilt, *Thomas Edison: Chemist*, 286.

69. Rosenblum and Associates, *Edison Winter Estate: Cultural Landscape Report*, II-11.

70. "Mr. Firestone and His Experts Confer with Thos. A. Edison."

Chapter 11. Inventor at Work and Play

1. "Have You Seen Him?" *Fort Myers Press*, January 24, 1925.

2. Baldwin, *Henry Ford and the Jews*, 210–40.

3. Lacey, *Ford, the Men and the Machine*, 211–14.

4. "Ford Returns from La Belle [*sic*]," *Fort Myers Press*, January 28; "Henry Ford Visits Labelle," *Fort Myers Press*, January 30, 1925.

5. Rosenblum and Associates, *Edison Winter Estate: Cultural Landscape Report*, II-12.

6. Nolan, *Fifty Feet in Paradise*, 220–21.

7. "Ford Promises Cooperation at Muscle Shoals," *Fort Myers Press*, February 6, 1925.

8. "Edison Recalls Early Days in City of Palms," *Fort Myers Press*, February 11, 1925.

9. Ibid.

10. "Edison's Prophecy," *Fort Myers Press*, February 7, 1925.

11. "Equipment of Edison Laboratory Bought by Ford for Museum," *Fort Myers Press*, February 19, 1925.

12. "Bids City Adieu," *Fort Myers Press*, February 21, 1925.

13. "Ford, Firestone and Edison Unite to Break Rubber Monopoly Now Held by Great Britain," *Fort Myers Press*, April 7, 1925; Rosenblum and Associates, *Edison Winter Estate: Cultural Landscape Report*, II-12.

14. "Ford, Firestone and Edison Unite to Break Rubber Monopoly Now Held by Great Britain."

15. "Climate Right for Rubber Says Expert," *Fort Myers Press*, March 19, 1925.

16. Josephson, *Edison: A Biography*, 471.

17. "Edison and Party Marvel at Progress of Collier County," *Fort Myers Press*, February 27, 1925.

18. "Thomas A. Edison Leaves for North This Afternoon," *Fort Myers Press*, April 16, 1925.

19. "Naples Florida, Issued by the Naples Company," brochure March 1888, Issued by The Naples Company. Reprinted by the Friends of the Collier County Museum, March 2000.

20. Jamro and Jamro, *The Founding of Naples*, 30–31.

21. Reynolds, *When Peacocks Were Roasted*, 10–15.

22. "Edison and Party Marvel at Progress of Collier County," *Fort Myers Press*, February 27, 1925.

23. "Barron Collier Tells the Fort Myers Press, in First Interview after His County Is Created, of Development Plans," *Fort Myers Press*, May 7, 1923.

24. Everglades was later known as Everglades City.

25. "Edison and Party Marvel at Progress of Collier County."

26. "Thomas A. Edison Leaves for North This Afternoon," *Fort Myers Press*, April 16, 1925.

27. "Diamond Dick, A Pharmacist Who Pals with Big League Players," *Modern Pharmacy*, April 1940; Sports section of the *Fort Myers Press* and *Tropical News*, from February through March, between 1925–1935.

28. Nolan, *Fifty Feet in Paradise*, 190.

29. Gannon, *Florida: A Short History*, 77.

30. Grismer, *The Story of Fort Myers*, 221.

31. Ibid., 224.

32. "Newton Baker Greets Edisons at Station," *Fort Myers Press*, February 5, 1926.

33. "Edison Is 79 Today; Plans Picnic Party," *The Tropical News*, February 11, 1926.

34. "Double Shift Makes Edison 120, Feels 50 on 79th Birthday," *Fort Myers Press*, February 12, 1926.

35. "Edison Wires New York Associates All about Fort Myers Cocoanuts," *Fort Myers Press*, February 12, 1926.

36. "No Flying Machines for Thomas Edison," *Tropical News*, February 16, 1926.

37. "Edison Visits Fair, Picture Is Snapped with Seminoles," *Tropical News*, February 24, 1926; "Edison and Mack in Crowd which Throngs Grounds," *Fort Myers Press*, February 25, 1926.

38. "Inventor Solves Gleason's Shoots," *Fort Myers Press*, February 25, 1926. Newspapers reported that Gleason threw a pitch with "plenty of smoke on it." Photographs of the event indicate otherwise.

39. "Edison's Grandson Slightly Injured by Family Auto," and "Daughter of Edisons Joins Family Party," *Fort Myers Press*, March 2, 1926; and "Edisons' Daughter Joins Sons Here," *Tropical News*, March 2, 1926. The newspaper mistakenly lists Ted Sloane as the injured party; Jack Sloane was hit. Personal communication from David E. Sloane.

40. "Lack of Oil Hits Concert as Edisons Drop the Films," *Tropical News*, March 2, 1926.

41. Newton, *Uncommon Friends*, 3–5.

42. "Firestone Is Skeptical But Interested in Edison Experiments with Rubber," *Fort Myers Press*, March 6, 1926.

43. "Ford May Be Here and Then Again He May Not Be Here," *Tropical News*, March 6, 1926;"Ford Party Lands at Ireland Dock," *Fort Myers Press*, March 9, 1926; "Ford Hears Champion Fiddler of Florida," *Tropical News*, March 9, 1926.

44. "Firestone and Fiddlers Precede Ford's Arrival," *Tropical News*, March 9, 1926.

45. "Mrs. Edison Praises Program Fort Myers Recreation Board," *Tropical News*, March 9, 1926.

46. "Rubber Tire Manufacturer Firestone Visits Henry Ford's Rubber Nursery," *Hendry County News*, March 26, 1926.

47. "Edison Park Statue to be Unveiled with Ceremony Wednesday," *Tropical News*, April 6, 1926; "Edisons to Attend Statue Unveiling at Park Entrance," *Fort My-*

ers Press, April 7, 1926; "Newton to Make Presentation with Mayor Accepting," *Fort Myers Press*, April 7, 1926; James D. and Eleanor Newton, interviews with the author, July 15, 1996.

48. Newton, *Uncommon Friends*, 6–7.

49. "Thomas Edison's 43rd Annual Visit to Fort Myers Ends This Afternoon," *Tropical News*, April 20, 1926.

Chapter 12. Rubber Research and Road Trips

1. Williams and Duedall, *Florida Hurricanes and Tropical Storms*, 17; and Gannon, *Florida: A Short History*, 83–84.

2. Grismer, *The Story of Fort Myers*, 230.

3. Newton, *Uncommon Friends*, 36–37.

4. "Souvenir booklet, The Edison Pioneers, Ninth Annual Meeting," February 11, 1927, EFWE.

5. "Edison Finds Beloved Palms Weather Storm," *Tropical News*, February 20, 1927.

6. "Edison Sees Success for Rubber Experiments," *Tropical News*, February 27, 1927.

7. "Edison Is Caught Napping as Blaze Perils Laboratory," *Fort Myers Press*, March 6, 1927.

8. "Thomas Edison Gives Ty Cobb Batting Lessons," *Fort Myers Press*, March 8, 1927.

9. "Edison Entertains Macks with Cigars and Gator Stories," *Fort Myers Press*, March 26, 1927.

10. "Venice All Agog as Edison Drives Up in Sports Car," *Fort Myers Press*, March 12, 1927.

11. "Edison Strives to Wrest Secret of Rubber from Florida Soils," *Venice News*, March 18, 1927.

12. "Edison Tours State Seeking Rubber Trees," *Fort Myers Press*, April 8, 1927.

13. "Edison Sees Self in Movies with President Harding," *Fort Myers Press*, April 14, 1927.

14. "Edison Ends Vacation in Excellent Health," *Fort Myers Press*, May 4, 1927.

15. "Mrs. Edison Urges City to Preserve Lower River View," *Fort Myers Press*, March 9, 1927.

16. "Editorial: Locating the Bridge," *Fort Myers Press*, March 11, 1927.

17. Undated reminiscence from Jared Treman Newman, [ca. 1927], Jared Treman Newman Papers, Rare and Manuscript Collections, Cornell University Library, Ithaca, New York.

18. MME to Jared Treman Newman, April 27, 1927, Jared Treman Newman Papers, Rare and Manuscript Collections, Cornell University Library.

19. "What Price Peace of Mind?" *Fort Myers Press*, April 6, 1927.

20. "Edison Finds Vacation in Excellent Health," *Fort Myers Press*, May 4, 1927.

21. John K. Small to TAE, January 9, 1928, John K. Small Collection, Florida State Archives, Tallahassee.

22. John K. Small to TAE, January 16, 1928, John K. Small Collection, Florida State Archives, Tallahassee.

23. "Edison Scientists to Brave Everglades on Rubber Hunt," *Collier City News*, January 26, 1928.

24. Charles A. Lindbergh, telegram to MME, February 3, 1928, EFWE, CEF.

25. "4000 School Children Attend Edison Party," *Fort Myers Press*, February 11, 1928, EFWE.

26. Ernest G. Liebold, "The Reminiscences of Ernest G. Liebold," January 1953, 1518, Oral History Section, Reminiscences Manuscripts Subsection, Benson Ford Research Center, Dearborn, Michigan.

27. *The American Eagle*, newspaper published by the Koreshan Unity, A. H. Andrews, Editor, Estero, Florida, February 23, 1928, 3.

28. "Henry Ford Makes Winter Home Here: Neighbor of Edison," *Fort Myers Press*, April 25, 1928.

29. Emil Ludwig, telegram to the Edisons, February 17, 1928, EFWE; *The American Eagle*, newspaper published by the Koreshan Unity, A. H. Andrews, Editor, Estero, Florida, February 23, 1928, 3.

30. "Ludwig Calls Edison 'Secret King' of U.S.," *Lexington Leader* (Lexington, Ky.), April 22, 1928.

31. Emil Ludwig, "Edison, Studie uber Genie und Character," *Die Neue Runschau*, January 1932, 52–69. Translated by Joachim Schatton.

32. Diary of Emil Ludwig, from Gordon Ludwig's transcripts of his father's yearly notebooks, in German shorthand, February 20, 1928, Schweizerisches Literaturarchiv (Literature Archive of Switzerland), Schweizerische Landesbibliothek, Bern, Switzerland.

33. *The American Eagle*, newspaper published by the Koreshan Unity, A. H. Andrews, Editor, Estero, Florida, February 23, 1928, 3.

34. Newton, *Uncommon Friends*, 17.

35. Minutes of the Valinda Literary Circle, Southwest Florida Museum of History.

36. "Mrs. Edison Urges Home as Occupation," *Fort Myers Press*, April 19, 1928.

37. "Henry Ford Visits LaBelle in New Model Ford Car," *Hendry County News*, February 24, 1928.

38. By March 5, 1928, Ford was in Sudbury, Massachusetts; see "Fords Will Visit New Trade School at Sudbury, Mass.," *Fort Myers Press*, March 6, 1928.

39. "Thomas A. Edison Motors to Miami on Tamiami Trail," *Miami Herald*, March 6, 1928, 1A.

40. "Rubber Culture Absorbs Edison While in Miami," *Miami News*, April 6, 1928.

41. Lief, *The Firestone Story*, 166.

42. "Thomas A. Edison Motors to Miami on Tamiami Trail."

43. "Motorcade to Bring 3,000 to Fort Myers," *Fort Myers Press*, April 17, 1928.

44. "Edison Estate Thrown Open to Visitors in Fort Myers," *Tropical News*, April 28, 1928.

45. Nerney, *Thomas A. Edison: A Modern Olympian*, 242.

46. "Old Laboratory of Edison's Will Come Down Soon," *Tropical News*, June 7, 1928.

47. MME, "Mixed Feelings," October 20, 1929, ENHS.

48. "Edisons Pack Up Preparing to Leave for North Tuesday," *Fort Myers Press*, June 12, 1928; "Edison Ends 45th Annual Visit to Winter Home in Fort Myers," *Tropical News*, June 13, 1928.

Chapter 13. A President Comes to Call

1. "Thomas A. Edison Due to Arrive Tonight on His 46th Annual Visit," *Tropical News*, January 16, 1929.

2. "Crowd of 200 Hails Inventor on His Arrival," *Fort Myers Press*, January 17, 1929.

3. "Edison Has Picture Taken but Ducks Inquiring Writers," *Tropical News*, January 18, 1929.

4. Marjory Stoneman Douglas, "Mrs. Thomas A. Edison, at Home," *McCall's Magazine*, October 1929.

5. "Handling Celebrities," *Fort Myers Press*, January 25, 1929.

6. William and Mary Miller Nichols to MME, February 5, 1929, CEF.

7. "Mr. Hoover's Visit," *Fort Myers Press*, February 6, 1929.

8. Ibid.

9. "Hoover to Join Edison in Motor Tour of Fort Myers," *Fort Myers Press*, February 7, 1929.

10. James D. Newton, interview with the author, July 15, 1996.

11. Newton, *Uncommon Friends*, 22–23; "Edison Celebrates 82nd Birthday with Hoover and Cronies," *Tampa Tribune*, February 11, 1929; "Edison Says Cost Bars Synthetic Rubber Making," *Fort Myers Press*, February 11, 1929.

12. "20,000 Acclaim Next President on Motor Tour," *Tropical News*, February 12, 1929.

13. "Henry Ford Arrives for Five Week Visit," *Tropical News*, February 8, 1929.

14. "The Big Day," *Tropical News*, February 12, 1929.

15. Grismer, *The Story of Fort Myers*, 257.

16. "Hoover Sees Edison on 82nd Birthday," *Fort Myers Press*, February 12, 1929.

17. "The Big Day," *Tropical News*, February 12, 1929.

18. "Hoover Sees Edison on 82nd Birthday."

19. Katheryn Miller Geraci, telephone interview with the author, January 1995.

20. "Edison Celebrates 82nd Birthday with Hoover and Cronies."

21. "New Sugar Industry at Clewiston Visited by Edison and Fort," *Fort Myers Press*, February 17, 1929; "Ford and Edison Spend Four Hours Here on Inspection of Southern Sugar Properties," *Clewiston News*, February 22, 1929.

22. MME to Dr. Hamilton Holt, February 11, 1929, Hamilton Holt Collection, Rollins College Archives and Special Collections.

23. "Edison Knocks off Work, Takes His Wife to Fair," *Tropical News*, February 22, 1929.

24. "Ford Joins 300 in Reviving Old 'Square' Dances," *Fort Myers Press*, March 5, 1929; "A Lesson in Dancing," *Tropical News*, April 16, 1929.

25. H. O. Knight, Royal Palm Council of Boy Scouts of America, to MME, April 1, 1929, EFWE.

26. "Mrs. Edison Plans Girl Scout Outing," *Tropical News*, June 11, 1929.

27. Forrest H. Johnson, Florida Flood Control Association, to MME, March 8, 1929, EFWE.

28. "Mrs. Edison Plans Safety Hill Sale," *Fort Myers Press*, March 7, 1929.

29. "Sunday School Lesson," made to the Young Men's Wesley Bible Class, April 14, 1929, Sidney Davis Collection, EFWE.

30. Grismer, *The Story of Fort Myers*, 257.

31. C. W. Carlton to MME, May 2, 1929. EFWE.

32. "Our Pioneers," *Tropical News*, April 9, 1929.

33. Multiple editorials, none with a byline but clearly written by MME, *Tropical News*, April 23, 1929.

34. "To the Ladies," *Tropical News*, April 24, 1929.

35. "Edison Forgets Work for Day, Makes First Try for Tarpon," *Tropical News*, May 19, 1929.

36. "Menge Pilots Edison on Everglades Tour," *Fort Myers Press*, May 28, 1929.

37. "Edison to End 46th Working Vacation at Home Here Today," *Tropical News*, June 13, 1929.

38. Letter to Dr. John W. Baird from MME, August 10, 1929, EFWE.

39. Rosamond Chadwick to MME and her reply in margin, September 14, 1929, EFWE.

40. "Edison Better After Serious Attack of Pneumonia Puts Life in Danger for 10 Days," *Fort Myers Press*, September 3, 1929, and "Doctor Reveals Edison Had Pneumonia; Ascribes His Recovery to Natural Vigor," *New York Times*, September 3, 1929.

Chapter 14. Honors and Exhaustion

1. Grismer, *The Story of Fort Myers*, 236–38.

2. Elizabeth Arias, "United States Life Tables," *National Vital Statistics Reports*, 53, no. 6 (November 10, 2004).

3. "Famed Inventor Ends Long Trip in Fine Fettle," *Fort Myers Press*, December 7, 1929.

4. "Stay Right Here, Sir," *Tropical News*, December 7, 1929.

5. Josephson, *Edison: A Biography*, 481.

6. "Problems for Henry Ford," *Tropical News*, September 8, 1929.

7. "The Santa Claus Fund," *Tropical News*, December 14, 1929.

8. "Edison to See Navy Fliers in Special Air Circus Today," *Tropical News*, January 5, 1930.

9. TE to MME, February 14, 1930, Book 27, CEF microfilm.

10. "Mrs. Edison Shoots 3 Holes of Golf and Becomes a Fan," *Tropical News*, February 1, 1930; "She Took to Golf," *Brooklyn Eagle*, January 31, 1930.

11. "Ford Joins Edison at Laboratory Here; Walks from E. End," *Fort Myers Press*, February 8, 1930.

12. "Edison on Birthday Feels More Than 83," *Tropical News*, February 11, 1930; "Thomas Edison and Wife Are Honored as Plaque Is Unveiled Here Today," *Fort Myers Press*, February 12, 1930.

13. Dr. Hamilton Holt, "Dedication of Thomas A. Edison Plaque at Fort Myers, Fla., February 11, 1930," Hamilton Holt Collection, Rollins College Archives and Special Collections.

14. "City Unveils Plaque in Honor of Edisons," *Fort Myers Press*, February 12, 1930.

15. "Edison Tours County Fair with Wife's Yellow Bunny; Goes Broke on Number 11," *Tropical News*, February 13, 1930.

16. "Ford Rides Merry-Go-Round for First Time Visiting Fair," *Fort Myers Press*, February 14, 1930.

17. "Greater Production Ford's Farm Relief," *Tropical News*, March 5, 1930.

18. Transcript of the address delivered by Dr. Hamilton Holt at Rollins College awarding Thomas Edison a Doctorate of Science, February 24, 1930, Rollins College Archives and Special Collections.

19. "Rollins Honors Thomas Edison with a Degree," *Fort Myers Press*, February 25, 1930; "Edison Receives Degree of Doctor of Science at Rollins College Today," *Orlando Sentinel*, February 24, 1930; "The Progress of the World," *Review of Reviews*, April 1930; "New Edison Honor," *The San Diego Sun*, March 8, 1930; "Edison Honored by Rollins College," *New York Times*, February 25, 1930.

20. "A Tribute to Mrs. Edison," *Fort Myers Press*, March 12, 1930.

21. "Cash Register Sings Merrily at Hill Store," *Fort Myers Press*, March 14, 1930.

22. "Edison Visited by Joe Chapple, Noted Writer," *Fort Myers Press*, March 15, 1930.

23. "Noted Botanist Visits Edison," *Fort Myers Press*, March 25, 1930; Letter to MME from John K. Small, February 3, 1930, series M83-2, carton 27, John K. Small Collection, Florida State Archives, Tallahassee.

24. "Thos. Edison Makes Trip to Everglades," *Fort Myers Press*, March 18, 1930.

25. "Edison Avers Rubber Plants Are Advancing," *Miami Daily News*, March 28, 1930.

26. "Edison Says Health Greatest Treasure," *The Miami Herald*, March 29, 1930.

27. Personals," *Fort Myers Press*, April 16, 1930.

28. "Edison Machine Is Ready Here to Run Rubber," *Fort Myers Press*, February 22, 1930.

29. "New Rubber Mill Ready for Testing," *Fort Myers Press*, April 11, 1930; "Golden Rod Will Furnish Rubber in Edison New Mill," *Clewiston News*, April 18, 1930.

30. "Edisons to Leave for the North Tomorrow Night," *Fort Myers Press*, June 10, 1930.

31. "Mrs. Edison Makes Hospital Donation," *Fort Myers Press*, April 12, 1930.

32. Israel, *Edison: A Life of Invention*, 456–57.

33. "Rotarians Hear Mrs. Edison at Weekly Meeting," *Fort Myers Press*, April 29, 1930.

34. "Mr. and Mrs. Edison in Yachting Party," *Tropical News*, April 13, 1930.

35. "Personals," *Fort Myers Press*, April 17, 1930.

36. "Edisons to Attend Girl Scout Rally at Beach Tonight," *Fort Myers Press*, April 25, 1930.

37. "Edison Visits Collier City," *Fort Myers Press*, May 12, 1930.

38. Untitled newspaper clipping from MME's clipping book, May 27, 1930, possibly the *Tropical News*, EFWE.

39. "Edison Feels Twenty Years Younger as He Boards Train After His 47th Year Here," *Fort Myers Press*, June 12, 1930.

40. Catherine Lawrence, Secretary Chautauqua Literary and Scientific Circle [C.L.S.C.] of Chautauqua, to MME, August 19, 1930, EFWE.

41. W. H. Reynolds, President, Fort Myers Chamber of Commerce, to MME, September 6, 1930, EFWE.

42. MME to W. H. Reynolds, September 19, 1930, EFWE.

43. Untitled article, *Newark Free Press*, October 20, 1930.

44. Sidney Davis to MME, December 16, 1930, EFWE.

Chapter 15. The Last Hurrah

1. "Edisons Start to Fort Myers Next Tuesday," *Fort Myers Press*, January 16, 1931.

2. "Edison on Way; Party Includes the Firestones," *Fort Myers Press*, January 21, 1931.

3. "Come in Special as Friends Wait at Wrong Depot," *Fort Myers Press*, January 22, 1931.

4. "Edison Absent from Shop but Work Goes On," *Fort Myers Press*, January 23, 1931.

5. MME to John Harvey Kellogg, February 8, 1931, John Harvey Kellogg Papers, Bentley Historical Library, University of Michigan.

6. Untitled and unsigned medical report written for the Edison family, August 5, 1931, EFWE.

7. Thanks to Dr. Matthew Greenston, Exeter, New Hampshire, for explaining the typical symptoms of Edison's illnesses.

8. "1-Hour Function to Open Edison Span on February 11," *Fort Myers Press*, January 24, 1931; "Bridge Dedication Plans Approved by Mrs. Edison," *Tropical News*, February 6, 1931.

9. "Edison Start to Fort Myers Next Tuesday," *Fort Myers Press*, January 16, 1931.

10. "Mrs. Edison Urges Red Cross Drive; Board to Consider," *Tropical News*, January 30, 1931.

11. "Edison Tells Interviewers Rubber Experiments Need 2 More Years," *Fort Myers Press*, February 12, 1931; "Edison, 84, Thinks Up Trend Has Begun," *New York Times*, February 12, 1931.

12. "Edison in Birthday Interview Says He Feels 'Pretty Good,'" *Tropical News*, February 12, 1931.

13. "Edison as Optimist," *Tropical News*, February 12, 1931.

14. Helen Stebbins, interview with the author, April 14, 2006.

15. "Carlton Coming for Dedication of New Bridge," *Fort Myers Press*, February 11, 1931; Virginia Halloway, interview with the author, December 5, 1995.

16. "Gov. Carlton Heads Notables Who Pay Honor to Inventor," *Fort Myers Press*, February 12, 1931.

17. "Mr. Edison's Birthday Cake to be Sold for Red Cross," *Tropical News*, February 14, 1931.

18. "Edison Cake Nets $107; Drive Now $118 from Goal," *Tropical News*, February 15, 1931.

19. "Ford Slips in Unheralded; Holds Reunion with Edison," *Tropical News*, February 20, 1931.

20. "Ford Spurns Sanibel Rum; Says He'd Dig Well First," *Tropical News*, February 22, 1931.

21. "Edisons Celebrate 45th Anniversary," *Fort Myers Press*, February 25, 1931.

22. "Edison, Talking from Here, Chief Insull Fete Speaker," *Tropical News*, March 1, 1931.

23. "Edison Rests While Visiting Firestone," *Tropical News*, March 12, 1931.

24. "Mrs. Thomas A. Edison at Miami Beach," *Newark Evening News*, March 12, 1931.

25. "Ford 'Stumps' Firestone; Chins Himself Six Times," *Tropical News*, March 14, 1931.

26. "Prosperity Is Up to People, Ford Asserts," *Fort Myers Press*, March 15, 1931.

27. Grismer, *The Story of Fort Myers*, 238–39.

28. "Edison Joins Large Crowd at Farewell," *Fort Myers Press*, March 24, 1931.

29. Cajeput trees are now known as melaleuca. Today millions of dollars are being spent on melaleuca eradication; the invasive tree has decimated native species.

30. "Edisons Will Assist in Trail Blazer Tree Planting Fete Today," *Fort Myers Press*, April 2, 1931; "Trail Blazers Set 200 Trees in Estero Fete," *Tropical News*, April 5, 1931.

31. "Thomas A. Edison to Receive Cup During P.T.A. Convention," *Tropical News*, April 7, 1931; "Edison Receives Cup as P.T.A. Convention Dedicates Oak Tree," *Fort Myers Press*, April 10, 1931.

32. "Edison Joins Schoolgirls Who Picnic on His Lawn," *Tropical News*, April 12, 1931.

33. "Edison Beats Talkie Craze by Silent Movies at Home," *Tropical News*, April 17, 1931.

34. "High School Girls Guests of Edisons," *Fort Myers Press*, April 18, 1931.

35. "Rotarians Honor Mothers Today in Special Program," *Fort Myers Press*, May 12, 1931.

36. "Mothers Day at Rotary Club Luncheon, Fort Myers, Fla., May 12, 1931," speech given by MME, EFWE.

37. "Rotarians Honor Mothers Today in Special Program," *Fort Myers Press*, May 12, 1931.

38. John K. Small to William Henry Meadowcroft, October 7, 1930, John K. Small Collection, Florida State Archives.

39. "Edison Says His Rubber Progress Is 'Satisfactory,'" *Fort Myers Press*, May 8, 1931.

40. "Edison Departs on Summer Trip to Jersey Home," *Fort Myers Press*, June 15, 1931.

41. "Edison Says His Rubber Progress Is 'Satisfactory.'"

42. "Edison Goes Out to Watch His Son Get Tarpon--Maybe," June 12, 1931 *Fort Myers Press*; "Son of Electrical Genius Catches Tarpon While Here," *Fort Myers Press*, June 15, 1931.

43. "Thomas A. Edison Is Given First Fort Myers Medal," *Fort Myers Press*, June 2, 1931.

44. "Beauty of Fort Myers Is Praised to All America When Edison Talks Over Radio," *Tropical News*, June 11, 1931.

45. "Edison Departs on Summer Trip to Jersey Home," *Fort Myers Press*, June 15, 1931; "Edison Closes 47th Annual Visit Tonight Departing for North," newspaper clipping, Mina Edison's Scrapbook, EFWE.

46. "Edisons to Leave Tomorrow after 48th Winter Season," *Fort Myers Press*, June 14, 1931.

47. "Edison and Wife Home after Winter in Florida," *New York Herald-Tribune*, June 16, 1931.

48. Lucius W. Hitchcock to MME, June 21, 1931; MME to Lucius W. Hitchcock, June 23, 1931, both in EFWE.

49. Sidney Davis to MME, July 8, 1931, EFWE.

50. "Edison, Ill, Collapses but Later Rallies," Associated Press story, August 1, 1931, "Edison" subject file, Southwest Florida Museum of History.

51. "Ford Visits Edison and Scouts Report Wizard Has Retired," *Fort Myers Press*, July 26, 1931.

52. "Edison Will Be Subject of City-Wide Prayer Day," *Fort Myers Press*, October 3, 1931.

53. Katherine Tipton Hosmer (Mrs. George E.) to MME, October 5, 1931, EFWE.

54. Lora V. Gault to MME, October 7, 1931, EFWE.

55. T.(?) Bakker to CE, October 7, 1931, EFWE; Charles Andrew Hafner to CE, October 8, 1931, EFWE.

56. Azel Price, interview with Mary Hanson, September 9, 1994, EFWE.

57. Newton, *Uncommon Friends*, 32.

58. MME, telegram to Mayor Fitch, October 18, 1931, EFWE.

Chapter 16. A Widow at Seminole Lodge

1. "Mourners Pause at Edison Bier While Minister Offers Prayer," Associated Press article, October 19, 1931, "Edison" subject file, Southwest Florida Museum of History; Josephson, *Edison: A Biography*, 483.

2. Baldwin, *Edison Inventing the Century*, 408; Israel, *Edison: A Life of Invention*, 462.

3. Newton, *Uncommon Friends*, 32.

4. Baldwin, *Edison Inventing the Century*, 410; Israel, *Edison: A Life of Invention*, 462.

5. Later Edison was re-interred at Glenmont, the Edisons' home in West Orange, New Jersey.

6. Baldwin, *Edison Inventing the Century*, 410.

7. Baldwin, *Edison Inventing the Century*, 412; "Edison Sons Avoid Fight over Estate," *New York Times*, February 26, 1931.

8. MME to Sidney Davis, December 14, 1931, EFWE.

9. "Mrs. Edison Gives Flowers to Sick as Cheer Tokens," *Fort Myers News-Press*, February 12, 1932.

10. "Edison Memorial Service Is Held," *Fort Myers News-Press*, February 12, 1932.

11. "Move Launched for an Edison Memorial Here," *Fort Myers News-Press*, January 25, 1932.

12. "Mrs. Edison Leaves New Jersey; Maybe Be Here This Evening," *Fort Myers News-Press*, February 24 1932.

13. "Mrs. Edison Presides at Meeting of Guild," *Fort Myers News-Press*, March 6, 1932.

14. "Firestone and Mrs. Edison Go to Sunday School Here," *Fort Myers News-Press*, March 21, 1932.

15. "Talk on Prohibition Given by Mrs. Edison," *Fort Myers News-Press*, April 12, 1932.

16. MME to Sidney Davis, October 17, 1932, Sidney Davis Collection, EFWE.

17. Grismer, *The Story of Fort Myers*, 240–43.

18. Newton, *The Invisible Empire*, 43.

19. "Tickets to Jubilee Singers Program Are Going Rapidly," *Fort Myers News-Press*, April 3, 1932; Robert E. Bennett, telephone interview with the author, October 25, 1995; Jeanette Perry, interview with the author, July 30, 1994; Bernese Davis, interview with the author, October 25, 1995.

20. "Mrs. Edison Loans Estate for Bird Studying Classes," *Fort Myers News-Press*, March 31, 1932.

21. "Filling Station Facing Edison Place Barred," *Fort Myers News-Press*, July 7, 1934.

22. "Mrs. Edison Is Wed to Edward Hughes," *New York Times*, October 31, 1935; "Mrs. Mina Edison to Wed Childhood Sweetheart Today," *Fort Myers News-Press*, October 30, 1935; Baldwin, *Edison Inventing the Century*, 412–13.

23. MME to Edward Hughes, February 8, 1938, EFWE, CEF.

24. Edward Hughes to MME, February 8, 1938, EFWE, CEF.

25. CE to MME, n.d., EFWE, CEF.

26. Henry M. Hughes to MME, January 12, 1939, EFWE, CEF.

27. Editorial, *Fort Myers News-Press*, February 28, 1936.

28. Edward Hughes to MME, November 8, 1938, EFWE, CEF.

29. Edward Hughes to MME, February 13, 1939, EFWE, CEF.

30. "Mrs. Edison Leaves Today," *Fort Myers News-Press*, May 2, 1940.

31. MME to Jay N. Darling, November 4, 1940, Papers of J. N. "Ding" Darling, University of Iowa Libraries, Iowa City.

32. Jeanette Perry, interview with the author, October 1995.

33. "Mrs. Mina Edison Here; Plans for New Library," *Fort Myers News-Press*, February 20, 1941.

34. Grismer, *The Story of Fort Myers*, 262, 264.

35. Population figures from report, by the City of Fort Myers, Florida, Office of the Mayor. Terms of Office and General Information, City of Fort Myers, October 6, 1995.

36. "Specifications of Labor and Materials Required for the Erection of a Memorial to Thomas Edison . . . by Eric Gugler and William E. Frenaye, Jr.," n.d., EFWE.

37. James D. Sturrock, Boynton Landscape Company, to MME, April 8, 1941; planting lists dated March 22 and April 7, 1941, both in EFWE.

38. Various drawings of plans for the library, EFWE.

39. "Edison Memorial Library Work to Start in June," *Fort Myers News-Press*, April 20, 1941.

40. Turner and Mulford, *Images of America: Fort Myers*, 101; Grismer, *The Story of Fort Myers*, 248.

41. Phone interview with Shirley Teger, widow of Leon Teger, who was reading from Leon Teger's unpublished memoir. Also Jeanette Perry's audio recording of Jeanette Perry's speech to the Royal Palm Yacht Club, March 20, 1992.

42. Untitled article, *Fort Myers News-Press*, April 14, 1942.

43. Chesley Perry, interview with the author, July 30, 1994.

44. Jeanette Perry, interview with the author, October 1995.

45. Jeanette Perry, interview with the author, July 30, 1994.

46. Shirley Teger, telephone interview with the author, January 2003.

47. "Mrs. Edison Praises Colored Veterans," *Fort Myers News-Press*, April 14, 1942.

48. Letter to Mrs. A. Stanley Hanson (Clara) from MME, March 23, 1941, EFWE.

49. Barbara Turner, "Miller Family Genealogy," 1995, EFWE.

50. "Pioneer in Autos; Leader in Production Founded Vast Empire in Motors in 1904, . . . Henry Ford is Dead . . ." *New York Times*, April 8, 1947.

51. "Mrs. Edison Here to Visit Friends," *Fort Myers News-Press*, April 9, 1942.

52. Robert Halgrim confirmed that after the real estate downturn, Mina Edison felt that the cost of a library was beyond her means. Robert C. Halgrim, interview with the author, April 29, 1993.

53. "Seminole Lodge Available for New University," *The Southwest Floridian*, March 24, 1945, EFWE.

54. "Mrs. Edison Here; Gopher Derby Is Delayed to Today," *Fort Myers News-Press*, February 14, 1947.

55. "Giant Parade to Highlight Events Today," *Fort Myers News-Press*, February 15, 1947; "25,000 Line Streets to See Huge Edison Light Parade," *Fort Myers News-Press*, February 16, 1947.

56. Ella Piper to MME, April 19, 1947, EFWE, CEF.

57. "Imogene" to MME, April 25, 1947, EFWE, CEF.

58. "Our 'First Lady,'" *Fort Myers News-Press*, February 14, 1947.

59. "City Gets Edison Place," *Fort Myers News-Press*, February 20, 1947.

60. Speech by MME on the dedication of Seminole Lodge to the city of Fort Myers, March 6, 1947, EFWE.

61. Madeleine Sloane Edison to MME, March 10, 1947, EFWE, CEF.

Bibliography

Libraries and Archives

American Academy of Arts and Letters, New York, New York
Benson Ford Research Center, Dearborn, Michigan
   Oral History Section, Reminiscences Manuscripts Subsection
Bentley Historical Library, University of Michigan, Ann Arbor, Michigan
Cornell University Library, Ithaca, New York
   Rare and Manuscript Collections
Edison and Ford Winter Estates, Fort Myers, Florida (EFWE)
   Sidney Davis Collection, Charles Edison Fund Collection, City of Fort Myers Collection
Edison National Historic Site, West Orange, New Jersey (ENHS)
State Library and Archives of Florida, Tallahassee
   John K. Small Collection
Henry B. Plant Museum, Tampa, Florida
Henry Ford Museum and Greenfield Village, Dearborn, Michigan (HFMGV)
Lakeland Library, Lakeland, Florida
   Herbert J. Drane Papers
Jacksonville Public Library, Jacksonville, Florida
Lee County Public Library, Fort Myers, Florida
Monroe County Clerk's Office, Key West, Florida
New York Public Library, New York, New York
   Richard Rogers Bowker Papers
Rollins College Archives and Special Collections, Lakeland, Florida
   Hamilton Holt Collection
Rutgers University, Archibald S. Alexander Library, Rutgers, New Jersey
   Papers of Thomas A. Edison
Schweizerisches Literaturarchiv, Schweizerische Landesbibliothek (Literature Archive
   of Switzerland, Swiss National Library), Bern, Switzerland.
Southwest Florida Museum of History, Fort Myers, Florida
University of Florida, Gainesville
   Florida Historical Map Collection
University of Iowa Libraries, Iowa City, Iowa

Interviews and Oral Histories

Bennett, Robert E. Telephone interview with the author, October 25, 1995.

Brantly, Awilda. Interview with Pam Miner, November 9, 2005, EFWE.

Davis, Bernese. Interviews with the author, June 17, 1995, and October 25, 1995.

Edison, Charles. Transcription of oral history conducted by Wendell Link, April 14, 1953, Edison National Historic Site.

Edison, Thomas. Interview, n.d. (ca. 1917), Edison General File, 1917, ENHS.

Geraci, Katheryn Miller. Telephone interview with the author, January 1995.

Gill, Estalina. Telephone interview with the author, March 2001.

Halgrim, Robert C. Interview with the author, April 29, 1993.

Halloway, Virginia. Interview with the author, December 5, 1995.

Harrell, Marie. Telephone interview with the author, March 2001.

Hill, Vivian. Telephone interview with the author, March 2001.

Holdsclaw, Linda. Telephone interview with the author, March 2001.

Johnson, Jacob. Telephone interview with the author, March 2001.

Newton, James D., and Eleanor Forde Newton. Interviews with the author, July 15, 1996, and numerous conversations from 1993 to 1998.

Oser, Marion Edison. Interview A-518, March 1956, ENHS.

Perry, Chesley. Interview with the author, July 30, 1994.

Perry, Jeanette. Interview with the author, July 30, 1994, and October 1995.

———. Audio recording of talk at the Royal Palm Yacht Club, March 20, 1992, Author's personal copy given by Jeanette Perry.

Price, C. Azel. Interview with Mary Hanson (audiotape), September 9, 1994, EFWE.

———. Interview with James H. Gassman, David Marshall, and Robert Beeson (videotape), June 25, 1999, EFWE.

Sherois, Carlisle ("Cobbie"). Interview with the author, June 20, 1995.

Sloane, Madeleine Edison. Interviews with Kenneth K. Goldstein, December 1, 1972, and March 13, 1973, ENHS.

Stebbins, Helen, Interview with the author, April 14, 2006.

Teger, Shirley. Telephone interview with the author, January 2003.

Warren, Lillian. Interview with Kathleen McKirk, n.d., ENHS

———. Interview with Kenneth Goldstein, July 3, 1973, ENHS.

Private Collections

David Edward Edison Sloane, private letters of Madeleine Edison Sloane and Last Will and Testament of Mina M. Edison, Hamden, Connecticut.

Charles Edison Fund, West Orange, New Jersey. Collections are currently dispersed to a number of repositories. Letters currently located at the Edison and Ford Winter Estates are designated CEF, EFWE in the endnotes. Other letters from this source are cited from the CEF microfilm.

Paul C. Spehr, collection of documents and information relating to W. K. L. Dickson, Bethesda, Maryland.

Published Sources

A. W. Bowen and Co. *The Progressive Men of the State of Montana.* Chicago: A. W. Bowen and Co., 1902.

Abbott, Karl P. *Open for the Season.* Garden City, N.Y.: Doubleday and Co., 1950.

Akerman, Joe A., Jr. *Florida Cowman: A History of Florida Cattle Raising.* Kissimmee, Fla.: Florida Cattlemen's Association, 1976.

Andrews, Allen H. *A Yank Pioneer in Florida.* Jacksonville, Fla.: Douglas Printing Co., 1950.

Arias, Elizabeth. "United States Life Tables." *National Vital Statistics Reports,* 53, no. 6 (November 10, 2004).

Baldwin, Neil. *Edison: Inventing the Century.* New York: Hyperion, 1995.

———. *Henry Ford and the Jews: The Mass Production of Hate.* New York: Public Affairs, 2001.

Barbour, George, M. *Florida for Tourists, Invalids, and Settlers.* New York: D. Appleton and Company, 1882.

Blanchan, Neltje. *Birds That Hunt and Are Hunted.* New York: Grosset & Dunlap, 1904.

Brauer, Norman. *There to Breathe the Beauty: The Camping Trips of Henry Ford, Thomas Edison, Harvey Firestone and John Burroughs.* Dalton, Pa.: Norman Brauer Publications, 1996.

Board, Prudy Taylor, and Esther B. Colcord, *Historic Fort Myers.* Virginia Beach, Va.: The Donning Company Publishers, 1992.

———. *Pages from the Past: A Pictorial Retrospective of Lee County, Florida.* Virginia Beach, Va.: Donning Company, 1990.

Braden, Susan R. *The Architecture of Leisure: The Florida Resort Hotels of Henry Flagler and Henry Plant.* Gainesville: University Press of Florida, 2002.

Brown, Robin C. *Florida's First People.* Sarasota, Fla.: Pineapple Press, 1994.

Brown, S. Paul. *The Book of Jacksonville: A History.* Poughkeepsie, N.Y.: A. V. Haight, 1895.

Collier, Peter, and David Horowitz. *The Fords: An American Epic.* New York: Summit Books, 1987.

Davis, Jack E., and Raymond Arsenault. *Paradise Lost? The Environmental History of Florida.* Gainesville: University Press of Florida, 2005.

Davis, T. Frederick. *History of Jacksonville, Florida and Vicinity, 1513–1924.* Jacksonville: Florida Historical Society, 1925

Douglas, Marjory Stoneman. "Mrs. Thomas A. Edison, at Home." *McCall's Magazine,* October 1929.

Edison, Thomas Alva. *The Diary and Sundry Observations of Thomas Alva Edison.* New York: Philosophical Library, 1948.

Ford, Henry, and Samuel Crowther. *My Life and Work.* Garden City, N.Y.: Doubleday, Page & Co, 1922.

Frisbie, Louise. *Florida's Fabled Inns.* Bartow, Fla.: Imperial Publishing Company, 1980.

Fritz, Florence. *Bamboo and Sailing Ships.* [Fort Myers, Fla.]: Florence Fritz, 1949.

Gannon, Michael. *Florida: A Short History.* Gainesville: University Press of Florida, 2003.

Gonzalez, Thomas A. *The Caloosahatchee: Miscellaneous Writings Concerning the History of the Caloosahatchee River and the City of Fort Myers, Florida.* Fort Myers Beach, Fla.: Southwest Florida Historical Society, 1982.

Grismer, Karl H. *The Story of Fort Myers: The History of the Land of the Caloosahatchee and Southwest Florida.* Southwest Florida Historical Society, 1949; reprint, Fort Myers Beach, Fla.: Island Press Publishing, 1982.

———. *Tampa: A History of the City of Tampa and the Tampa Bay Region of Florida.* St. Petersburg, Fla.: St. Petersburg Printing Company, 1950.

Hendrick, Ellwood. *Lewis Miller: A Biographical Essay.* New York: G. P. Putnam's Sons, 1925.

Hendry, Ella Kathryn. *Front Porch Stories: Tales of the Hendry Family, Pioneers in Florida's Peace River Basin.* Port Charlotte, Fla.: Jonathan Wilson Sandige Publications, 2000.

Israel, Paul. *Edison: A Life of Invention.* New York: John Wiley & Sons, 1998.

Jamro, Ron, and Gerald L. Jamro. *The Founding of Naples.* Naples, Fla.: Friends of the Collier County Museum, 1985.

Josephson, Matthew. *Edison: A Biography.* New York: John Wiley & Sons, 1959.

King, Edward. "Pictures from Florida." *Scribner's Monthly Magazine,* November 1874.

Lacey, Robert. *Ford, the Men and the Machine.* Boston: Little, Brown and Company, 1986.

Lief, Alfred. *The Firestone Story: A History of the Firestone Tire & Rubber Company.* New York: Whittlesey House, 1951.

Ludwig, Emil, "Edison, Studie uber Genie und Character," *Die Neue Runschau* (January 1932): 52–69.

Mannering, Mitchell. "Thomas A. Edison and His Triumphs," *National Magazine.* December 1914.

McIver, Stuart. "Tarpon House." *Florida Sportsman,* March 1985.

McKay, Donald E., ed. *Pioneer Florida.* 2 vols. Tampa, Fla.: Southern Publishing Company, 1959.

Missall, John, and Mary Lou Missall. *The Seminole Wars: America's Longest Indian Conflict.* Gainesville: University of Florida Press, 2004.

Nerney, Mary Childs. *Thomas A. Edison: A Modern Olympian.* New York: Harrison Smith and Robert Haas, 1934.

Newton, James D. *Uncommon Friends: Life with Thomas Edison, Henry Ford, Harvey Firestone, Alexis Carrel, & Charles Lindbergh.* San Diego, Calif.: Harcourt Brace and Company, 1987.

Newton, Michael, *The Invisible Empire: The Ku Klux Klan in Florida.* Gainesville: University Press of Florida, 2001.

Nolan, David. *Fifty Feet in Paradise: The Booming of Florida.* San Diego, Calif.: Harcourt Brace Jovanovich, 1984.

Reynolds, Dorris. *When Peacocks Were Roasted*. Naples, Fla.: Enterprise Publishing, 1999.

Rosenblum, Martin Jay. *Edison Winter Estate: Historic Structures Report*. Fort Myers, Fla.: Edison Ford Winter Estates Foundation, January 2002.

Rosenblum, Martin Jay, and Associates. *Edison Winter Estate: Cultural Landscape Report*. Fort Myers, Fla.: City of Fort Myers, February 2002.

Rowe, Anne E. *The Ideal of Florida in the American Literary Imagination*. Baton Rouge: Louisiana State University Press, 1986.

Simonds, William Adams. *Edison: His Life, His Work, His Genius*. New York: Blue Ribbon Books, 1934.

Smoot, Tom. *The Edisons of Fort Myers: Discoveries of the Heart*. Sarasota, Fla.: Pineapple Press, 2004.

Ste. Claire, Dana. *Cracker: The Cracker Culture in Florida History*. Daytona Beach, Fla.: Museum of Arts and Sciences, 1998.

Steiger, Ernst. *Steiger's Education Directory for 1878*. New York: E. Steiger, 1878.

Tebeau, Charlton, W. *A History of Florida*. Coral Gables, Fla.: University of Miami Press, 1971.

Turner, Gregg. *A Short History of Florida Railroads*. Charleston, S.C.: Arcadia Press, 2003.

———, and Stan Mulford. *Images of America: Fort Myers*. Charleston, S.C.: Arcadia Press, 2000.

Vanderbilt, Byron M. *Thomas Edison: Chemist*. American Chemical Society, 1971.

Venable, John D. *Mina Miller Edison: Daughter, Wife, and Mother of Inventors*. East Orange, N.J.: Charles Edison Fund, 1961.

———. *Out of the Shadow: The Story of Charles Edison*. East Orange, N.J.: Charles Edison Fund, 1978.

Vincent, George E. *Theodore W. Miller, Rough Rider*. Akron, Ohio: Privately printed, 1899.

Watts, Steven. *The People's Tycoon: Henry Ford and the American Century*. New York: Alfred A. Knopf, 2005.

Williams, John M., and Iver W. Duedall. *Florida Hurricanes and Tropical Storms, 1871–2001*. Gainesville: University Press of Florida, 2002.

Wynne, Lewis N., and James J. Horgan. *Florida Pathfinders*. Tampa, Fla.: Saint Leo College Press, 1994.

———. "Naples Florida, Issued by the Naples Company, R. G. Robinson, Gen'l Manager," pamphlet, March 1888. Reprinted by the Friends of the Collier County Museum, Naples, Florida, March 2000.

———. Population figures from the City of Fort Myers, Florida. *Terms of Office and General Information*, Report, Office of the Mayor, City of Fort Myers, October 6, 1995.

———. *Decennial Census of the United States*, U. S. Bureau of the Census available at www.census.gov.

Index

Page numbers in italics refer to illustrations

Abbott, Karl, 56
Adams, Queenie, 170, 182
Arcade Theater, 106, 109–10, 129, 143, 171
Armeda, Nicolas "Nick," 5, 47, 116
Assumhachee (Seminole guide), 110
Atlantic Coast Line Railroad: Edison's private
    Pullman, 67, 70, 106; map, *59*; service in
    Fort Myers, 59–60, 63,77; station in Fort
    Meyers, *88*, 112
Atlantic Seaboard, 182

Bartow, Fla., 5, 27
Baseball, 119, 122, 126–27, *158–59*, 172
Bassler, B. W., 18, 198n.46
Batchelor, Charles, 30
Bell, Alexander Graham, 2
Bell Telephone, 2–3
Bellview Hotel, 53
Bergmann & Company, 15, *37, 38*
Bessie (friend), 81
Big Cypress wilderness area, 76–79, *77*, 80
Bogue, Lucy, 97, 102, 171
Bradford Hotel, 63, 108, 119
Bradshaw, Dr. Hammond, 125–26
Broward, Napoleon B., 66, 71
Bryan, William Jennings, 120, *121*
Burroughs, Jetty, 184
Burroughs, John, 74, 75, 78–81, 98
Burton, Willard. *See* Edison, William

Cajeput trees, introduced, 172, 221n.29
Calibron, 180
Caloosahatchee River: bridges, 60, *89*, 113, 129,
    152, 167, 170; cattle trade, 5; description,

6–7, *7*, 54–55; Edison family excursions,
    63–64, *64*, 71, 80; effects of dredging, 66,
    71; photograph, *93*
Campbell, T. B., 58
Campsall, Frank, 115, 128, 134
Capling, George, 105
Captiva Island, Fla., 63, 72
Carlton, Gov. Doyle E., 170
Carson, Frank, 78
Cedar Key, Fla., 4
Chadwick, Rosamond, 144
Chappel, Joe, 150
Chautauqua Institute, 16, 31, 152, 182
Civil War, 3, 6, 10, 152
Cleveland, Pres. Grover, 8–9
Cleveland, Stafford C., 9, 17, 22
Clewiston, Fla., 141, *141*
Cobb, Ty, 127, *159*
Colgate, Margaret, 82
Colgate, Muriel, 82, 184
Colgate, Richard, 82
Collier, Barron, 111, *111*, 118, 152
Coolidge, Pres. Calvin, 147
Cornapatchee (Seminole guide), 110
Cracker, use of term, 49, 142, 196n.39

Daniels, Josephus, 99
Darrow, Clarence, 120
Davis, Bernese, 184
Davis, Sidney, 152, 175, 179
A Day with Thomas A. Edison, 143
Dickson, William Kennedy Laurie, 46
Disston, Hamilton, 12, 64
Douglas, Marjory Stoneman, 132

Doyle, Tina, 106

Drane, Herbert J., 11

Dynamo: at the estate, 16, 29, 30, 42, 44, 102; manufacture by Edison, 2; at Seminole Canning Co., 47

Eastman, George, 173

Edison, Beatrice (daughter-in-law), 180, *189*

Edison, Carolyn Hawkins (daughter-in-law), 99, 101–3, 130, 109, 174, 187

Edison, Charles (son): activities after father's death, 180; April Fool's Day prank, 83; camping trips and excursions, 78, 79, 81; childhood, 51, 52, 53, 60–61; death, 180; engagement and wedding, 101–2; fishing skills, 60–61, *93*, 109, 174; inheritance, 179; music skills, 76; photographs, *93*, *96*; radio manufacture, 151; visits to estate, 58, 60–61, 63, 76, 83, 84, 109, 187

Edison, Edith (cousin), 53. *See also* Potter, Edith

Edison, Madeleine (daughter): childhood, 44, 51, 52, 53, 58; on the disadvantages of guests, 75, 76; education, 63; engagement and wedding, 73, 83; Model T excursion, 81; *Ode to Captain Menge*, 65; photograph, *96*; "Rules for Guests at Seminole Lodge," 71–72; visits to estate prior to marriage, 60, 63–64, 67

Edison, Marion "Dot" (daughter): childhood, 2, 3, 14, 19, 23, 26; relationship with father, 29; relationship with step-mother, 14, 24, 29, 32. *See also* Oeser, Marion Edison

Edison, Mina Miller (wife): depiction in husband's doodles, *41*; estate responsibilities, 44,45, 69, 105, 175, 181–82; family responsibilities, 29, 31, 46, 63, 101–2, 177; golfing, 147; "home executive," promotion of term, 133, 185; and husband's career and privacy, 24, 28–29, 126, 129, 132, 138, 145; journalism, 142

—community activities: articles on, 132, 173, 186; ban on billboards, 133, 179, 181; bible class, 142, 152, 181; for black citizens, 181, 185; bridge, 129; charity, 146, 150, 167, 171, 179; city planning, 104, 142; country club, 67; fish stocking, 72–73; gardening groups, 181, 185; to honor pioneers, 142;lectures,

142, 173, 181, 185; library and museum, 67, 183, 185; music, 123; networking, 55, 66, 108; parks, 113–14, 123; protection of Seminole lands, 181; statue, 122; support for enlisted men, 184–85; Valinda Literary Circle, 133, 142, 152, 167, 175, 181

—life: wedding, honeymoon, and move to the estate, 19–27; reactions to new home, 23; first pregnancy and miscarriage, 29, 31, 42; second pregnancy, Madeleine, 42, 44; fourth pregnancy, Theodore, 51; death of brother, sister, and father, 51–52; at birth of grandson, Michael, 166; 45th wedding anniversary, 171; during husband's last days, 175–77; remarriage, 182–83; death, 187; photographs, *91*, *95*, *96*, *156*, *164*, *188–91*; relationship with husband, 24, 31–32, 77; state and national activities, 142, 172. *See also* Miller, Mina

Edison, Sam (father), 45, 46

Edison, Theodore (son): activities after father's death, 180; care of father, 174; childhood, 51, 52, 58, 60, 67, 68; death, 180; golfing, 147; inheritance, 179; photographs, *95*, *96*; radio manufacture, 151; visits to estate, 58, 60, 67, 79, 116

Edison, Thomas, Jr. (son): care of father, 174; childhood, 2, 131; death, 180; inheritance, 179, 180; marriage, 51; photograph, *189*; questionable behavior, 29, 46, 51

Edison, Thomas Alva: birthday interviews, 116, 120–21, 139, 148, 167–69; boats, 58, 60, 67, 105, 113; camping, 76–79, 80; estate (*See* Thomas A. Edison Estate); film about, 143; funeral and burial, 178–79, 223n.5; hunting, 3, 31–32, 54–55; investment in the community, 67–69, 97–98, 105; legacy, 187, 192–93; Morse Code skills, 1, 17; museums, 116, 126, 136, 180; photographs, *90*, *95–96*, *154–65*; political activism, 110–11; private railroad car, 67, 70, 106; purchase of former Gilliland estate, 66; relationship with Mina, 24, 31–32, 77; relationship with the neighbors, 68–69, 73, 103–4, 116, 129, 136, 192; scientific research (*See* Research of Thomas Edison); storytelling ability, 128; views, 120–21, 130, 139, 148, 167–69

—fishing: on decline in fish populations, 97; in later years, 142, 174; outings, 54–55, 57–58, 59, *93*, 108; quest for a tarpon, 42, 60–61
—health issues: colds and pneumonia, 28, 29–30, 144, 145; dizziness, 31; ears and hearing, 5, 28, 29–30, 31, 62, 82, 126, 128, 140, 143, 170; exhaustion, 145–53, 166–67, 174; final collapse, coma, and death, 175–77; heart condition, 28, 29–30; kidney dysfunction, diabetes, and ulcers, 167
—life: childhood, 1; marriage to Mary Silwell, 2, 3, 12; exploratory trip to Fla., 3–11; meeting Mina, 14; courtship of Mina, 16–17; wedding, honeymoon, and move to the estate, 19–27; betrayal by Gilliland, 43–45; meeting Ford, 76; camping trip to Big Cypress, 76–79, *77*; 81st birthday, 131; 82nd birthday, 138–41; 83rd birthday and plaque dedication, 147–49, *161*; 84th birthday and bridge dedication, 167–71; 45th wedding anniversary, 171; death, 177
Edison, William Leslie (son), 2, 29, 31, 51, 179, 180
Edison Birthplace Museum, 180
Edison Botanic Research Corporation, 134–35, 176
Edison Bridge, *89*, 113, 152, 167, 170
Edison Machine Works, 30
Edison Park subdivision, 119, 122, 123–24, 125, 140
Edison Pioneers, 120, 125
Edison Portland Cement Company, 59, 179, 180
Edison's Daughter, 180
Elcar, 110
Electrolier, 15, 16, 30, *37*
Estate in Fort Myers. *See* Seminole Lodge; Thomas A. Edison Estate
Evans, Col. E. L., 59
Evans, Edward, 106
Evans, Maj. James, 10, 45
Everglades: canalization and drainage, 12, 66, 71, 98; conservation issues, 181
Edison family excursions: 63–64, *64*, 118; road development, 110

Fairlane, Mich., 98
Firestone, Harvey: airplane for charity event, 150; death, 185; at Edison's 83rd birthday, 147, 149, 161; and Edison's rubber research, 114, 117, 122–23, 134–35, 176; at Edison's 81st birthday, 131; Edisons' visits to, 101, 134, 171; film of camping trip, 129; Miami home, 101, 110, 134, 150; photographs, *156*, *163*, 188; and Pres. Hoover, 140; rubber research, 150; trip to Calif., 98; visits to estate, 110, 122–23, 147, 149, 171
Firestone, Idabelle, 101, 140, 149, 150
Firestone, Roger, *163*
Firestone, Russell, *188*
Fitch, Josiah H., 170
Florida: agriculture, 7; cattle industry, 5, 6, 7, 69, 196n.39; effects of the Depression, 144, 145, 172, 181; and the Gilded Age, xvii, 3, 52; growth in the 1920s, 119; hurricanes, 105, 125; railway system, 4, 22, 27, 52, 53, 57, *59*, 59–60, 63, 174; road system, 110, 111, 113, 117, *134*, 135–36; western counties, *111*, winter tourism, 3. *See also specific cities*
Florida Everglades. *See* Everglades
Florida wildlife: birds, 7, 21, 54–55, 57, 109, 113, 119, 143, 184; decline in bird populations, 79–80; decline in fish populations, 72–73, 97; fish, 5, 109; marine life, 5, 57; reptiles, 6, 21, 54, 78
Floweree, Elizabeth, 55, 103
Ford, Clara: camping and fear of snakes, 78, 79; dancing, 142; move to Fairlane, Mich., 98; and Pres. Hoover, 140; wanting to go to Fla., 130; winter home (*See* The Mangoes)
Ford, Edsel, 78, 80, 81
Ford, Henry: background, 75; camping trip, 78, 79; death, 185; on Edison's death, 178; at Edison's 83rd birthday, 147; and Edison's rubber research, 114, 117, 134–35, 176; Golden Jubilee of Light, 146; lawsuit against, 115, 129–30; love of old-fashioned dances, 121, 142; meeting Edison, 76; Model T given to Edison, 81, *160*, 171; move to Fairlane, Mich., 98; Muscle Shoals project, 107, 112, 115; photographs, *87*, *88*, *156*, *161–62*, *188*; political activism, 110–11; and Pres. Hoover, 140; rubber research, 115–16, 123, 134; trip to Calif., 98; visits to estate, 74–75, 78, 79, 80–81; winter home (*See* The Mangoes)

Fort Myers, Fla.: airport, 122; bridge dedication, 167, 170; city planning Round Table, 104, 142, 146; description, 7, 8, 50; Edison Bridge, *89*, 113, 152, 167, 170; Edison's first visit, 7–11; Edison's legacy in, 192; fire department, 57; fires, 57, 67, 74; growth, 103–4, 113, 119, 142; history, 6, 10; hotels (*See* Fort Myers Hotel; Shultz Hotel); infrastructure, 112; libraries, 67, 183, 185; military bases, 184; and Mina Edison (*See* Edison, Mina Miller, community activities); Philadelphia Athletics, 119, 122, 126–27, *158–59*, 172; photograph, *92*; plaque for the Edisons, 144, 147, 149, *161*; promotion by Edison, 83–84, 97–98, 113, 121; railway service, 59–60, *88*; reactions to Edison's move to, 10, 12–13, 18; relationship with the Edisons, 68–69, 73, 103–4, 116, 129, 136, 192; road system, 110, 111, 113; road to Edison estate, 22, 23, 53, 68–69, 84, 192; segregation, 108, 112, 181; Seminole Lodge deeded to, 187, 192; skyscrapers, 112; telephone service, 49
—celebrations: centennial, 49; Christmas, 8, 146; Edison Pageant, 186, *191*; Edison Park dedication, 123–24; Edison's birthdays, 131, 147–49, *161*, 167–71; Edison's memorial, 179; Edison's plaque dedication, 147, 149, *161*; Pres. Hoover's visit, 140; welcome, 26–27, 75, 106, 109, 112
—electrification: bridge lights, 170; expectations for Edison, 16, 27, 28, 30, 32, 42–43, 49; expectations for McGregor, 47; by Gardner, 47–48; lighting prior to, 27, 28; street lights, 112
Fort Myers Hotel (Royal Palm Hotel): as base for visitors, 54, 55, 56, 63; depiction, *85*; funding for electrification of cannery, 47; grand opening, 48; purchase by Tootie Terry, 67; swimming pool, 70
Foxworthy, Mrs. J. E., 59
Frierson boardinghouse, 17
Frink, Alden, 14, *34*

Gardner, A. A., 47–48
Gilded Age, xvii, 3, 52
Gilliland, Ezra T.: betrayal of Edison,

43–45; cottage in Mass., 13; estate plans and construction, 12–18, 23–26, *25*; estate sold to McGregor, 47 (*See also* McGregor Plantation; Poinciana); exploratory trip to Fla., 3–11; friendship with Edison, 13–14, 19, 22, 26; hobbies, 3, 16; *Lillian* steam launch, 16, 17; move into new home, 23; research, 2–3, 43
Gilliland, Lillian, 3, 13–14, 19, 23, 26
Gleason, Kid, 122, 127
Glenmont. *See* West Orange, N. J., Glenmont home
Great Depression, 144, 145, 172, 181
Greenfield Village, Mich., 146
Grove, Lefty, 119, 127

H. B. Plant steamer, 53, 57, *86*
Haldeman family, 118
Harding, Pres. Warren G., 129
Hawkins, Carolyn (daughter-in-law). *See* Edison, Carolyn Hawkins
Heitman, Gilmer, 106
Heitman, Harvie E.: Arcade Theater, 106, 109–10, 129, 143, 171; Bradford Hotel, 63, 108, 119; death, 107; as Edison's business agent, 66, 68, 69, 71, 100, 103; friendship with Tootie Terry, 73; general store, 51; Lee County Packing House, 74; packing house after fire, 74; stables, 54
Henry Ford Museum, 116, 126, 136
Hibble, Len, 78
Hibble, William, 43–44, 45
Hill, Flossie, 113, 133, 150, 174
Hitchcock, Grace. *See* Miller, Grace
Holt, Hamilton, 147, 149–50, 175
Hoover, Herbert, Jr., 140
Hoover, Lou, 140, 178
Hoover, Pres. Herbert, 137–38, 140–41, 147, *156–57*, 169, 179
Huelsenkamp, C. J., 9–10, 12, 13
Hughes, Edward Everett (Mina's second husband), 182–83, *190*
Hurricanes, 105, 125, 126

Insull, Samuel, 171, 175
Inventions. *See* Research of Thomas Edison
Isaacs, Philip, 55–56

Jacksonville, Fla., 19–20
James McCutcheon & Company, 15, *36*
Johnson, Preacher "Bob," 106

Kellogg, Dr. John Harvey, 76, 167
Kellow, R. W., 100–101, 102
Kennebec Framing Company, 15, *35*
Keystone Hotel, 9, 23
Key West, Fla., 5, 9, 101, 117–18, *118*, *155*

LaBelle, Fla., 63, 115–16, 123
Laboratories. *See* Menlo Park, N. J.; Thomas
    A. Edison Estate, laboratory for electrical
    research; Thomas A. Edison Estate, labora-
    tory for rubber research; West Orange,
    N. J., laboratory
Lake Okeechobee, Fla., 63–64, *64*, 71, 98,
    125
Lee County Fair, 122, 142, 149
Lee County Packing House, 74
Lehmann, Theodore, 46
Lindbergh, Charles, 131
Louise (Mina's maid), 23
Ludwig, Dr. Emil, 132–33
Ludwig, Elga, 132

Mack, Connie, 119, 122, *158–59*
Mallory, W. S., 59
The Mangoes: Ford's purchase, 98; Ford's
    visits, 106–8, 109, 123, 132–33, 134, 147, 171;
    photograph, *87*
McGraw Company, 180
McGregor, Ambrose M., 47, 49, 51, 69. *See also*
    McGregor Plantation
McGregor, Bradford, 47, 58, 63
McGregor, Tootie, 47, 55, 58, 62. *See also* Terry,
    Tootie McGregor
McGregor Plantation, 47, 63
Melaleuca. *See* Cajeput trees, introduced
Menge, Capt. Fred: death, 185; excursions, 55,
    63–64, 80, 117; friendship with Edison, 103,
    113, 142–43, 174; friendship with Edison's
    grandsons, 109; *Ode to Captain Menge*, 65;
    rubber research, 114; *Thomas A. Edison*
    steamer, 57, 74, *86*
Menge, Conrad, 55, 57
Menlo Park, N. J., 1–2, 15, 31, 146

Miami, Fla., 101, 110, 125, 134, 140, 150. *See also*
    Tamiami Trail
Milan, Ohio, 1, 180
Miller, Grace (sister-in-law): girls' school ad-
    ministrator, 63; golfing, 147; Tamiami Trail
    excursion, 171; visits to estate, 53, 57, 60, 179,
    187; visit to military base, 184
Miller, Ira (brother-in-law), 67
Miller, Jane "Jennie" (sister-in-law), 51, 60, 97
Miller, John V. (brother-in-law), 105, 185, *188*
Miller, Lewis (brother-in-law), 185
Miller, Lewis (father-in-law), 14, 16, 24, 26–27,
    31–32, 52
Miller, Mary (sister-in-law), 185
Miller, Mary Valinda (mother-in-law), 24,
    26–27, 57–58, 63, 133
Miller, Mina (wife), 14, 16–17. *See also* Edison,
    Mina Miller
Miller, Theodore (brother-in-law), 51
Minnie (Henry Ford's cousin), 109
Morse code, 1, 17
Moye, M. E., 59
Muscle Shoals project, 107, 112, 115
Mussolini, Benito, 169

Naples, Fla., 113, 117–18, *118*
National Geographic Magazine, 146
Native Americans. *See* Seminole Indians
Newton, James D., 122–25, 127, 128, 131, 138

Oak Place School, 63
Ocklawaha River, 21–22, *39*
Ode to Captain Menge, 65
Oeser, Marion Edison (daughter), 100, 151, 179,
    180. *See also* Edison, Marion "Dot"
Oeser, Oscar (son-in-law), 100
O'Neill, Hugh, 48
Ott, Frederick: April Fool's Day prank, 83;
    death, 185; as estate employee, 106, 124, 126,
    127, 166, 174; excursions, 59, 60–61, 71, 117;
    purchase of laboratory equipment, 102;
    rubber extraction research, 151; unveiling
    of commemorative plaque, 147
Ott, John, 178

Palatka, Fla., 21, 22
Panic of 1893, 46

Pavese, Mike, 167

Pavese, Rocco, 109

Perkins, Col. J. P., 12, 24

Perry, Jeanette, 185

Philadelphia Athletics, 119, 122, 126–27, *158–59*, 172

Photographs, *85–96, 154–65, 188–91*

Piper, Dr. Ella, 108, 133, 186

Plant, Henry B., 52. *See also* Bellview Hotel; *H. B. Plant* steamer; Tampa Bay Hotel

Poinciana, 55, 66

Potter, Edith (cousin), 106, 117, 125, 128, 179. *See also* Edison, Edith

Proctor & Company, 69

Prohibition, 121, 148, 168, 171

Punta Gorda, Fla., 50, 57, 59

Punta Rassa, Fla., 5–6, 17, 66, 81, 171

Randolf, John, 83

Research of Thomas Edison: aviation anti-fog device, 169; battery, 56, 60, 62; chemical analyses, 67; electric lighting and system, 2, 10, 15, 16, 24; iron ore production, 31, 46, 47, 51; magnetism and motor design, 30, 31, *40*; military-oriented, 99–100; motion pictures, 46, 58, 84; patents from, 2, 20, 31, 56; phonograph, 1, 43, 58, 82, 84, 105, 151, 168; railway truck, 22; stock ticker, 1, 2; telegraph, 1, 5, 20, 24; telephone, 1, 2–3; *vs.* time with the family, 2, 20, 24, 30, 31

—rubber: dedication to, 134, 149, 151, 166; extraction from plants, 117, 135, 141, 151, 166, 174, 177; with Firestone and Ford, 114, 134–35, 176; first tires, 135; plant species, 117, 126, 128–29, 131, 135, 139, 148, 151, *165*, 169; production cost analysis, 117; views on synthetic, 139, 173–74

Rockefeller, John D., 49

Rollins College, 147, 149–50, 175

Rommel, Eddie, 119

Roosevelt, Pres. Franklin D., 181

Roosevelt, Pres. Theodore, 51

Royal Palm Hotel. *See* Fort Myers Hotel

Rubber. *See* Ford, Henry, rubber research; Research of Thomas Edison, rubber

St. Augustine, Fla., 3, 20

St. James hotel, 19, 20

Sanford, Fla., 22

Sanibel Island, Fla., 55, 63, 66, 72, 103, 171

Sapiro, Aaron, 115, 129, 130

Scarth, Sidney, 122

Scopes, John T., and the Scopes Trial, 120, 121

Seaboard Air Line, 174

Seminole Canning Company, 47

Seminole Indians: Everglades land conservation, 181; fort as defense against, 152; guides, 110; history, 8; at Lee County Fair, 122; monitored by soldiers at Fort Myers, 6

Seminole Lodge: daily life, 75–76, 83; deeded to Fort Myers, 187, 192; home named, 57; impact of Fort Myers growth, 103–4; improvements, 69–70; photographs, *92, 94, 95, 154*; rules for guests, 71–72

Shultz, George, 6, 47, 66, 67

Shultz Hotel (Tarpon House), 6, 17, 31, 47, 66, 67

Silver Springs, Fla., 22

Silwell, Mary (wife), 2, 3, 12

Simmons, Al, 119

Sloane, David (great-grandson), 180

Sloane, John (son-in-law), 73, 83

Sloane, John "Jack" Edison (grandson), 103, 109, 119, 122, 180

Sloane, Madeleine Edison (daughter): biography, 180; birth of fourth child, 166; death, 180; engagement and wedding, 73, 83; establishment of Edison Birthplace Museum, 180; inheritance, 179; visits to estate, 53, 63, 71, 75-76, 78-84, 103, 122, 187. *See also* Edison, Madeleine

Sloane, Michael Edison (grandson), 166

Sloane, Peter Edison (grandson), 122

Sloane, Ted Edison (grandson), 103, 109, 119

Sloane, Thomas (grandson), 180

Small, Dr. John K., 130–31, 150, 173

Smith family, 103

Spanish American War, 51, 179

Stadler, Josephine, 175

Stadler, Sen. C. A., 108

Stock market, 46, 144

Stout, Dot, 59

Stout, Frank M., 126, 166
Stulpner, Ewald, 45, 58, 67, 69, 100
Summerlin, Samuel, 8, 10, 13
Summerlin House, 6, 17
Summerlin property, 10–11, 12–13
Suwanee, 55
Symington, James, 45–46

Tamiami Trail, 111, 112, *134*, *135–36*, 171, 172
Tampa, Fla., 11, 22, 52–53. *See also* Tamiami Trail
Tampa Bay Hotel, 52, *85*
Tarpon House. *See* Shultz Hotel
Tate, Alfred, 44
Teger, Leon, 184
Ten Thousand Islands, 118
Terry, Gen. M. O., 62, 66, 73
Terry, Tootie McGregor, 62, 67, 69, 73. *See also* McGregor, Tootie
Thomas A. Edison, Inc., 180
Thomas A. Edison Estate: costs, 14–15, *34–36*; description, 12, 18, 23, 54, 82; dock and pier, 17, 43, 58, 67, 102, 105; electrification, 30, *37*, *38*, 44, 60; family move into, 23–27; fire, 126; Friendship Walk, 175; furnishings, 15; Gilliland property, 43–45, 47, 66 (*See also* McGregor Plantation; Poinciana); laboratory for rubber research, *163*, 166, 176; landscaping, 17, 18, *25*, 25–26, 47; map, xix; open house for the community, 136; open to the public after Edison's death, 181–82; pets, 99; plans and construction, 12–18, 23–26, *25*; renovations and improvements, 58, 67, 69–70; rules for guests, 71–72; seawall issues, 69, 98, 104, 129; Seminole Lodge (*See* Seminole Lodge); swimming pool, 70; as a university, proposal, 185; water supply and indoor plumbing, 44, 58; winter visits 1885–1947, xi–xiv
—laboratory for electrical research: dismantlement, 102–3, 116, 126, 130, 136, 138, *162*; purchase by Ford, 136, 138, 146, *162*; set up, supplies, and electrification, 15, 16, 18, 29–30

Thomas A. Edison steamer, 57, 74, *86*
Thompson, Eli, 17, 22, 24, 26
Thompson, Sam, 78
Thorp, Bessie, 59
Timeline: Mar. 1885, 1–11; Apr. 1885 – Feb. 1886, 12–18; Feb. – Mar. 1886, 19–27; 1887–1888, 28–41; 1888–1899, 42–50; 1900–1904, 51–61; 1905–1913, 62–73; 1914–1915, 74–84; 1916–1920, 97–104; 1921–1924, 105–14; 1925–1926, 115–24; 1927–1928, 125–36; Jan. – Oct. 1929, 137–44; Dec. 1929 – 1930, 145–53; Jan. – Sept. 1931, 166–77; Oct. 1931 – 1947, 178–87
Tinstman, Ben E., 103, 105
Tinstman, Nellie, 103
Tires, rubber, 135, 171
Towles, Capt. W. H., 68–69
Trailblazers, 110, 172
Travers, Julia, 66
Travers, R. I. O., 66

Ukkelberg, Harry, *188*
U.S. Department of Agriculture, 176

Vivas, Joseph, 17

W. R. Wallace and Company, 70, 71
West Orange, N. J.: Edison's funeral, 178–79; Glenmont home, 31, 46, 68, 175, 178, 185, 187; laboratory, 42, 84, 102, 178; Winter visits to Fort Myers, xi–xiv. *See also* Seminole Lodge; Thomas A. Edison Estate
Winthrop, Mass., 13
Wood, William Halsey, 31, 42
World Industrial and Cotton Centennial in New Orleans, 2–3, 14
World War I, 84, 98–100, 101
World War II, 183–85

Zeeman, Hans, 100–101
Zeeman, Mrs., 100

Michele Wehrwein Albion, a former curator at the Edison and Ford Winter estates, writes freelance articles and reviews children's books. She lives with her family in New Hampshire and visits Southwest Florida regularly.